Multiculturalism from the Margins

Multiculturalism from the Margins

Non-Dominant Voices on Difference and Diversity

Edited by
DEAN A. HARRIS

*Prepared under the auspices
of Bifocal Publications*

BERGIN & GARVEY
Westport, Connecticut • London

Library of Congress Cataloging-in-Publication Data

Multiculturalism from the margins : non-dominant voices on difference
 and diversity / edited by Dean A. Harris.
    p.   cm.
    Includes bibliographical references and index.
    ISBN 0–89789–449–9 (hc : alk. paper).—ISBN 0–89789–455–3 (pbk.)
    1. Pluralism (Social sciences)—United States.
  2. Multiculturalism—United States. 3. United States—Race
relations. 4. United States—Ethnic relations. 5. Minorities—
United States. I. Harris, Dean A.
  E184.A1M843   1995
  305.8′00973—dc20   95–13442

British Library Cataloguing in Publication Data is available.

Library of Congress Catalog Card Number: 95–13442
ISBN: 0–89789–449–9
    0–89789–455–3 (pbk.)

First published in 1995

Bergin & Garvey, 88 Post Road West, Westport, CT 06881
An imprint of Greenwood Publishing Group, Inc.

Printed in the United States of America

The paper used in this book complies with the
Permanent Paper Standard issued by the National
Information Standards Organization (Z39.48–1984).

10 9 8 7 6 5 4 3 2

Contents

Acknowledgments

The conception, development, organization, and final publication of this collection has been a long and arduous task covering a time span of almost three years. I suspect that one of the lessons to be learned from all the time and energy expended on such projects is that whatever monetary rewards are reaped from books of this type, they will never sufficiently replenish the psyche and body of that expenditure. Hence, the motivation behind them should never be solely any hoped for material rewards, but rather should include some other factors. I am glad, then, that I began this, my first book project, with the motivations of an educator pursuing the dreams those of us afflicted (blessed?) with such bugs have: The desire not only to share knowledge, but also to infect others with the excitement of learning and the feeling of mastery that comes of deep and broad understanding. I turn to those who infected me with their own enthusiasm for their vocation and its media in a later paragraph. First however, I would like to acknowledge those directly involved in the production of the book.

Apart from any ambitions and perseverance on my part, this project would still be stuck in its infancy but for the support of the fourteen educators who believed in my vision enough to invest some of their precious time in this venture. Special thanks go to Iris Marion Young, first for her wonderful book, which was the initial inspiration for this collection, and secondly for her willingness to adapt one of the essays from that book for the general reader. I don't know that she knows how much was riding on her willingness to participate. My thanks are generous and, as long as this book stays in print, broadcast wide and far.

My appreciation also goes out to the other contributors for their accessibility, their eagerness to share their work with a readership that normally may never encounter such work, and their promptness during this long collaboration: Cheryl Zarlenga Kerchis, John Garcia, Lucius Outlaw, Robert Dawidoff, Isidro Ortiz, Paula Timmerman, María Lugones, Joshua Price, Edward Chang, Angela Oh, Jessie Owens Smith, and Mary Jane Collier. And thanks to Carolyn Murray for her involvement in this and past projects, and for her on-going encouragement.

Many current educators can look back on their education history and point to certain teachers and mentors who were inspirational and instrumental in turning them on to the life of the educator. Two I would like to mention and thank have close ties to the University of Chicago. James Coleman, who in his office and later on the streets of Hyde Park talked with me of the sociological mind spawned in my own mind a desire to dig deeply into the social. And thanks to Greg Schneider, who years ago got a college student focused on the periodic table of elements and Van Halen to begin thinking critically about his surroundings. He spun me around and pushed me onto an exhilarating path that is forever branching in myriad ways, and has no end.

And lastly, I offer my admiration, indebtedness, and love to my wife, who for the past two years has seen me for too many nights finish with the dishes and then walk right back into the office to conspire with, so she says, my other wife—my computer. Thanks for your understanding, your patience, and your encouragement.

Introduction

The recently published and highly regarded books by Charles Taylor (*Multicultural-ism*), Robert Hughes (*Culture of Complaint*), Arthur Schlesinger, Jr. (*The Disuniting of America*), and Richard Bernstein (*Dictatorship of Virtue*) have certainly been an aid to those of us grappling with the numerous issues surrounding what has come to be called multiculturalism. Yet, as much as I would like to be as complimentary as possible of the scholarship supporting each book, I can't overlook the fact that each of the authors is lightly complected and male, which says to me that probably none of them can speak first person about a personal history of minority group oppression and marginalization—with the possible exception of Mr. Bernstein. This fact I find extremely informative of how really open we U.S. Americans are to the truly radical and frightening, yet exhilarating demands and consequences of cultural pluralism and equality. The corollary question being, then: why have there been so few books produced by major publishing houses that disseminate the conflicting opinions of historically marginalized voices? Is it mere coincidence that, but for maybe Cornel West, the only authors big publishers will place their names behind are those of white males? Are there not any books written by authors of color of sufficient quality to warrant publication? Do we find it too easy to think that there aren't?

Practically speaking, the answer is that white males are major readers of nonfiction, and they tend to read books written by white males (and there is no dearth of such books). Publishers like to make money, hence they cater to the desires of one of the largest reading (and spending) audiences—white males. The problem for multiculturalism being: it is not white males but rather members of historically oppressed and marginalized groups who are critiquing society and the dominant culture for being exclusionary and authoritarian, yet one of the primary means of knowledge dissemination—books—is not disseminating these critiques! Want to learn about Chicana political theory? Go read a book or article written by a white scholar or commentator. Does that make sense? How can one legitimately participate in a discussion when the arguments of both sides are being defined and enunciated by only one side? We Americans know more about Afrocentrism from George Will and Arthur Schlesinger, Jr., than from Maulana Karenga or Molefi Asante. In effect then, *radical* multiculturalism is being co-opted and redefined by those most privileged, and those with the most to lose in the debate.

In a 1994 essay, Frances Aparicio argues that "proponents of multiculturalism have repeatedly dismissed ethnic and cultural specificity as too 'particularist'" and "too conflictive, too divisive, or perhaps too ethnocentric. . . . When powerful white scholars speak for and on the behalf of people of color, multiculturalism becomes valid."[1] In effect, this watered-down multiculturalism has been repackaged and made palatable for the majority at the expense of those most affected by myopic *mono*culturalism. Certainly each of the above-mentioned authors supports a multicultural nation, but each most definitely has a different opinion of just what that means because, among other things, each opinion is affected by the writer's racial, gender, and class perspective. If that is the case, then how can anyone claim to have properly adjudicated between conflicting sociocultural perspectives when those already wielding the most power are defining the issues for both sides for our consumption?

In response to the current mainstream monologue on multiculturalism, this book is an attempt to provide a space for authors of color to share their thoughts and ideas on diversity, difference, pluralism, privilege, and ethnicity. In aggregate, the essays are meant to speak toward the attempt by white scholars to reserve to themselves all power to define these terms, though the essays do not take up directly any specific arguments made by Taylor, Hughes, Bernstein, or Schlesinger. Nevertheless, whether speaking as a Korean male or female, Latina or Jewish male, or as an African American man or woman, each writer is attempting to validate a marginalized perspective and its corollary arguments for what they are, and not for what they have been described and defined as being by privileged mainstream writers.

Your attitude right now (suggested by your willingness to pick up this book) may be similar to that of my own a few years ago when this project was conceived. At that time the so-called "culture wars" were only just beginning to be reported in the popular media. I was working in an office during the day and spent my evenings spelunking through a variety of books and magazines for the sheer enjoyment of learning without even the remotest thought of publishing a book on anything. Through my reading, I am continually reminded of the breadth of my ignorance, and, as I am prone to do, eventually latch onto some subject that seduces me and attempt to read everything about it I can get my hands on. For some reason I got hooked onto race and power and have been engrossed in those subjects for the past four years. Being a "white heterosexual male" negotiating the early part of the decade, upon encountering the issues and arguments surrounding diversity, I found myself facing a wall of people and ideas that simultaneously pinched my social justice nerve and my ignorance nerve, and also elicited a fear response. Difference, domination, oppression, privilege, discrimination, and diversity, among others, were all words for which new connotations were being created and which tugged at me from opposing directions. At the beginning of my education the only thing I was sure of was that I knew nothing of what the arguments were about, yet understood that the outcome was of monumental significance.

Since my initial introduction to the spectrum of issues covered in this book, my enthusiasm for them has never wavered. There is just so much to learn about so many provocative things—most having major ramifications for my physical and psychological well-being and future as well as this country's future. But rather than becoming overwhelmed by the myriad issues that attempt to completely rethink the creation and future of every artifact of culture, I decided I would be better off initially to focus on issues I already had an interest in and see how race and gender affected them, and continue to affect them. I think that approach is the healthiest one to take, for there is no way physically or politically to become an *authority* on race or gender; that is one of the central planks of multiculturalism. There is just too much to learn and too many people to get acquainted with. In the end, what we must rely on to broaden our horizons as much as possible are the avenues of dialogue we create and sustain, reasoned discussion, openness to multifarious experiences, a willingness to experiment and question our individual interests, and a supportive and well-functioning democracy.

Before introducing the contents of the individual essays, I want to touch a bit upon a fulcrum that the debate over multiculturalism can be said to be balancing on. That balancing point concerns differing opinions about the extent to which current and historical racism decides political and economic placement in American society. It is an important debate, for *if* it can be successfully argued that a level playing field has been established and that all persons and peoples have equal access to the means to power and influence, then radical multiculturalism's persuasiveness will have been severely undermined, if not completely destroyed. The contributors to this text will be arguing in differing ways that such arguments are indefensible and extremely deceptive.

Michael Omi and Howard Winant, in their book *Racial Formation in the United States,* and Ruth Frankenberg in her book *White Women, Race Matters,* plot out a history of American racism.[2] They theorize three phases spanning our history from the founding of the colonies to the contemporary period. The first phase, which dominated discourse up through the first decades of this century, assumed biological bases for race. Blacks, Native Americans, Asians, Mexicans (to a lesser extent), and others were biologically different from whites and, as the equation determined, inferior to them. Such an assumed superiority over "colored" people justified all sorts of political and economic inequities, such as slavery and the theft of Native American lands. This phase is characterized by what Frankenberg terms "essentialist racism," for proponents held that there were essential—biological—differences between whites and "others" that could neither be denied nor changed.

The second phase, which came to the fore in the 1920s, de-emphasized biological difference and instead looked to cultural and social differences as indicators to whites of appropriate behavior toward people of color. This change allowed for the creation of a discourse of assimilation that is still prevalent today. It now mattered less that an Asian might have some "germane" biological differences than it did that there seemed to be some pretty large cultural differences separating whites from, say, Korean immigrants. But, whereas biology is pretty hard to change, cultural practices can be modified, discarded, and embraced. Through the gradual process of assimilation, then, it was thought that persons of color could gain access to some of the benefits historically set aside for whites only. It was reasoned that if the field were leveled for all races via assimilation, then only *individual* successes and/or failures would determine an individual's lifecourse. Thus, a highly charged and deterministic social milieu gave way to an environment supposedly based solely on merit. Frankenberg, however, argues that this phase suffers from what she calls "color- and power-evasiveness"—two symptoms of which are the call for racial color-blindness and an unwillingness on the part of the empowered cultural elite to discuss real structural power shifts.

In response to this evasiveness a third phase emerged during the 1960s and 1970s that Frankenberg says is based on "race-cognizance." While the second phase was based upon racial similarity—whether inborn or acquired—the third, as was the first, is based on difference. The first phase, articulated by *whites*, assumed differences between the races that were genetically determined. In contradistinction, the third phase, articulated by *peoples of color,* argued racial differences that were socially and culturally based. This phase is termed "race-cognizant," because peoples of color were (and still are) arguing that race has in the past mattered and continues to do so today. The effects of historical racism are still with us today and exert considerable influence on the lifecourses of peoples of color *and* whites. One simple example: the Social Security Act mandated that insurance be extended to workers to protect against unemployment, disability, and old age. But the act excluded farm workers and domestic household laborers from coverage—sectors that employed two-thirds of all employed Blacks. Would the exclusion have been codified if whites served in those sectors to the proportion that Blacks did? How does that exclusion, then, affect Blacks living today? How did the inclusion of the majority of working whites under the act privilege them?

Today, by arguing for the immediate creation of a racially color-blind society, socially entrenched whites reveal their belief that the historical effects of racism are no longer with us. For them, their privileged status and the marginalized, exploited, and powerless status of a disproportionate number of persons of color are no longer relevant issues to be discussed. They claim that during this century a meritocracy was created in this country that can account for, and determines, the economic and political placement of each and every member of this society, no matter what color. In addition, any sort of toleration—let alone celebration—of difference will only result in exacerbating the continuing fragmentation of what is left of this nation's "cultural center," the bread box that contains all that is worth saving and fighting for. This collection of essays is a response to just such claims. And the best place to start the discussion is with the first essay cowritten by Cheryl Zarlenga Kerchis and Iris Marion Young.

This book consists of eleven chapters. The key chapter is the first, on difference. It is an adaptation of the first chapter of Iris Marion Young's text *Justice and the Politics of Difference.* It is the proper starting point for this book, for that book was the starting point for my own journey that resulted in the publication of this collection. There is much more to that book than just an investigation of difference. But an understanding of difference is the route a reader of this book must pass through, negotiating all the numerous bumps and hurdles of individual and group identity, before arriving at the fork that demands that one make a navigational choice: provincialism (not a through street) or multiculturalism (freeway—or maybe toll road).

Kerchis, who has adapted Young's chapter for inclusion in this collection, weaves two threads throughout the chapter. She places the two threads in tension with each other to show how the legacy of the first thread, the "ideal of assimilation," has guided this country though its five-hundred-year history, bringing us to the point where to continue developing as a nation and as individuals we must exchange that worn and weakened thread for a stronger one: a "politics of difference." As Kerchis makes clear, the ideal of assimilation simultaneously obfuscates already present realities of difference and similarity yet highlights some differences and turns them into identifying features used for the purposes of exclusion and demonization. When we typically speak of difference, we place ourselves in the role of speaker, judge, and keeper-of-the-normal, thereby creating the Other as totally different. Thus, for example, heterosexuals, as self-appointed ajudicators of legitimate sexual orientation, demonize homosexuals, bisexuals, and the transgendered, turning them into the Other, all the while ignoring the fact that they too are looking for love, affection, and attention; have aspirations, dreams, and fears; are expressing their individuality; and vote and speak, just as heterosexuals do. We humans are similar in many ways, and we are different in many ways. But why are some privileged to judge and others allowed only the capacity to be judged? Kerchis argues that we are discovering that the legacy of the ideal of assimilation is isolation and conformism, and a close-mindedness to all that difference has to offer us in our daily lives as citizens, relatives, friends, and peers.

In chapter 2 John A. Garcia tackles the meanings of "multiculturalism." The popular media would have you believe that multiculturalism is a recent movement of peoples of color to gain freedom, recognition, and power in an effort to bring down all that this country has fought to create, sustain, and export to other countries. Our laws, which have created a relatively safe and orderly place to work, live, and play; our history, which supposedly includes the stories of those of import and influence; our "representative" government, which serves us all equally; and our sovereign state are all, we are told, under attack by radicals who are promoting schism by emphasizing the differences of race, gender, ableism, and so on.

Garcia argues that, in fact, multiculturalism has been a reality for a long time. Though, as María Lugones will argue in chapter 7, the influence that multiculturalism has exerted to the present can be more accurately characterized as "ornamental." Ornamental multiculturalism is the sort that provides a space for restaurants serving Indian cuisine but won't let an Indian American serve in an elected office, let alone influence this country's methods for governing. Unfortunately, U.S. American multiculturalism is tempered (some might say emasculated) by white supremacy, Western standards of law, value, and worth, and cultural domination. Garcia's call to combat this dilution of diversity is to argue for what he terms "corporate pluralism." Only then will our society, cultural artifacts, government and process of governing work as though each of us is involved.

How successfully this country has utilized the talents of individuals from minority groups is the topic Lucius T. Outlaw covers in chapter 3 as he surveys recent African-American history. African Americans have been struggling for centuries trying to make this country their home: should they remain living in a country that enslaved them and raped their homeland, and attempt to forge some sort of life as a minority racial group? How should they deal with the early Constitutional equivocation as to their humanity: are they human or are they but three-fifths human? What is the best means to flourish economically: through integrating and assimilating their needs and wants, or through developing a unique economic niche and focusing on "buying Black?" In some fashion or another, these questions, whether in the minds of African Americans or in the minds of whites, are still relevant today. It is a moral abomination that the way racial minorities are often treated in this country can only stem from an ideology that holds that they are not totally human and therefore cannot rightfully lay claim to the rights and privileges that others enjoy and the Constitution guarantees.

Although it would not be accurate to say that the rights movements of women, racial minorities, and the disabled have accomplished all that they set out to accomplish and thus it is in some way time to move on to the claims of another historically oppressed group, another group is raising its voice and forcing its way onto the airwaves and our brain waves. In 1994 Michael Nava and Robert Dawidoff published a book entitled *Created Equal: Why Gay Rights Matter to America.* Although prior to reading the text I knew that I was in support of protecting the rights of gays and lesbians to all that heterosexuals have granted themselves and benefit from, I could never have argued the case as well as I could after reading the book. The offspring of their writing collaboration is wonderfully accessible, yet thoroughly informative on the collection of issues that have come to be called "gay issues," though upon finishing reading the interview, you may come to the conclusion that those issues are not merely gay ones. Since it is not possible to reprint the entire book here as chapter 4, we have included an interview with Professor Dawidoff as an overview of some of the key issues of the book.

Take note of one of the kernels in the interview: that when encountering the arguments for and against the protection of rights for queers, it is crucial to differentiate between those arguments that are germane and those that are not. As you will read, the fact that this process is skipped by so many on both sides of the issues—as well as by queers themselves—is a monumental source of frustration for apologists. One would think that a careful consideration of pertinent arguments and counterarguments would be a basic intellectual activity on the part of those engaged in the discussion. One of Dawidoff's arguments is that those opposing so called "gay rights" are less concerned with intellectual consistency and rigor, and more concerned with . . . well, you'll see.

"To subjugate or persecute by unjust or tyrannical use of force or authority. To weigh heavily upon. To overwhelm or crush." Such is the definition of "oppress" according to *The American Heritage Dictionary.* It is a good one, though merely a starting point for Iris Marion Young. Chapter 5, which is entitled "Five Faces of Oppression," is an adaptation of the chapter of the same name from her book that was the inspiration for this collection of essays. Beginning first with a discussion of what is meant by "social group," she argues that for many theorists such groups do not exist. One might think a discussion on the existence of social groups merely pedantic, yet when it comes to, for example, granting affirmative action benefits, a fleshed-out concept of social groups is required for deciding which individuals have standing and which do not. Might gays and lesbians, due to their oppressed and minority status, be allowed to benefit from affirmative action policies? What about pedophiles?

The lengthiest section of the chapter is an in-depth consideration of oppression. Young theorizes five types of oppression and discusses the differences between them and the characteristics of each; she also provides illustrations of how minority groups are and have been affected by each "face." The following chapter, chapter 6, considers these five faces in light of Chicano/Chicana history. It provides numerous examples of the sometimes subtle and other times overt workings of and strategies behind powerlessness, cultural imperialism, exploitation, violence, and marginalization—the five faces of oppression.

Chapter 7 is also an extension of Young's chapter on oppression. "To experience cultural imperialism means to experience how the dominant meanings of a society render the particular perspective of one's own group invisible at the same time as they stereotype one's group and mark it out as the Other."[3] In this chapter, cowritten by María Lugones and Joshua Price, the authors tackle "dominant culture," the force behind cultural imperialism. Through a combination of traditional argumentation and first-person testimony, Lugones and Price engage our reason and our emotions in an effort to communicate the cultural and personal damage wreaked upon non-dominant cultures by dominant cultures and peoples. In addition, in spite of (though also due to) that domination and subordination, members of dominant cultures hurt themselves by inhibiting the voicing of—let alone the implementation of—ideas that could jump-start progress and aid intercultural and interpersonal understanding. In the provocative last half of the chapter, the authors show how we are stalling human progress by founding our understanding of people, issues, and institutions on an unsustainable triumvirate of certainty, simplicity, and agreement. The only way to move beyond this unholy alliance supporting domination and cultural imperialism is to embrace an alternate set of cognitive bases.

Their exploration of simplicity and complexity is not the only provocative surprise in this essay. Your encounter with chapter 7 will also require an open and inquiring mind due to the languages used by the authors. Small parts of the essay are not written in English, and translations are not provided. I would ask that upon encountering them (assuming you can't read the passages), you think about your initial reaction to them and consider your solution to the problem of incomprehension—all within the context of the ideas expressed and the arguments made in the essay.

In chapter 8 Edward T. Chang and coauthor Angela E. Oh show how April 29, 1992, affected Koreans living in the Los Angeles area. April 29, or what Koreans call

Sa-ee-Gu, was the first day of unrest following the Rodney King trial. That day, the aftermath of the riots, and the subsequent trials left an indelible mark on the Korean community in Los Angeles, and one that will not be erased any time soon. Chang and Oh argue that even in the enlightened 1990s, the way Koreans are treated is but an extension of their treatment throughout the century. The Korean experience of emigration to the West and the subsequent attempt to create a viable life for themselves has a number of similarities to that of African Americans and Latino/Latinas. They too have been called "lazy, dirty, unskillful, heavy smokers, and . . . not . . . orderly [in the way they live their lives]."[4] They too have had an extremely difficult time getting noticed and winning the proper respect and rights incumbent upon citizenship while simultaneously dealing with being stereotyped as "oriental," that is, subservient, quiet, predatory, sagelike, and skilled in kung-fu. This chapter is a good introduction to Korean Americans and their history in this country. The authors have much hope for the community, but are also aware of the challenges inflicting those that choose to remain in what can sometimes be a hostile environment.

Do some free association with some of your white friends and relatives, and start with the word "race." Don't be surprised if the most common response is "Blacks." In this country the word race is synonymous with Black, and only sometimes connotes Asian or Latino. It is often closely associated with poverty, also. For years I had in my file cabinet a file marked Race/Poverty in which I kept articles about poverty and about Black issues. One fact of life for whites in this country is the *un*acknowledged status of their color as a race. Ever heard something close to these sentiments emanate from your radio or television? "Blacks can be grouped into a race as can Asians, Latinos, Native Americans, and so forth, but whites are really individuals. We are to be treated as individuals. If we choose to be a member of a group, it is a *voluntary* association. Our color—white—is merely a color. Sure, one can gather a bunch of white people together and claim that a group of whites has been formed, but the color white, unlike the color black or brown, says nothing about the individual." If this sounds rational and sensible to you, then chapter 9, coauthored by Carolyn B. Murray and J. Owens Smith, should be a bumpy ride.

Whiteness and white privilege are hot topics these days. It has only been within the past decade that whiteness has been placed on the surgery table of academe and made ready for dissection and deconstruction—and none too early. In the first half of this chapter, Smith tackles the policy side of white privilege. In a discussion of a variety of governmental policies, such as the National Labor Relations Act of 1935 and the Davis-Bacon Act of 1952, he shows how enacting these laws sustained and reinforced white privilege and the subordination of Blacks in the workplace and the wider society. From Smith's perspective, seemingly neutral and helpful policies are now judged to have been biased toward a certain group—and more often than not that group was white people.

In the second half of the essay, Murray, a psychologist, considers the psychological bases of the invisibility of whiteness to whites. Why is it that whites believe Blacks are lazy and violent? Is discrimination a natural process, or is it something that can be avoided? And what of the psychological sources of stereotyping? Taken together, these two arguments encompassing white privilege make for a fascinating investigation into the workings of the human psyche and white supremacy.

This collection concludes with a consideration of communication. We have as U.S. Americans, among other policies, those of affirmative action to thank for the increasing number of minorities represented in business, government, and education compared to thirty years ago and earlier. Because of this nation's long (and still continuing) history of white supremacy, white people are only now having to learn how to live and work peacefully, productively, and respectfully with persons of color. Due to that fact the final chapter of this book focuses on intercultural communication. Before reading Mary Jane Collier's chapter you may not believe that communication is so complicated. Each of us probably believes that he or she is a fairly competent communicator (there are just a lot of stupid people out there who are poor listeners, right?). But, in fact, we all have much to learn about communication. Author Deborah Tannen has gained quite a bit of notoriety of late because of her thoughtful books on communication differences between the sexes. Mediocre and non-competent communication is easy and ubiquitous. Skilled interlocution, on the other hand, is something one must learn. I think Collier's thoughts, stemming from her own research on intercultural communication, are the perfect, if you will, commencement address, upon the completion of your reading. As the last thing you read in the book, I hope its contents will be the first things you put to good use and the last things you forget—forget, that is, because they have become so much a part of your daily routine.

1

Social Movements and the Politics of Difference

Cheryl Zarlenga Kerchis and Iris Marion Young

There was once a time of caste and class when tradition held that each group had its place in the social hierarchy—that some were born to rule and others to be ruled. In this time of darkness, rights, privileges, and obligations were different for people of different sexes, races, religions, classes, and occupations. Inequality between groups was justified by both the state and the church on the grounds that some kinds of people were better than others.

Then one day, a period in the history of ideas known as the Enlightenment dawned, and revolutionary ideas about the equality of people emerged. During the Enlightenment, which reached its zenith in Europe in the eighteenth century, philosophers called into question traditional ideas and values that justified political inequality between groups. They declared that all people are created equal because all people are able to reason and to think about morality. They also argued that because all people are created equal, all people should have equal political and civil rights.

The ideas of Enlightenment thinkers have marked the battle lines of political struggle in the United States for the past two hundred years. The Revolutionary War was fought on Enlightenment principles, and our Constitution was based on the principles of liberty and equality. In the beginning, however, the vision of liberty and equality of our founders (as well as most Enlightenment philosophers) excluded certain groups. Women did not have equal political and civil rights, and African Americans were enslaved. Inspired by the ideals of liberty and equality, women and African Americans engaged in a long and bitter struggle for political equality. By the 1960s, the battle for legal equal political and civil rights was won, though the struggle for equality in all walks of life continues.

Today in our society, prejudice and discrimination remain, but in many respects we have realized the vision that the Enlightenment thinkers set out. Our laws express rights in universal terms, that is, applied equally to everyone. We strive for a society in which differences of race, sex, religion, and ethnicity do not affect people's opportunities to participate in all aspects of social life. We believe that people should be treated as individuals, not as members of groups, and that their rewards in life should be based on their individual achievement—not on their race, sex, or any other purely accidental characteristic.

Though there is much to admire in this vision of a society that eliminates group differences, it has its own limitations, which contemporary social movements have called into question. Just as Enlightenment social movements challenged widely held traditional ideas and values that justified oppression in their time, today's social movements are challenging widely held ideas about justice that justify oppression in our time. These social movements criticize the idea that a just society is one that eliminates group differences under the law and guarantees equal treatment for all individuals. The central question they wish to ask is this: is it possible that the ideal of equal treatment of all persons under the law and the attempt to eliminate group differences under the law in fact perpetuates oppression of certain groups?

In this chapter, we will argue that the answer to this question is yes. In our argument we will first discuss the ideal of justice that defines liberation as the transcendence of group difference. We call this the *ideal of assimilation*. This ideal usually promotes the equal treatment of all groups as the primary way to achieve justice. In this discussion, we will show how recent social movements of oppressed groups in the United States have challenged this ideal of assimilation. These movements believe that by organizing themselves and defining their own positive group cultural identity they will be more likely to achieve power and increase their participation in public institutions. We call this positive recognition of difference the politics of difference, and explain how it is more likely to aid in the liberation of oppressed groups.

In the second part of the chapter, we will discuss the need to change the way we think about group differences in order to have a politics of difference that leads to the liberation of oppressed groups. We will explore the risks associated with a politics of difference, in particular, the risk of recreating the harmful stigma that group difference has had in the past. To avoid this restigmatizing of groups, we will argue for a new and positive understanding of difference that rejects past exclusionary understandings of difference.

In the final part of this chapter, we will consider practical issues of policy and representation in relation to a politics of difference. First, we will discuss the issue of group-neutral versus group-conscious policies. By this we mean policies that treat all groups in the same way (group-neutral) versus policies that treat different groups differently (group-conscious). We will discuss two specific cases in which group-conscious policies are needed to ensure fairness to disadvantaged groups. Lastly, we will argue for group representation in American social institutions including governmental and non-governmental institutions. We will explain how group representation promotes justice, suggest the kinds of groups that should be represented, and give some examples of group representation within some already-existing organizations and movements in the United States.

LIBERATION FOR OPPRESSED GROUPS THROUGH THE IDEAL OF ASSIMILATION

The Ideal of Assimilation and Equal Treatment of Social Groups

What strategy of reform is most effective for achieving the liberation of oppressed groups? If we desire a non-racist, non-sexist society, how can we get there? One strategy for achieving this society is to pursue what we call an ideal of assimilation. The ideal of assimilation as a strategy for the liberation of oppressed groups involves the elimination of group-based differences under the law. Thus, in a truly non-racist, non-sexist society, a person's race or sex would be no more significant in the eyes of the law than eye color or any other accidental characteristic. People would have different physical characteristics (such as skin color), but these would play no part in determining how people treated each other or how they were treated under the law. Over time, people would see no reason to consider race or sex in policies or in everyday activities, and group-based differences by and large would no longer matter.

Many contemporary thinkers argue for this ideal of assimilation and against the ideal of diversity that we will argue for later in this chapter. And there are many convincing reasons to support such an ideal. Perhaps the most convincing reason is that the principle of equal treatment of groups provides a clear and easily applied standard of equality and justice for use by courts and government institutions that deal with issues of race and sex discrimination. Under a standard of equal treatment, any discrimination whatsoever on the basis of group differences is considered illegal. Any law, regulation, employment practice, or government policy that treats persons differently on the basis of the race or sex is labelled unjust. The simplicity of this principle of equal treatment makes it a very attractive standard of justice.

There are two other convincing reasons to support the ideal of assimilation and the principle of justice as equal treatment. First, the ideal of assimilation may help to change the way people think about group differences. It treats classifications of people according to accidental characteristics like skin color or gender as arbitrary, not natural or necessary. Some people happen to be Black. Some are female or Hispanic or Jewish or Italian. But these differences do not mean that these people have different moral worth or that they necessarily aspire to anything different than anyone else in political life, in the workplace, or in the family. By suggesting that these categories are not important, the ideal of assimilation helps us realize how often we limit people's opportunities in society (because they are Black, female, and so on) for arbitrary reasons. Second, the ideal of assimilation gives individuals a great deal of choice in their lives. When group differences have no social importance, people are free to develop themselves as individuals, without feeling the pressures of group expectations. If I am a woman, I can aspire to anything I wish to and not feel any special pressure to pursue or settle for, for instance, one occupation versus another.

The ideal of assimilation, which calls for equal treatment of groups and the elimination of group difference in social life, has been extremely important in the history of oppressed groups. Its assertion of the equal moral worth of all persons (regardless of their group characteristics) and the right of all to participate in the institutions of society inspired many movements against discrimination. There is no question that it continues to have considerable value in our nation today, where many forms of discrimination against groups persist.

Contemporary Challenges to the Ideal of Assimilation

Since the 1960s, a number of groups have questioned the value of this ideal of assimilation and equal treatment. Is it possible, they have asked, that this ideal is not truly liberating for some oppressed groups? Instead of seeking to eliminate group difference, they wonder, would it not be more liberating for groups to organize themselves and assert their own positive group cultural identity? These groups see a politics of difference as opposed to a politics without difference as a better strategy for achieving power and participation in the institutions of social and political life. In the next section, we will discuss the efforts of four contemporary social movements to redefine the importance of group difference and cultural identity in social and political life in a way that they find more liberating.

The African American Movement

In the 1960s, with the enactment of the Civil Rights Act of 1964, the Voting Rights Act of 1965, and numerous lawsuits spawned by these new laws, African Americans won major victories that declared racial discrimination in politics and the workplace illegal. Despite these successes, however, criticisms of the civil rights strategy emerged from within the African American community in the form of the Black Power movement. Black Power leaders criticized the civil rights movement for three reasons: they were unhappy with the civil rights movement's goal of integration of African Americans into a society dominated by whites; they criticized the movement's alliance with white liberals and instead called upon African Americans to confidently affirm their cultural identity; and they criticized the movement for not encouraging African Americans to organize themselves on their own terms and to determine their political goals within their own organizations.

Instead of supporting integration with whites, Black Power leaders called on African Americans to strengthen their own separate and culturally distinct neighborhoods as a better means of obtaining economic and political power. In sum, they rejected the ideal of assimilation and the suppression of group difference in political and economic life. In its place, they advocated self-organization and a strengthening of cultural identity as a better strategy for achieving power and participation in dominant institutions.

In recent years, many of the ideas of the Black Power movement have resurfaced among African Americans. Despite the legal protections won during the civil rights era, African American economic and political oppression persists. In economic life today, African Americans experience unemployment rates more than twice those of whites and poverty rates more than three times those of whites. And they still face substantial discrimination in educational opportunities, business opportunities, and the housing market.

What has happened since the 1960s? Why the persistence of inequalities almost forty years after *Brown v. Board of Education*, and almost thirty years after the Civil Rights and Voting Rights acts? Many African Americans argue that the push toward integration by the civil rights movement had unintended negative effects on the African American community. While civil rights protections opened the doors of opportunity for some African Americans, those left behind were made worse off. Many African Americans have been assimilated into the middle class and no longer associate as closely with poor and working class African Americans. As a consequence, African American solidarity has been weakened, and in many neighborhoods African American businesses, schools, and churches have been hurt by the exodus of middle-class African American families. Hence, once again, many African American leaders are calling for a rejection of the goal of integration and assimilation and are calling upon African Americans to organize themselves and seek economic and political empowerment within their own neighborhoods.

Another legacy of the Black Power movement that lives on today is the assertion of a positive Black cultural identity. The "Black is beautiful" movement that emerged in the 1960s celebrated a distinct African American culture and struggled against the assimilation of that culture into the dominant culture of American society. In their clothing and hairstyles, members confidently asserted their own cultural styles and rejected the narrow definition of style and beauty of the predominantly white culture. Since that time, African American historians and educators have sought to recover the rich history of African America and have retold the stories of African American writers, artists, musicians, inventors, and political figures, who received little attention in the history textbooks of white America. And they have subsequently fought with school boards across the nation to ensure that respect for African American history and culture is integral to the history curricula under which every student in this country is educated.

All of these examples reflect a rejection of the idea that assimilation of African Americans into the dominant culture of America is a desirable goal. They instead reflect a desire for an alternative politics of difference through which African Americans can gain their fair share of power and increase their participation in social, political, and economic life in America without shedding their own self-determined group cultural identity.

The American Indian Movement

Not long after the Black Power movement emerged in the 1960s, a movement with similar ideals arose among Native Americans. American Indian Movement leaders called for Red Power, which, like Black Power, rejected the assimilation of Native

American peoples that had been the goal of government policies toward Indians throughout the nineteenth and twentieth centuries. In many ways, their rejection of the dominant culture and its values was even stronger than that of Black Power.

The American Indian Movement claimed a right to self-government on Indian lands
and struggled to gain a powerful Indian voice in the federal government branch responsible for policy making toward Native American peoples—the Bureau of Indian
Affairs. They went to the courts to fight for land taken away from them. They also used
the court system to fight for Indian control of natural resources on reservations that
were being exploited by mining companies and other corporations.

Like Black Power, Red Power also extended its struggle beyond political and economic issues. Red Power advocates wanted to restore and strengthen cultural pride
among Native Americans. In the last twenty years, Native Americans have struggled
to recover and preserve elements of their traditional culture such as religious rituals,
crafts, and languages that have been ravaged by the government's policy of Indian
assimilation.

The Gay and Lesbian Movement

The gay and lesbian movement that emerged in the 1960s began, much like the
African American movement of that period, as a struggle for equality and civil rights.
Gay-rights advocates wanted to protect gay men and lesbians from discrimination in
government institutions and in employment. The movement strived for the ideal of
assimilation and equal treatment that we have talked about throughout this chapter.
They asked society to recognize that gay people are no different from anyone else in
their aspirations or moral worth, and that they too deserve the same protections under
the law extended to all other U.S. citizens.

Over time, however, many members of the gay and lesbian movement came to
believe that the achievement of civil rights alone would not liberate gay men and
lesbians from the discrimination they faced in society. Though they had achieved some
legal victories, gay men and lesbians were still often harassed, beaten up, and intimi-
dated by heterosexuals who disapproved of their gay "lifestyle." It seemed the dominant culture could tolerate gays and even extend limited legal protection to gay people
as long as they kept their sexuality a *private* matter. But *public* displays of gay lifestyles
were (and still are) often met with hostility and violence. For many gay men and lesbians, concealing their sexuality and lifestyles in a private world is just as oppressive as
the public and explicit discrimination they often face in institutions.

Today, most gay and lesbian liberation groups seek not only equal protection under
the law but also group solidarity and a positive affirmation of gay men and lesbians as
social groups with shared experiences and cultures. They reject the ideal of assimilation that suppresses group differences in political and social life and makes these differences a purely private matter. They refuse to accept the dominant heterosexual
culture's definition of healthy sexuality and respectable family life, and instead have
insisted on the right to proudly display their gay or lesbian identity. Like the other

groups mentioned above, they have engaged in a politics of difference that they find more liberating than the politics of assimilation.

The Women's Movement

Until the late 1970s, the aims of the contemporary women's movement were for the most part those of the ideal of assimilation. Women's movement members fought for women's civil rights and the equal treatment of and equal opportunity for women in political institutions and the workplace. The movement strived to eliminate the significance of gender differences in social life. Women and men were to be measured by the same standards and treated in the same way in social institutions. Women's rights advocates saw any attempt to define men and women as fundamentally different in their aspirations for successful careers outside the home as just another means of oppressing women and limiting their opportunity to participate in the male-dominated spheres of government and business. This strategy of assimilation was extremely successful in undermining traditional ways of thinking about sex differences and women's roles. The idea that women naturally aspired to less in terms of participation in politics and the workplace was finally overturned.

Despite these successes, however, many in the women's movement grew uncomfortable with this strategy of assimilation, which defined equality as the elimination of sex differences in social life. Since the late seventies, a politics of difference has emerged from within the women's movement that rejects the goals of gender assimilation. The first signs of this rejection were seen among women who advocated feminist separatism.

Feminist separatists believed that women should aspire to more than formal equality in a male-dominated world. They argued that entering the male-dominated world meant playing according to rules and standards that men had set up and had used against women for centuries and across cultures. Instead of trying to measure up to male-defined standards, they called for the empowerment of women through self-organization and the creation of separate and safe places where women could share their experiences and devise their own rules of the game. In such separate and safe places, women could decide for themselves what was socially valuable activity instead of uncritically accepting the values and activities of a male-dominated society. One of the outcomes of this separatism was the creation of women's organizations and services to address the needs of women that have historically received little attention from male-dominated society. The organizations formed in this period include women's health clinics, battered women's shelters, and rape crisis centers, all of which today continue to improve the lives of many women.

Some of the ideas of this separatist movement are reflected in the recent work of feminist philosophers and political thinkers. Unlike earlier feminist thinkers, these women question the idea that women's liberation means equal participation of women in male-dominated political institutions and workplaces. While they do not suggest that women withdraw from such institutions, they suggest that society ought to rethink the value of femininity and women's ways of approaching human relations. These theorists suggest that women tend to be socialized in a way that, in comparison with men, makes them more sensitive to other's feelings, more empathetic, more nurturing of others and the world, and better at smoothing over tensions between people.

They argue that this more caring, nurturing, and cooperative approach to relations with other people should not be rejected out of hand by feminists as limiting women's human potential or their ability to contribute to the world. They suggest that women's attitudes toward others and toward nature constitute a healthier way to think about the world than the competitive and individualistic attitudes that characterize male-dominated culture in the Western world. By holding on to these values, women can help to transform institutions, human relations, and the interaction of people with nature in ways that may better promote people's self-development within institutions and better protect the environment.

Thus, a political strategy that asks women to give up the values of caring or nurturing in order to succeed in the workplace or in politics not only undervalues what women have to contribute to those spheres, but undermines the possibility of transforming male-dominated institutions in a way that will result in a healthier society as a whole. To resolve this dilemma, then, the politics of assimilation needs to be replaced by a politics of difference that makes it possible for women to participate fully in social and political institutions without suppressing or undervaluing gender differences.

WHY IS THE POLITICS OF DIFFERENCE LIBERATING?

The Importance of Group Difference in Social Life

All of the social movements discussed above have offered an alternative view of liberation that rejects the ideal of assimilation. In their assertion of a positive sense of group difference, these social movements have put forth an ideal of liberation that we will call the politics of difference. In their view, a just society does not try to eliminate or ignore the importance of group differences. Rather, society seeks equality among social groups, requiring each to recognize and respect the value of the experiences and perspectives of all other groups. No group asks another to give up or hide its distinct experiences and perspectives as a condition of participation in social institutions.

Is a politics of difference really necessary? Are group differences really that important? Many political philosophers deny the importance of social groups. To them, the notion of group difference was created and kept alive by people who sought to justify their own privilege and the oppression of specific groups. Some theorists agree that there are important differences among groups that affect the way people see themselves and others, but they see these differences as undesirable. The ideal of assimilation either denies the importance of social groups or sees them as undesirable.

In contrast, we doubt that a society without social groups is possible *or* desirable. Today, whether we like it or not, our society is structured by social groups that have important consequences for people's lives. Social groups do affect the way people see themselves and others in both positive and negative ways. People form their identities—their sense of who they are—in part through their membership in social or cultural groups. There is nothing inherently bad about people identifying with certain groups. Attachment to an ethnic tradition, language, culture, or set of common experiences has always been a feature of social life. The problem for a democratic nation occurs when group membership affects people's capacities to participate fully in our social institutions. In the United States today, some groups are privileged while others are oppressed. The politics of difference offers a way of retaining the positive, identity-affirming aspect of group difference while eliminating the negative aspect—the privileging of some groups over others.

The Oppressive Consequences of Ignoring Group Difference

None of the social movements that we have discussed deny the claim that the strategy of eliminating group difference and treating all groups the same has helped improve the situation of oppressed social groups. On the contrary, each of these social movements at one time pursued such a strategy. But why did they eventually begin to question its effectiveness in eliminating group oppression? Why was assimilation called into question?

Many of these social movements of oppressed groups found that the achievement of formal equality under the law did not put an end to their disadvantaged position. Even though in many respects the law is now blind to group differences like sex and race, certain groups continue to be oppressed while other groups are privileged. Many forms of oppression, such as racial slurs, are more subtle, yet they are just as corrosive than the more easily identifiable forms of overt and intentional discrimination. They persist in the structure of institutions that make it difficult for members of disadvantaged groups to develop their capacities. Oppression also exists in forms of everyday interaction and decision making in which people make assumptions about the aspirations and needs of women, African Americans, Hispanics, gay men and lesbians, and other groups that continue to be oppressed. The idea that equality and liberation can only be achieved by ignoring group differences has three oppressive consequences for disadvantaged social groups.

First, ignoring group difference disadvantages groups whose experience and culture differ from those of privileged groups. The strategy of assimilation aims to bring excluded groups into the mainstream of social life. But assimilation always implies coming into the game after it has already begun, after the rules and standards have already been set. Therefore, disadvantaged groups play no part in making up the rules and standards that they must prove themselves by—those rules and standards are defined by privileged groups. The rules and standards may appear to be neutral since they are applied equally to all groups. In actuality though, their formation was based only upon the experiences of privileged groups—oppressed groups being excluded from the rule-making process.

If such standards are applied equally to all groups, why do they then place some groups at a disadvantage? The real differences between oppressed groups and dominant groups often make it difficult for oppressed groups to measure up to the standards of the privileged. These real differences may have to do with cultural styles and values or with certain distinct capacities (for example, women's capacity to bear children). But quite often these differences are themselves the result of group oppression. For example, the long history of exclusion and marginalization of African American people from the economic and educational systems of this country has made it very difficult for many of them to gain the levels of educational attainment and technical skills that whites have. Yet, despite this history of oppression, they must compete for jobs on the basis of qualifications that are the same for all groups, including historically privileged groups.

The second oppressive consequence of ignoring group difference is that it allows privileged groups in society to see their own culture, values, norms, and experiences as universal (shared by all groups) rather than group specific. In other words, ignoring group differences allows the norms and values that express the point of view and experience of privileged groups to appear neutral and uncontroversial. When the norms and values of particular privileged groups are held as normal, neutral, and universal, those groups that do not adhere to those norms and values are viewed by society as deviant or abnormal. This issue is discussed in more detail in the chapter "Five Faces of Oppression."

When groups that do not share the supposedly neutral values and norms of privileged groups are viewed as deviant or abnormal, a third oppressive consequence of ignoring difference is produced. Members of those groups that are viewed as deviant often internalize society's view of them as abnormal or deviant. The internalization of the negative attitudes of others by members of oppressed groups often produces feelings of self-hatred and ambivalence toward their own culture. The ideal of assimilation asks members of oppressed groups to fit in and be like everyone else, yet society continues to see them as different, making it impossible for them to fit in comfortably. Thus, members of groups marked as different or deviant in comparison to privileged groups are caught in a dilemma they cannot resolve. On one hand, participating in mainstream society means accepting and adopting an identity that is not their own. And on the other, when they do try to participate, they are reminded by society and by themselves that they do not fit in.

The Liberating Consequences of the Politics of Difference

We have given three reasons why a strategy of assimilation that attempts to ignore, transcend, or devalue group differences is oppressive. We would now like to turn to the politics of difference and to explain the ways in which it is liberating and empowering for members of oppressed groups. The key difference between the politics of difference and the politics of assimilation lies in the definition of group difference itself. The politics of assimilation defines group difference in a negative way, as a liability or disadvantage to be overcome in the process of assimilating into mainstream society. In contrast, the politics of difference defines group difference in a positive way, as a social and cultural condition that can be liberating and empowering for oppressed groups. There are four ways in which this positive view of difference is liberating for oppressed groups.

First, a politics of difference that defines group difference in a positive way makes it easier for members of oppressed groups to celebrate and be proud of their identity, which the dominant culture has taught them to despise. In a politics of difference, members of oppressed groups are not asked to assimilate, to try to be something they are not. They are not asked to reject or hide their own culture as a condition of full participation in the social life of the nation. Instead, the politics of difference recognizes that oppressed groups have their own cultures, experiences, and points of view that have positive value for themselves *and* society as a whole. Some of their values and norms may even be superior to those of more privileged groups in society.

Second, by recognizing the value of the cultures and experiences of oppressed groups, the politics of difference exposes the values and norms of privileged groups as group specific, not neutral or universal. The politics of difference recognizes that the values and norms of privileged groups are expressions of their own experience and may conflict with those of other groups. In the politics of difference, oppressed groups insist on the positive value of their own cultures and experiences. When they insist on this, it becomes more and more difficult for dominant groups to parade their norms and values as neutral, universal, or uncontroversial. It also becomes more difficult for dominant groups to point to oppressed groups as deviant, abnormal, or inferior.

Thus, for example, when feminists assert the positive value of a caring and nurturing approach to the world, they call into question the competitive and individualistic norms of white male society. When African Americans proudly affirm the culture and history of Afro-America, they expose the culture and history of white society as expressing a particular experience—only *one* part of America's story. When Native Americans assert the value of a culture tied to and respectful of the land, they call into question the dominant culture's materialism, which promotes pollution and environmental destruction. All of these questions posed by oppressed groups suggest that the values and norms of dominant groups comprise one perspective, one way of looking at the world, that is neither neutral, shared, nor necessarily superior to the ways of oppressed groups.

When we realize that the norms and values of privileged groups are not universal, it becomes possible to think about the relation between groups in a more liberating way. Oppressed groups are not deviant with respect to privileged groups. They simply differ from privileged groups in their values, norms, and experiences, just as privileged groups are different from them. Difference is a two-way street; each group differs from the other; each earns the label "different." When the relations among groups are defined this way, we eliminate the assumption of the inferiority of oppressed groups and the superiority of privileged groups and replace it with a recognition and respect for the value of the particular experiences and perspectives of all groups.

Third, by asserting the positive value of different groups' experiences, the politics of difference makes it possible to look critically at dominant institutions and values from the perspective of oppressed groups. In other words, the experiences and perspectives of oppressed groups provide critical insights into mainstream social institutions and values that can serve as a starting point for reform of those institutions and values. For example, by referring to their members as "brother" or "sister," African Americans engender in their traditional neighborhoods a sense of community and solidarity not found in the highly individualistic mainstream society. As mentioned earlier, feminists find in the human values of nurturing and caring a more superior way of approaching social and ecological relations than the competitive, militarist, and environmentally destructive approach of male-dominated society. The politics of difference takes these critiques by oppressed groups seriously, as a basis for reform of dominant institutions. Such critiques shed light on the ways that dominant institutions should be changed so that they no longer reinforce patterns of privilege and oppression.

Fourth, the politics of difference promotes the value of group solidarity amidst the pervasive individualism of contemporary social life and the politics of assimilation. Assimilationist politics treats each person as an individual, ignoring differences of race, sex, religion, and ethnicity; everyone should be treated equally and evaluated according to his or her individual effort and achievement. It is true that under this politics of assimilation many members of oppressed groups have achieved individual success, even by the standards of privileged groups. However, as we have already learned, many groups continue to be oppressed despite the individual success of some group members. For example, over the last thirty years, Blacks have increased their representation in well-paying occupations such as law, medicine, and engineering. Yet they are still very much underrepresented in these fields and overrepresented in less well-paying occupations like orderlies, taxicab drivers, and janitors. That is why oppressed groups refuse to see these individual successes as evidence that group oppression has been eliminated. Instead of celebrating the success of some of their members, they insist that the celebration wait until their whole group is liberated. In the politics of difference, oppressed groups, in solidarity, struggle for the fundamental institutional changes that will make this liberation possible. We will discuss some of these changes later in the section, "Group Representation in Participatory Democracy."

By now, the distinctions between the politics of assimilation and the politics of difference should be clear. Some people might object to the way we have made these distinctions. We anticipate that the strongest objection will be that we have not presented fairly the advantages of a politics of assimilation that strives to transcend or get beyond group differences. Many who support the politics of assimilation do recognize the value of a pluralistic society in which a variety of lifestyles, cultures, and associations can flourish. We do not, however, take issue with this vision of a pluralistic society. What we emphasize is that this vision does not deal with fundamental issues that suggest the need for the politics of difference.

As we have repeated throughout this chapter, we think it is counterproductive and dishonest to try to eliminate the public and political significance of group difference in a society in which some groups are more privileged than others. The danger in this approach is that group differences get pushed out of the sphere of public discussion and action and come to be seen as a purely private or non-political matter. When this happens, the problem of oppression of some groups tends to go unaddressed in our public institutions, and patterns of privilege and oppression among groups are reinforced. The politics of difference that we advocate recognizes and takes seriously the public and political importance of group differences, and takes the experiences of oppressed groups as a starting point for reform of our public institutions. The goal of this politics of difference is to change our institutions so that no group is disadvantaged or advantaged due to its distinct culture or capacities, thus ensuring that all groups have the opportunity to participate fully in the nation's social and political institutions.

REDEFINING THE MEANING OF DIFFERENCE IN CONTEMPORARY LIFE

The Risk of Restigmatizing Oppressed Groups

Many people inside and outside the liberation movements we have discussed in this chapter are fearful of the politics of difference and its rejection of the politics of assimilation. The fear of many is that any public admission of the fact that groups are different will be used to justify once again the exclusion and separation of certain kinds of people from mainstream society. Feminists fear that the affirmation of values of caring and nurturing that are associated with motherhood will lead to a call for women to return to the kitchen and the home, places where it is claimed those values can best be utilized.

African Americans fear that an affirmation of their different values and experiences will lead again to a call for separate schools and communities, "where they can be with their own kind." Many in these groups are willing to accept the fact that formal equality (treating everyone the same under the law) reinforces current patterns of advantage. This, they say, is preferable to a politics of difference that risks the restigmatization of certain groups and the reestablishment of separate and unequal spheres for such groups.

We are sympathetic to these fears. It certainly is not unusual in political life for one's ideas, actions, or policies to have unintended negative effects because others have used them to justify ends different from those intended. Nevertheless, we believe that this risk is warranted since the strategy of ignoring group differences in public policy has failed to eliminate the problem of group oppression; the same patterns of privilege and oppression continue to be reproduced. All of which begs the question, Is there a way to avoid this risk of restigmatizing groups and rejustifying their exclusion?

We believe there is a solution, and it depends on redefining the meaning of difference itself.

Rejecting the Oppressive Meaning of Difference

In order to avoid the risk of recreating the stigma that oppressed groups have faced in the past, the meaning of difference itself must be redefined. In other words, we must change the way people think about differences among groups. In the politics of difference, the meaning of difference itself becomes an issue for political struggle.

There is an oppressive way of understanding difference that has dominated Western thinking about social groups for many centuries. This meaning of difference, which we will call the essentialist meaning, defines social groups in opposition to a normative group—typically the dominant social group. The culture, values, and standards of one social group provide the standards against which all other groups are measured.

The attempt to measure all groups against some universal standard or norm generates a meaning of difference as dichotomy, a relation of two opposites. Thus we have paired categories of groups—men/women, white/Black, healthy/disabled, rich/poor, young/old, civilized/uncivilized, to name a few. Very often, the second term in the pair is defined negatively in relation to the first. Those in the second category are defined as lacking valued qualities of those in the first. There are rational men, and there are irrational women. There are productive, active young people, and there are feeble old people. There is a superior standard of humanity, and there is an inferior one.

This way of thinking about difference as a good/bad opposition in which groups are defined in relation to a supposedly universal norm has oppressive consequences. Some groups are marked out as having different natures, which leads quickly to the assumption that they therefore must have different aspirations and dispositions that fit them for some activities and not others. It also leads to the argument that because nature is static, change is impossible. Women are defined as lacking men's rationality, which justifies their exclusion from high-ranking positions in business and government. People with disabilities are seen as unhealthy or helpless, which justifies isolating them in institutions.

The essentialist meaning of difference just described lies at the heart of racism, sexism, anti-Semitism, homophobia, and other negative attitudes toward specific groups. In these ideologies only the oppressed groups are defined as different. When oppressed groups are thought of as having fundamentally different natures from the "normal" group, it becomes easier for the "normal" group to justify excluding those groups from mainstream institutions and communities. On the other hand, once it is admitted that all groups have some things in common and that no group represents a universal or "normal" standard, it becomes more difficult to justify any group's exclusion from political and social life.

Redefining Difference as Variation

The politics of difference rejects the essentialist definition of difference, which defines it as deviance from a neutral norm and holds that some groups have essentially different natures and aspirations. In the politics of difference, however, group difference is seen as ambiguous and shifting, without clear categories of opposites that narrowly define people. Difference represents variation among groups that have similarities and dissimilarities. Groups are neither completely the same nor complete opposites. In the politics of difference, the meaning of group difference encompasses six key principles:

1. *Group difference is relational.* We can only understand groups in relation to each other. Group differences can be identified when we compare different groups, but no group can be held up as the standard of comparison. Thus, whites are just as specific a group as African Americans or Hispanics, men just as specific as women, able-bodied people just as specific as people with disabilities. Difference does not mean a clear and specific set of attributes that a group shares, but means variation and heterogeneity. It appears as a relationship between groups and the interaction of groups with social institutions.

2. *Group difference is contextual.* That difference is contextual simply means that group differences may be more or less relevant depending on the context or situation in which they come up. In any context, the importance of group difference will depend on the groups being compared and the reasons for the comparison. For example, in the context of athletics, health care, or social service support, wheel chair-bound people are different from others in terms of the special needs they might have. But in many other contexts, these differences would be unimportant. In the past, people with disabilities were often excluded and segregated in institutions because their physical difference was seen as extending to all their capacities and all facets of their lives. Understanding difference as contextual eliminates this oppressive way of thinking about difference as all-encompassing.

3. *Group difference does not mean exclusion.* An understanding of difference as relational and contextual rejects the possibility of exclusion. No two groups lie exclusively outside each other in their experiences, perspectives, or goals. All groups have overlapping experiences and therefore are always similar in some respects.

4. *Members within a group share affinity for each other, not a fixed set of attributes.* Groups are not defined by a fixed set of characteristics or attributes that all group members share. What makes a group a group is the fact that they have a particular affinity for each other. The people I have an affinity for are simply those who are familiar to me and with whom I feel the most comfortable. Feelings of affinity develop through a social process of interaction and shared experience. People in an affinity group often share common values, norms, and mean-

ings that express their shared experience. No person's affinities are fixed: a person's affinities may shift with changes in his or her life. Likewise, group identities may shift over time with changes in social realities. Group affinity is further discussed in the chapter "Five Faces of Oppression."

5. *Groups define themselves.* Once we reject the idea that groups are defined by a set of common, essential attributes, groups are left to define for themselves what makes their particular group a group. This process of *self*-definition is emancipating in that it allows groups to reclaim a positive meaning for their difference and to decide collectively what they wish to affirm as their culture. Thus, the culture of oppressed groups is no longer defined by dominant groups in negative relation to mainstream culture. Many social movements of oppressed groups have begun this process of redefining their group identity for themselves. Both African American and Native American social movements have sought to redefine and reaffirm their cultural distinctiveness, often reclaiming from the past traditional values and norms that have meaning for them today. Some gays and lesbians are reappropriating the term "queer" and redefining it themselves.

6. *All groups have differences within them.* Our society is highly complex and differentiated, and no group is free of intragroup difference. For instance, a woman who is African American and a lesbian might identify with a variety of social groups—women, African Americans, lesbians. A woman who is Hispanic and heterosexual might have different affinities. Within the context of a social movement such as the women's movement, these differences between women are potential sources of wisdom and enrichment as well as conflict and misunderstanding. Because there is a potential for conflict within groups among persons who identify with more than one group, groups, like society as a whole, must also be attentive to difference.

RESPECTING DIFFERENCE IN POLICY

In this section, we will discuss the kinds of policies called for by the politics of difference. This discussion depends on two key assumptions. The first is that our nation should strive for social justice in its political and social institutions. We define social justice as the realization of institutions that allow all people to develop and exercise their capacities, express their experiences, and participate in determining their actions and the conditions of their action. By this definition, institutions are unjust when they (1) limit some people's capacity for self-development or (2) prevent some people from participating in determining their actions or the social conditions of their actions. Thus, social justice is concerned with creating institutional frameworks that permit members of all social groups to flourish, and reform those that systematically prevent some people's self-development or participation.

An important goal of social justice is social equality. Social equality does not refer to the condition of everyone having an equal amount of social goods (like public services, schooling, health care) or material goods. Rather, it refers to the condition of full participation and inclusion in society's institutions and the opportunity for all people to develop and exercise their capacities and pursue their goals.

In our society, we have granted formal equality (equal treatment under the law) for members of all groups, with the exception of gay men and lesbians. Gay people have won some protections under the law, but these are not as comprehensive as those granted other groups. As we have demonstrated throughout this chapter, the achievement of formal equality has not put an end to the oppression of certain groups. Men continue to be more privileged than women, whites more privileged than African Americans and Hispanics, and so on. These persistent patterns of privilege and oppression suggest the need for a new approach to public policy that recognizes, encourages, and accommodates group difference rather than ignoring it.

Group-Neutral and Group-Conscious Policies

One of the key debates about policies to promote social equality concerns the issue of whether group-neutral or group-conscious policies are more effective in promoting equality. Group-neutral policies are those that ignore group differences and treat all groups according to the same laws and standards. Equal civil rights is an example of a group-neutral policy. Group-conscious policies, on the other hand, are those that recognize that some groups are more disadvantaged than others and offer special rights and protections to members of oppressed groups. Affirmative action is one kind of group-conscious policy.

Among liberation movements of oppressed groups, there is considerable disagreement about whether group-neutral or group-conscious policies should be pursued. Debates about this issue within these movements have been long and sometimes divisive. In this section, we argue that group-conscious policies are needed to undermine persistent patterns of privilege and oppression among different social groups. Later, we will illustrate through a discussion of two policy issues (pregnancy rights and workplace equality for women, and language policies for non-English speakers) how group-conscious policies undermine oppression.

But first, we must clarify the arguments against group-neutral policies. Why are policies that treat groups equally sometimes oppressive? There are two reasons. First, such policies rely on rules and standards that are presumed to be neutral and universal. All competitors for jobs or other social positions are measured according to these rules and standards. However, these rules and standards often are not neutral. They presume that the capacities, values, and experiences of dominant groups are shared by all groups. Groups that do not share these capacities, values, and experiences are disadvantaged as a result of these neutral rules and standards. This does not mean that some groups are inferior to others. Different capacities may be the result of long periods of discrimination or exclusion. For example, African Americans are disadvantaged by formally neutral rules and standards for jobs because they have been excluded and marginalized in the economic and educational systems for centuries. Women are disadvantaged by formally neutral standards for admission to engineering programs because for decades schools have reinforced gender stereotypes that women cannot excel as well as men in math and science.

Group-neutral policies also disadvantage some people because they fail to recognize the persistence of discrimination and negative attitudes toward oppressed groups, even when the law declares them equal and such attitudes illegal. Though the law may be blind to difference, in everyday interactions, people make assumptions about certain group members based on prejudice and stereotypes. Group-neutral policies tend to push such issues into the realm of private interaction. Yet private interactions like job interviews, credit applications, or real estate transactions impact significantly the lives of people who face persistent prejudice.

Despite these negative consequences of group-neutral policies, many people continue to support them. Some rules and standards may not be truly neutral, but an effort should be made to make them so. Though it may be possible in some cases to devise rules and standards that are truly neutral (that disadvantage no group), in many cases it is not possible. The cases we discuss later suggest that truly neutral policies are very difficult to achieve. But even if such policies were possible, they do not deal with the problem of negative attitudes and stereotypes that persist despite formal legal equality. The politics of difference argues that these negative attitudes cannot be eliminated by ignoring group difference, but rather can only be challenged by the positive recognition of the value of oppressed groups' cultures and experiences.

For example, television programs often present oppressive stereotypes of women, African Americans, Hispanics, and Native Americans. A group-neutral policy might seek to eliminate such stereotypes from television programs. However, merely eliminating negative portrayals does not deal with the need for many more positive and interesting portrayals of women and people of color that express their own experiences and self-perceptions. Remedying this problem might require active policies to encourage much greater participation by women and people of color in the creative processes of television than exists today.

Some people who support group-neutral policies and the assimilationist ideal of equal treatment are willing to accept group-conscious policies as a temporary means of reducing inequality among social groups. They often support affirmative action policies as a remedy for past discrimination and as a way of helping oppressed groups "catch up" to more privileged ones. We argue, however, that such temporary group-conscious policies conceive of social equality too narrowly. Group-conscious policies should be seen not only as a means of reducing inequality in the distribution of jobs or other social goods. They must also affirm the positive value of the culture and experience of oppressed groups. In other words, groups cannot be socially equal unless their specific culture and experience is recognized and respected as socially valuable by other groups.

A Dual System of Rights

Earlier in this chapter, we discussed the risk associated with the politics of difference and its recognition and affirmation of group differences. There is a danger that the implementation of group-conscious policies will restigmatize oppressed groups and lead some people to justify once again the exclusion of such groups from social institutions. How can group-conscious policies avoid this danger? One way is through a dual system of rights in which group-specific rights stand alongside the general civil and political rights guaranteed to all people.

Under such a system, any attempt to use group-conscious policies to exclude certain groups from participation in institutions or to justify discrimination against them will continue to be illegal under civil rights laws. Group-conscious policies are permitted only when they *promote* inclusiveness—that is, when they enhance oppressed groups' opportunities to participate fully in social and political institutions. Thus, the politics of difference calls for two sets of rights: a general system of rights that are the same for everyone, and a system of group-specific rights and policies that might vary for different oppressed groups. We will now consider two cases in which a set of group-specific policies is necessary to promote social equality: pregnancy rights and women's equality in the workplace, and language policy and bilingual education.

Pregnancy Rights and Women's Equality in the Workplace

Are women's interests best promoted through sex-neutral or sex-conscious public policies? In recent years, this question has been the subject of heated debate within the women's movement. Much of the debate has focused on the issue of women's equality in the workplace, and more specifically on the pregnancy and childbirth rights of working women.

Many feminists argue that women's interests are best protected when the law treats pregnancy and childbirth like any other temporary "disability" that male or female workers may face. Thus they push for the inclusion of pregnancy leaves and benefits within sex-neutral leave and benefit policies that apply to all workers. Pregnancy leaves and benefits then become the same as leaves and benefits for any illness that requires extended absence from work. As a consequence, pregnancy policies tend to vary widely from employer to employer and often depend on the generosity of employers' leave and benefit policies toward all workers.

Why are feminists reluctant to argue for special treatment of pregnant workers? Past experience makes them fearful that employers will use special classifications like pregnancy as an excuse for excluding and disadvantaging women. One can imagine the excuses that might be made. Women cannot be promoted as quickly because their childbearing capacity makes them likely to be absent from work for long periods. Women cannot be trained for certain jobs that are dangerous because they might one day become pregnant. In the politics of difference, however, these excuses would not be justified. Pregnancy policies would stand alongside general civil rights protections that would make such exclusion illegal.

In our view, the equal treatment approach to pregnancy is inadequate to ensure women's full participation in the workplace. Not only does it imply that women have no special right to leave and job security when having a baby, it also treats pregnancy itself as a disability. We object to the classification of pregnancy as a disability. Pregnancy and childbirth are normal conditions of normal, healthy women. They should not be stigmatized as unhealthy or as deviant from male-defined workplace norms of good health and attendance at work. Treating pregnancy and childbirth in this way also suggests that the only reason pregnant women have a right to miss work is the physically inability to do their jobs.

This conception of pregnancy fails to recognize that pregnant women have special needs that go beyond being unable to work. Childbearing itself is socially necessary work, and women need time to carry out that work. A woman ought to have the right to enough leave time to establish breast feeding with her child and to develop a relationship and routine with her child if she chooses. Pregnancy policies that attempt to encapsulate pregnancy under some sex-neutral category of disability tend to ignore these special needs, and, as a consequence, deny women sufficient time with their newborn children.

The politics of difference recognizes and affirms these special needs and calls for policies that allow women the opportunity to bear children without giving up the right to self-development in the workplace. At a minimum, this would require employers to offer more generous leave policies designed explicitly for women having children. It might also involve considerable restructuring of workplace policies to ensure that women are not disadvantaged by their capacity to bear children. A number of steps that employers might take in that direction include providing day care in or near the workplace, giving women the option of working part-time in the first year of their child's life, or allowing women to work from home when feasible. Because it is unlikely that most employers will take such action on their own, women should press for group-conscious policies that alter male-dominated institutions in accordance with their needs.

Language Policy and Bilingual Education

In 1986, the majority of voters in California supported a referendum declaring English the official language of that state. The ramifications of this policy are not clear, but it does mean that the state has no obligation to print ballots and other public literature or provide services in any other language but English. The California referendum spawned numerous movements across the country to declare English the official language of the United States, especially in areas with large populations of people whose first language is not English.

Many proponents of this movement justify it on the grounds that it saves the government money. However, what lies behind it is a not-so-subtle appeal to national unity and the assimilation of linguistic minorities. Many proponents of this movement see non-English-speaking people as a threat to the cultural identity of the nation. They argue that the nation cannot survive without a common identity shared by all citizens—a common language being one of the most important foundations of such a common identity. A society that includes many cultures and languages within it will certainly be beset by conflict, divisiveness, and ultimately disintegration, the argument goes. Establishing English as the official language supports a common national identity and encourages non-English speakers to assimilate more quickly.

There are several reasons why this assimilationist policy is wrong. First, it is unrealistic. The United States has always had sizeable linguistic and cultural minorities and will continue to for some time. In the past twenty-five years, there has been a huge influx of Latin Americans and Asians into this country. Their numbers are large and growing. In many public school districts across the nation (including San Antonio and Phoenix), Hispanic children comprise the majority of all students.

Second, the idea of one cultural and linguistic identity to which all must aspire is oppressive. It asks people to transform their sense of identity in order to "make it" in mainstream life. This is an unreasonable requirement of citizenship, and one which many linguistic minorities have rejected. For example, many Latino groups have maintained their distinct culture in this country, even some whose members have lived here for several generations. Though some members have assimilated, others have not and maintain strong ties to Mexico, Puerto Rico, and other Latin American countries.

Third, the idea of a single, common, national culture does not succeed in its stated aim of creating a harmonious nation. While it is true that societies with many linguistic and cultural groups often experience conflict, divisiveness, and civil war, the primary cause of such conflict is not group difference itself, but the relations of domination and oppression among groups, which produce resentment and hostility. Holding up the dominant culture as the norm only makes conflict worse because it allows dominant groups to devalue the experiences and perspectives of oppressed groups.

The issue of language is particularly important in education policy. In 1974, the Supreme Court ruled that the state had an obligation to remedy the English language deficiency of its students so that they would have an equal opportunity to learn all subjects. However, the court did not specify what types of education programs should be implemented. In the United States today, bilingual education is a controversial issue, especially in those districts with large linguistic minorities. The Bilingual Education Act of 1978 set aside funds for use by schools in developing bilingual education programs, but most non-English-speaking students still do not receive programs that meet their linguistic needs.

Presently, nearly all the programs that have been implemented throughout the public school system are assimilationist in intent. That is, they strive to bring students up to par in English, but do little to help the student maintain and develop his or her first language. Some programs, such as English as a Second Language, provide no instruction in students' first language and often are taught by persons who cannot speak that language. In other programs, often called immersion programs, students are instructed mainly in English but by a bilingual teacher who can question students in both languages. The third and least common type of programs are transitional programs in which some courses are taught in students' native language, with English instruction introduced gradually as students become more proficient.

Most Americans support programs for students with limited English in order to help them learn English. However, the more such programs instruct in a native language, the more they are considered by English speakers to be unfair and special treatment of minorities and a waste of taxpayer's money.

The last model, and what we believe to be the preferable model for bilingual education, bilingual-bicultural maintenance programs, is rarely practiced in the United States today. Bilingual-bicultural maintenance programs attempt to accomplish two goals: (1) develop and reinforce students' knowledge of their native language and culture, and (2) train them to become proficient in English. These programs do not ask students to leave behind their native language and culture in order to succeed in school. Instead, they respect the value of this language and culture and strive to maintain it, even as students become more proficient in English.

In the politics of difference, bilingual-bicultural maintenance programs are preferable to those that expect students to assimilate. This does not mean that students should not become proficient in English. Proficiency in English is a vital condition of full participation in American society. There are, however, different ways to achieve that proficiency, and we recommend programs that allow students to hold on to their linguistic and cultural identities as they become proficient in English.

In both the cases of pregnancy rights and bilingual education, we have argued for a set of group-conscious policies that both affirm group differences and seek to ensure that groups are not disadvantaged in pursuing self-development and full participation in social institutions. The set of group-specific policies and rights needed to ensure this participation is not the same for every oppressed group, but depends on the specific situation and specific institutional context. Group-specific policies and rights are warranted when they are needed to promote social justice—to protect a group's cultural autonomy and to address its needs as an oppressed minority.

GROUP REPRESENTATION IN PARTICIPATORY DEMOCRACY

Why Group Representation Is Needed

We have argued throughout this chapter that the possibility of full participation in social and political life for all people is a requirement of a just society. In our democracy, however, groups do not participate on an equal basis. Some groups are more privileged than others, in terms of wealth, organizational resources, and political power. Because the experiences and perspectives of dominant groups are taken to be the norm, the voices of oppressed groups often go unheard, or when they are heard, they may be deemed deviant or abnormal.

There is a good deal of evidence to support the notion that some groups have a harder time being heard in the political process than others. One key problem is that women, African Americans, Hispanics, and gay people are underrepresented in legislative bodies at the state level and in Congress, and hold few high-level positions in government. Even at the local level, oppressed groups have difficulty expressing their interests. A number of studies of public forums and town meetings have found that women, African Americans, working-class, and poor people tend to participate less and have their interests represented less than whites, middle-class professionals, and men. White middle-class men typically assume roles of authority and are usually more practiced at public speaking. Women, old people, and poor people often find it more difficult to get to public meetings because of responsibilities in the home or lack of transportation. And even when they do attend, they are hesitant to speak out of fear that they may not be articulate enough or that others will not take them seriously.

In these and other cases, the relations of privilege and oppression between groups have an effect on public participation, even though the nation claims to be blind to difference. Some groups are consistently heard more than others because of the wealth, organizational resources, and power they possess. Because privileged groups often dominate public discussion of political issues, we need to have some mechanisms to ensure that the voices of oppressed groups are heard.

We offer the following principle as a solution: in any public forum or discussion of political issues, whether at the federal, state, regional, or community level, the institutions concerned should provide mechanisms for the recognition and representation of the voices and perspectives of oppressed or disadvantaged groups in the community. In order for group representation to be effective, it should be implemented in accordance with three principles:

1. Oppressed groups should have access to institutions and public resources to support the self-organization of group members so that they can empower themselves collectively and decide together what their interests are in a particular context.
2. Institutions concerned should facilitate and provide resources for group analysis and development of policy proposals in contexts where decision makers are required to take group perspectives into consideration.
3. Oppressed groups should have group veto power over policies that affect them directly, such as abortion rights policy for women or land use policy for Indian reservations.

Specific representation for oppressed groups in the decision making processes of our democracy would promote justice more effectively than current democratic procedures in which some groups are consistently heard more than others. There are four ways in which group representation promotes justice.

First, it assures more fairness in setting the public agenda and hearing opinions about matters on that agenda. Some groups are socially and economically more privileged than others and have the financial, personal, and organizational resources to enable them to speak and be heard. As a result, discussion of policy issues is often distorted and biased because the ideas and perspectives presented are those of the privileged. Specific representation of oppressed groups helps to correct this distortion because it gives voice to the perspectives and priorities of oppressed groups, resulting in more inclusive dialogue.

Second, because group representation ensures that both the privileged and the oppressed have an opportunity to be heard, it better ensures that all needs and interests in society will be given consideration in democratic discussions. In many political discussions today, privileged groups do not advance the interests of oppressed groups— partly because they do not understand those interests and partly because their privilege depends on the continued exclusion and oppression of some groups. While groups may share many needs that all groups can express, often their difference means that they have specific needs that are best expressed by them. Thus, group representation facilitates the public expression of needs by those who tend to go unheard in many forums. It also reduces the possibility that certain groups can be excluded from key elements of social life. When groups are guaranteed representation, they may feel more comfortable calling for group-specific policies to address their needs. Representation helps ensure that any group-specific policies enacted are designed to help them, not hurt them.

Third, group representation helps all groups to understand each other's needs since it forces them to discuss their needs in terms of an appeal to justice. In other words, groups must give reasons for their needs in terms that other groups can understand and recognize as legitimate. Such a process makes it more difficult for privileged groups to pass off their self-interests as legitimate social needs. Demands for public action to meet needs are tested in a public discussion in which groups confront the opinion of other groups who may have very different needs. In a process of discussion in which all groups participate and give reasons for their needs, it is more likely that self-interest, rather than justice, will be exposed as the motivation behind the needs of the privileged.

Finally, group representation promotes just outcomes of public action because it increases social knowledge and practical wisdom in policy making. How is social knowledge increased by group representation? Groups have different needs, interests, and goals as well as different communities and experiences. As a consequence, they have different knowledge bases. A certain group may know more about an institution or a place than another. Because of its particular experience, a certain group may have a better understanding of the likely impact a public policy may have on a particular place or group of people than another group may have. By including all group perspectives in public discussions, we will be more likely to arrive at wise and just decisions.

Which Groups Are Represented?

Some people will surely object to the principle of group representation offered here on the grounds that in a society as complex as ours, hundreds of groups would demand to be represented. However, in the politics of difference, only certain kinds of groups would require representation. There are two criteria. First, the principle of group representation applies only to *social* groups, not interest groups or ideological groups. A social group is a collective of people who have affinity for one another because they share a set of experiences or a way of life. Members of a social group take themselves to be different from at least one other group in terms of their culture or experiences. We have talked about many social groups throughout this chapter: Native Americans, women, and gay men and lesbians, among others.

In contrast, an interest group is an association of persons who join together to promote a particular goal or policy with respect to a specific issue or set of issues. Mothers Against Drunk Drivers (MADD) is an example of an interest group. An ideological group is a group of persons who share political beliefs. Nazis, socialists, feminists, and anti-abortionists are ideological groups. Neither of these kinds of groups is a social group. Further discussion of social groups can be found in the chapter "Five Faces of Oppression."

Second, the principle of group representation we advocate calls for representation only for oppressed or disadvantaged social groups. Privileged groups are already represented, in the sense that their voice and experience tend to dominate public discussions. The chapter "Five Faces of Oppression" provides criteria for determining whether a group is oppressed and therefore whether it deserves special representation.

Implementing a Principle of Group Representation

So far, we have limited our discussion of group representation to political institutions and public decision making. Though we certainly advocate group representation in representative bodies at all levels of government, the principle of group representation should not be restricted to government institutions. Social justice requires a much wider implementation of democratic principles than currently is the case in American society. Put simply, people should have the right to participate in the making of rules and policies of any institution with authority over their actions. This principle extends beyond government to the workplace, schools, social service organizations, community groups, and other social institutions. It also applies to oppressed groups themselves. The decision-making bodies of women's groups should include representation of African American and Hispanic women. African American and Hispanic groups should give representation to African American and Hispanic women.

The principle of group representation called for here is not the equivalent of proportional representation. Proportional representation is a system of representation used in many other countries that allocates seats in a representative body to various groups in proportion to their numbers in the electorate. In other words, a group that is 20 percent of the electorate would be entitled to 20 percent of the seats. Proportional representation of oppressed groups may sometimes be too much or too little to accomplish the aim of having the needs of such groups met. For example, if the members of Congress were elected by a system of proportional representation, an election might result in no seats for Native Americans, since they comprise such a small part of the population. On the other hand, allocating half of all seats in representative bodies to women might be more than is required to have their needs addressed and might make it more difficult for other groups to be represented.

There are some precedents for the kind of group representation we advocate within contemporary social movements. Many political organizations, unions, and feminist groups have established formal caucuses within them for African Americans, Latinos, women, gay men and lesbians, people with disabilities, old people, and others whose perspectives might go unheard without specific representation. Some of these organizations even require members of disadvantaged groups to be represented in their leadership bodies.

A number of mainstream organizations have also implemented a principle of group representation. The National Democratic Party has rules requiring the representation of women and people of color as delegates to national conventions. Many nonprofit agencies require representation of women, blacks, Latinos, and people with disabilities on their boards of directors. And some corporations have even instituted limited representation of oppressed social groups on their boards and in corporate discussions.

Some might argue against a principle of group representation on the grounds that it would exacerbate conflict and divisiveness in public life and make it impossible to reach decisions. Especially if groups had veto power over policies that fundamentally affected them, there would be no hope of getting anything done in politics. We offer three counterarguments to this objection.

First, the objection that nothing would get done assumes that there will be irresolvable conflicts of interest among groups. But this is not so. Groups may have different perspectives about some issues, but they may often be compatible, and a general discussion concerning them may improve everyone's understanding of a problem. Second, group representation has the potential to decrease conflict, not increase it. Patterns of privilege and oppression among groups are the real source of conflict among groups. Group representation can help to change those patterns by equalizing the ability of groups to express their needs and be heard. Thus, over time, group representation should diminish certain kinds of conflict. Finally, even if group representation did stall decision making sometimes, in many cases stalled decisions would be more just than the continued systematic silencing of some voices in political life.

Implementing principles of group representation in national and local politics in the United States or in particular institutions such as factories, offices, universities, churches, schools, and social service agencies will obviously require creative thinking and flexibility on the part of all who participate in these institutions. We have no simple formulas to offer, and there are few models to follow. But this difficulty does not lead us to abandon the idea. Already there are social movements in this country that have implemented group representation in their organizational structures. It remains to be seen whether they will push the issue of group representation in national political institutions onto the public agenda.

CONCLUSION

This chapter relies on a handful of clear principles, which we will summarize here. Social justice requires democracy. People should be involved in collective discussion and decision making in all the settings that ask for their obedience to rules—workplaces, schools, neighborhoods, and so on. Unfortunately, these social and political institutions privilege some groups over others. When some groups are more disadvantaged than others, ensuring democracy requires group representation for the disadvantaged. Group representation gives oppressed groups a voice in setting the public agenda and discussing matters on it. It also helps to ensure just outcomes of the democratic process by making sure that the needs and interests of all groups are expressed.

Throughout this chapter, we have asserted that the ideal of a society that eliminates, transcends, or ignores group difference is both unrealistic and undesirable. Justice in a society with groups requires the social equality of all groups, and mutual and explicit recognition and affirmation of the value of group differences. The politics of difference promotes social equality and undermines group oppression by affirming the value of group difference, attending to group-specific needs, and providing for group representation in social institutions.

The challenges faced by such a politics are formidable. While many public and private institutions have begun to recognize the value of diversity, demands for a real voice for oppressed groups in decision-making processes are often met with fear and hostility. Still, we are hopeful that a politics of difference may be on the horizon. The United States is becoming more diverse, not less. Women and minorities comprise increasing proportions of the labor force and their needs are more and more difficult for employers and public officials to ignore.

However, demographic changes alone are unlikely to induce substantive policy change. Politics matters. While oppressed groups are increasing their representation in political institutions, social movements of oppressed groups will continue to play a critical role in shaping attitudes and dialogues about change and mobilizing the public to act. It is our hope that the ideas in this chapter provide a source of inspiration to social movements. The politics of difference is an alternative vision of politics that challenges the assumption that the present system is the only or best system. It is not meant as a blueprint for change, but as a starting point for dialogue. It provides a standpoint from which we can identify forms of injustice in our current institutions and explore different strategies to remedy them.

2

A Multicultural America: Living in a Sea of Diversity

John A. Garcia

For many years, the changing demographic fabric of the United States has been the subject of much public discourse and debate. At the same time, issues of lifestyle preferences and challenges to traditional views about gender, race and ethnicity, and class roles have raised central questions revolving around what it means to live in America. Demographic projections indicate a near majority of the U.S. population will be of minority origin by 2040. Within this context, ideas of multiculturalism, diversity, unity, balkanization, the United States as a melting pot, and assimilation have filled the news and print media as well as many books exploring the meaning and consequences of these ideas. This chapter serves to explore the critical facets of multiculturalism that extend beyond the development of curriculum and symposia in our educational institutions.

In this chapter I want to focus on the meaning of multiculturalism in our modern society. Why do the varying responses to multiculturalism take the form they do? How will the demographic imperatives of the future translate into societal redefinitions of power relations, cultural dominance versus heterogeneity, and institutional arrangements based on multicultural group status? Any discussion of multiculturalism must also consider the meaning of "difference" in modern society. The transformation of this nation into a multicultural society could result in a nation that voluntarily and openly accepts and garners the benefits of contributing traditions, values, philosophies, and behaviors. This trend, though, is struggling against a social structure that has been perceived to be grounded upon a dominant culture and value system. Thus, multiculturalism and difference are challenging cultural and ideological supremacy and upsetting the sense of naturalness and neutrality that infused most peoples' sense of modern society.

The U.S. American ethos values individualism, egalitarianism, equality of opportunity, and emphasis on Western cultures, among other things. These values have historically been ingredients of a pervasive American tradition that serves as a cultural core that all members of society (citizens or not) internalize, thus ensuring societal stability and gradual change. Indigenous populations like Native American tribes were brought into the American social system via conquest. They have either remained isolated Native Americans or they have conformed to the "American tradition." Succeeding waves of immigrants have undergone a similar acculturation and assimilation process in which acquisition of and dependence upon a national ideology is attained. The predominance of the American "melting pot" thesis is represented by the acceptance of an adaptation process encountered by all groups entering American society.

With a diversity of cultural as well as racial and ethnic groups continually entering the United States (voluntarily or involuntarily), group differences are acknowledged, but in transitional terms. That is, group members are expected to internalize American values within the first generation. Their own group traditions and values are to be replaced in a short period of time. Although characterization of group difference in reference to values, attitudes, language, or behaviors may be compared neutrally, in reality, too often supremacy is the result of such a comparison. Being different from the dominant culture implies incompatibility, inferiority, and non-integration into the wider social sphere. Thus, multiculturalism is believed to represent, at minimum, a challenge, but more likely a threat to the foundation of this country's "greatness" and strength.

DEFINING MULTICULTURALISM

The definition of multiculturalism requires consideration in addition to an analysis of its relevance to contemporary American society. The most prevalent view of multiculturalism is rooted in race and ethnicity. Multiculturalism is a sustained effort by racial and ethnic groups to recover, preserve, and achieve recognition for their distinct cultural identities from society at large. Clearly then, multiculturalism represents a resistance to the cultural amalgamation of the American "melting pot," which limits the number of pathways leading to successful integration. Assimilation is viewed as the only option available for members of minority racial and ethnic groups.

An additional facet of multiculturalism broadens this view and promotes public awareness of human diversity. This latter view would incorporate gender, sexual orientation, and lifestyle alternatives that are deemed outside the purview of traditional American values. In this light, seeing society comprised of interdependent peoples, some of whom are challenging what is acceptable in mainstream culture, gives rise to a subversion of that mainstream culture. However specifically or broadly the term multiculturalism is defined, an empowering process is central to the accomplishment of a multicultural nation.

The debate, then, over bringing to fruition a multicultural society centers around costs and negative consequences. That is, racial and ethnic groups are seen as weakening core values and the cultural system by refusing to blend in and accept the dominant ideology and culture. Multiculturalists are also perceived to be a direct challenge to national loyalty: ethnic preservationists are insubordinate to the central political system, and their weakened loyalty undermines both social and political stability. Antagonists of multiculturalism argue that even multiple loyalties (i.e., to one's own racial and/or ethnic group, gender, sexual orientation, national polity, etc.) serve to minimize the central social and political fabric that ensures national pride, advancement, and international domination. Hence, members of multicultural groups are seen as opponents of mainstream society, patriotism, and world domination.

The assault on multiculturalism has been carried out in the name of patriotism and supremacy in a competitive global community. True loyalty to the nation is characterized by heightened national chauvinism and a claim for U.S. superiority over all other nations. Consider the claim made by William J. Bennett (secretary of education during the Reagan administration) regarding any changes in college and university humanities curricula. As secretary of education, he argued against changing the traditional Western civilization curriculum because, he claimed, Western societies formulated the social standards which all peoples throughout the world have embraced, or if they haven't yet, ought to. The introduction, review, and integration of non-Western ideas, values, and aesthetics would be incompatible with patriotism and national chauvinism.

Indeed, the impact of incorporating multiculturalism into the dominant values system could well challenge patriotism in the sense that loyalty entails an individual's sense of superiority over all individuals and nations of the world. An understanding of different cultures, traditions, belief systems, histories, and ideas and perspectives is a worthy goal and should be integrated into our value system. Within such a developing multicultural society, the open interchange and interaction could produce educational, business, social, intellectual, and possibly interfamilial ties within situations in which issues of superiority among peoples and nations would no longer be relevant.

Thus the issue should not be whether the United States is moving toward a multicultural society or not, but how multiculturalism fits within the social and political institutions and processes. We are a nation comprised of persons from many different countries, with many different cultural traditions and values, mother tongues, and psychological senses of one's own history. At the same time, all groups undergo cultural transformation to assume some characteristics and identification with the dominant culture and institutions. With this discussion, the inclusion of the concept of American pluralism will be extended beyond the current paradigm of liberal pluralism.

LIBERAL AND CORPORATE PLURALISM

One of the primary areas of contention in the United States deals with formal, legal recognition and distributive rewards based on minority status. For the most part, official governmental actions have not recognized *groups* as special categories eligible for benefits or targeted sanctions. The idea of freedom of choice allows each person to work out his or her differences and goals such that banding together is voluntary. As a result, racial and/or ethnic associations, residential patterns, and cultural practices, or the absence of them, are the result of individual and voluntary action.

In this context, the only basis for governmental intervention is the prevention of differential treatment or discrimination based on individual and/or group characteristics. The formal protections in law and the Constitution identify such categories as previous conditions of servitude, race, national origin, gender, and so forth. Even though ascriptive traits are identified in individual terms, legal protections are typically applied to members of a group. Legislation that deals with open housing, fair employment practices, voting rights, public accommodations, and education serve to ensure that freedom of choice is available to all members of society. This does not necessarily mean that government is endorsing or mandating integration or even that group rights should supersede individual rights. Rather, it is ensuring the existence of an environment that will live up to the ideals of equality, freedom, opportunity, and individual worth when the rest of us are failing to live up to these ideals. The actions of government incorporate principles of liberal pluralism which recognize the disparity between American values and the opportunities available to racial and ethnic group members.

The activism and turmoil of the 1960s heightened the awareness of the disempowered status of minority groups in American society when formal demands by racial and ethnic groups for full implementation of the American dream were pressed. Recognition of cultural groups serves to alter prevailing power relationships and assert the intrinsic value of non-dominant cultures within the American mainstream. Formal standing within the polity postulates group rights and status in terms of both political power and economic rewards. Some scholars have identified this type of pluralism as "corporate pluralism." If this political condition exists, a distributive formula is subsequently created that defines group membership as a critical factor in individual outcomes. The state defends group as well as individual rights.

While corporate pluralism does not exist in this country, affirmative action policies could be considered an antecedent. Government-mandated and court-upheld affirmative action policies of the past twenty-five years in employment, education, athletics, and government contracts can be viewed as a step toward corporate pluralism. Proponents of these steps consider them short-term and compensatory techniques to remedy the accumulated effects of discrimination. Yet the active desires and demands of multicultural groups do represent sustained efforts to alter existing power relationships and ensure more equal status by formalizing group recognition within the policies of political institutions.

Thus a critical dimension within the discussion of the multicultural debate is the status of individuals and group membership in American society. Individual rights, freedoms, responsibilities, and obligations are widely established within the American ethos and legal principles. On the other hand, official group rights and privileges are largely foreign to the American system. Groups can have protective status from discriminatory practices, but distributive rewards based on race and ethnicity are seldom mandated. Therefore, how the American legal system deals with according group rights, in addition to individual rights, is an area for potential contention and redefinition.

Cultural differences among racial and ethnic groups and how social and political institutions deal with such differences lies at the heart of societal tensions. What is the role of institutions in defining the maximum amount of freedom groups and individuals warrant while minimizing ancestral heritage as a consideration? The American ethos would dictate giving individuals who are from racial and ethnic groups the maximum amount of freedom of choice. At the same time, though, there would neither be any bonus points given for racial and/or ethnic persistence nor penalties extracted for drawing away from racial and/or ethnic membership. There would not be any inherent promotion of one multicultural group over another.

This public policy position maintains that the American ethos serves as the dominant national character and mode. Liberal pluralism would be tolerant of differences as long as they were perceived in as neutral a manner as possible. The role of multicultural groups would be to keep the political system honest so that violations of neutrality would be raised and challenged.

A court case that exemplifies the questioning of the neutrality of difference is the "separate but equal" principle represented in the *Plessy v. Fergusson* decision. The case held that as long as comparable facilities and services existed, separation of persons by race was deemed consistent with the American ethos. Yet the debate and evidence presented sixty years later in *Brown v. Board of Education of Topeka* documented that segregating individuals by race established differences that engendered perceptions of superiority and inferiority, and caused stigmatization. As a result, the "separate but equal" principle had established inequalities based on race. With this decision and through the efforts of the NAACP and other organizations, a more neutral ground was established regarding group difference. The lesson to be learned, therefore, is that the liberal pluralist perspective of maintaining a neutral policy on difference might require that multicultural groups serve as watchdogs, advocates, and challengers to public policies that might impose or perpetuate institutional sanctions against a non-neutral notion of difference.

Corporate pluralism places a high value on cultural diversity. It actively encourages ethnic and racial preservation. It assumes that groups can play a major role in bringing about social justice. In this way, the presence of many and diverse multicultural groups in the United States represents a mosaic of cultural subpatterns that coexist under some overall framework of national integration and harmony. Therefore, the plentiful cultural mosaic provides a richer cultural life for everyone.

Advocates of multiculturalism do not merely emphasize moral and philosophical imperatives for the reconfiguration of the social order. Multiculturalism goes far beyond an appreciation for, the maintenance of, and better understanding of diverse cultures and groups; it focuses on the empowerment of racial and ethnic groups. Public policies that establish group rights and promote group differences should be viewed as proper goals for political institutions. Such an approach would engender an idea of difference that is more inclusive, less value laden, and non-hierarchical. In this way, individuals in society would not use difference as an inducement to judgments of superiority over other persons and groups, but rather they would appreciate and understand the differences that do exist as well as the commonalties that connect all neighbors.

LANGUAGE PERSISTENCE AND PUBLIC POLICY

The persistence of language groups presents another controversy for opponents of multiculturalism. What will be the official language policy for the conduct of public affairs and discourse? The American tradition has followed a practice of de facto monolingualism. For the past ten years, referendum efforts in many states have enacted "official English" legislation. These referenda typically mandate English usage in the educational system and for all legal documents and procedures. No other language is given official standing. These referenda serve to legitimate and reinforce institutional monolingualism and the expectation that full citizenship requires acceptance of English as one's mother tongue. However, supporters don't necessarily endorse hostile actions toward non-English groups that teach or maintain their mother tongue. Non-English-language maintenance can be taught at home or in private cultural schools for cultural and non-official purposes.

While this position characterizes the current situation, pressures for bilingual educational programs, bi- or multilingual court interpreters, and public records like ballots and notices have also been recent policy developments. These programs have been justified, in a legal sense, as fulfilling due process protections or making possible transitional assistance until better command of English is achieved. Therefore, the presence of other languages does not necessarily constitute elevating languages other than English into official status.

The recognition of a group's language as well as group status raises some other concerns about the impact of multiculturalism on the American ethos. Individualism and individual rights are deeply embedded in the American tradition. A person's achievements are based on individual initiative, abilities, perseverance, and performance (referred to as individual meritocracy). Such a view emphasizes the centrality of individualism and upward mobility, and one's achievements are seen as the result of individual efforts. In this context, political institutions and processes serve to prevent discriminatory practices that would impede an individual's effort to excel.

The tension for greater recognition of multiculturalism lies with individual and group rights. This can be illustrated by the distinction between equality of opportunity and equality of results. American values and policies dictate an "even playing field" for all members of society so that individual talents and differences can be realized. The goal of equality of results is based on the overall status of groups in the larger social structure. A person's economic status, access to political representation, and access to program participation is compared with that of individuals from other racial and ethnic groups and the "dominant" group. Any disparities across groups can result in governmental intervention to equalize group status.

Advocates of multiculturalism emphasize not only moral and philosophical imperatives for the reconfiguration of a different social order; they also demand the empowerment of multicultural groups. Promoting group rights as well as individual rights and affirmative public actions to protect and encourage the expression of difference, are seen as appropriate tasks of government.

Opponents of multiculturalism would contend that the current generation of majority-group members should not be expected to pay for the sins of previous generations. Majority-group backlash signifies a direct challenge to the greater incorporation of multiculturalism and a return to the myth of individual meritocracy. Antagonists see such pressures as undermining fundamental values, processes, and principles of the American democratic experiment. On the other hand, corporate pluralism would actively support multilingualism. Multicultural groups would have the right to maintain their ancestral languages and would be encouraged to do so. Having only one official language for the polity would not be the case. In fact, all members of the nation would be encouraged or perhaps compelled to become bi- or multilingual.

MULTICULTURALISM: A SOCIETY'S ADAPTATION OR NOT

I began this chapter by trying to discuss multiculturalism in American society in terms of its critical features and fundamental challenges to the American ethos. The reality of the changing demography of this nation implants the long-term presence of racial and ethnic groups and the dynamic processes that preserve and perpetuate cultural differences. The myth of the American melting pot has been scrutinized and dismantled. Group social identities do persist beyond the first generation of multicultural groups, and the dominant society's responses and actions toward them helps to accent the differences. I have tried to suggest that the issues revolving around multiculturalism extend over and above intergroup cultural understanding and respect. The issue of multiculturalism also confronts the prevailing social order of power relationships, defining and interpreting the meaning and value of American life and the empowerment of multicultural groups more distant from the dominant culture. As a result, I defined multiculturalism in two interrelated ways. The first focuses on racial and ethnic groups and their efforts to promote, preserve, and achieve recognition as contributing members of the social and institutional fabric of this nation. I also included a broader definition of multiculturalism to include the broadest range of the human diversity (i.e. diversity based on gender, sexual orientation, lifestyle alternatives, etc.). The purpose of this chapter in the context of this book is to discuss multiculturalism at the macro level. That is, I chose not to focus on the aspects of multiculturalism and the educational system that deal with teaching diversity and broadening understanding. While an understanding of diverse peoples is central in any discussion of multiculturalism, I decided to direct my discussion to the role of sociopolitical institutions and dominant cultural values in relation to racial and ethnic groups.

As a result, I introduced the ideas of dominant culture, assimilation, American ethos, liberal and corporate pluralism, and group status. Basically, I tried to establish that this country's efforts to deal with differences (especially racial, linguistic, and cultural ones) have been influenced by ideas of supremacy, pervasive Western standards of worth, and domination for conformity. It comes as no real surprise that tensions and clashes arise over the perceived notions of multiculturalism that this process entails. Individuals who desire cultural and ideological uniformity reintroduce the tenets of mandatory conversion of all racial and ethnic groups to accept and internalize all aspects of the dominant culture. My introduction of the concept of pluralism serves to more accurately represent the diverse sociocultural fabric that has existed and still exists in this nation. Pluralism is based upon the existence of identifiable groups with their own special interests. Thus, a primary role of sociopolitical institutions is to reflect and implement democratic processes that include access, interest articulation, and participation in the decision-making process. Liberal pluralism recognizes group differences but does not intervene in the maintenance or dismantling of multicultural groups. It serves to protect the opportunity to continue group membership and impose sanctions against discriminatory practices.

In contrast, I juxtaposed the model of corporate pluralism with liberal pluralism. The former incorporates racial and ethnic groups more formally into the institutions and policy outcomes of the polity. Formal recognition, distribution of rewards and allocations, and ensuring official group status become appropriate activities of government. This approach to the formal incorporation of multiculturalism appends group rights to accompany the tradition of individual rights. In addition, formal incorporation would suggest a reconfiguration of power relationships such that multicultural groups achieve some basic paradigm shifts with the American ethos. That is, institutionalization of group recognition and rights, inclusion of multicultural systems into the dominant culture (systems that are currently marginalized), and an ideology of difference that is more neutral and intrinsically positive would be concrete examples of a new social order in America. The empowerment of multicultural groups would be a primary force if such institutional changes were realized.

So what contribution does this chapter provide in the extensive review, analysis, and advocacy for or opposition to multiculturalism? My perspective is intended to suggest that public discourse and institutional responses are the critical contexts for dealing with multiculturalism. Very basic assumptions and challenges to the ideological and institutional configuration of this sociopolitical system are intertwined with the examination of multiculturalism. The diversity that exists in this country already (racially and ethnically) will continue to be even more evident in the twenty-first century. How we will maintain a positive level of tolerance for diversity, at a minimum, seems quite clear in light of certain principles within the corpus of the American ethos as well as legal traditions. The remaining question may center more on whether the further inclusion and expansion of the American ethos would strengthen the fabric of this nation's foundation. An understanding of multicultural groups and their values serves as a first step to bridge preconceptions of superiority and moral righteousness. At the same time, public discourse and evaluation of this country's strengths and weaknesses in light of the multicultural realities could serve as a bridge to reconcile long historical tensions: such discourse could also examine the impact of more multicultural groups joining this society. Inclusiveness, relational differences, mutual respect and understanding, and empowerment would seem to be very critical ingredients in American institutional responses to the positiveness of the diversity of peoples and cultures under one nation.

3

Racial and Ethnic Complexities in American Life: Implications for African Americans

Lucius T. Outlaw

A TROUBLED BEGINNING

Though well over two hundred years old, the United States of America is still an experiment in nation making. The goal of the experiment is expressed in the Latin phrase that appears on the nation's seal and coins: *e pluribus unum*, "out of many, one." That is, to forge a stable, long-lasting nation-state in which justice for all prevails, one that provides for domestic peace and tranquillity out of a population of diverse races, ethnicities, and nationalities with different cultures and life orientations and sometimes conflicting and incompatible beliefs, values, orientations, and agendas. In founding the nation, guidelines were set forth by principles expressed in such documents as the Declaration of Independence, the Constitution, and the Bill of Rights. These principles characterize citizenship and the grounds of representative government in terms that were to have no regard for supposedly "morally irrelevant" factors such as race, creed, color, or national origin (or sex, as would be required explicitly later), since "all men" were said to be created in the image of God and thus equally endowed with certain capacities (reason being the most important) and rights. Even so, in reality citizenship was restricted to property-owning white males and denied to women of European descent, Native Americans, and enslaved African and African-descended peoples. (The exclusion of persons of African descent required the extraordinary and convoluted step of declaring them to be, by virtue of their race, but three-fifths human and thus "by nature," not the *kind* of beings who could ever become fit for citizenship.) Though from this troubled beginning there would be years of dedicated struggle by principled men and women of all races and ethnicities to overturn these exclusions, it would take the decade of Civil War and Reconstruction, the 1860s, to produce the constitutional amendments that would pave the way for full citizenship for women of European descent and persons of African descent, and later for others. Still, the full achievement and enjoyment of the rights, privileges, benefits, and responsibilities of citizenship for those once excluded is yet to be achieved, as opposition to doing so continues to be a forceful factor in national political life in various ways.[1]

We continue, then, to be haunted by contradictions that were made constitutionally sanctioned features of American life at the nation's founding. The declaration of freedom from the supposed tyranny of King George and the injustice of taxation without representation was based upon God-given "natural rights of Man." And yet, supporters of freedom and natural rights continued enslaving and otherwise oppressing Africans and other peoples and subjecting white women to male domination and exclusion from public political life. The contradictions were institutionalized in invidious, hierarchical, and rank-ordering distinctions among peoples in the body politic on the basis of their race, ethnicity, gender, or social and economic class. Well into the twentieth century, racial segregation and discrimination against women would be sanctioned by law at the federal, state, and local levels.

Throughout the history of this country, much of our political life has, therefore, been shaped by efforts to overcome these injustices and to realize full citizenship and the pursuit of material well-being and happiness for those free, willing, and able to pursue them. From the late nineteenth through the middle of the twentieth centuries, the pursuit of justice and equality for all (whether in integrating or assimilating new immigrants into the nation or overcoming the injustices of racial apartheid and other forms of discrimination and integrating those so victimized into the body politic) has been guided generally by a widely shared consensus that a United States citizen is a person whose identity is shaped by distinctive core values of the modern, American enlightenment. These core values, elaborated and made a defining part of American political life through the political philosophy of liberalism, define each citizen as "essentially" (thus, all citizens equally) free, rational, autonomous, and created in the image of God. As such, all principles and laws are meant to apply equally to all persons without regard for their race, creed, color, sex, or national origin. Further, these laws and principles are thought to rest on a singular form of rationality, present as a capability (at least potentially) in each normal adult person. This reasoning capability, when exercised properly, determines the norms for all human activities that are good and right. Reason, then, is suppose to provide guidance for determining the norms and values for private and public life and the progressive development of the nation. Thus has it been thought by many that the United States of America is the fullest realization of freedom and progress in human history. However, in the racialized context of the developing nation, it was still the case that white Americans were said to be the particular people—the particular race—in whom this mission of progress was embodied, to whom it was entrusted, and who would provide leadership for the rest of the nation's and world's peoples, educating them regarding the meaning of freedom and happiness and how to achieve both. Thus the success of this experiment in building a nation of one out of many was thought to require white (racial) supremacy. Life in America, therefore, was organized accordingly to the greatest extent possible.

A TROUBLED PRESENT

Opposition to white supremacy and racial oppression has defined much of African American life throughout our presence in the New World. More recently (the 1950s to the mid-1970s), opposition took the form of the civil rights and Black Power movements. Both were fueled by several sources: the proclamations and promises of the guiding philosophy of liberalism, motivations from African and African American legacies—religious life in particular—and motivating energies released by the learning experiences, as well as full knowledge and appreciation of the contributions of Black soldiers and others to two world wars and the Korean War, fought to "make the world safe for democracy." These were movements of determined men and women, young and old, white as well as Black, to gain full freedom for Black people. They emerged at a time when the self-proclaimed historic mission of America, given even greater impetus by the enormity of the nation's unmatched global military and economic powers after the wars, was being challenged. It was challenged first by competition from European nations, which, once war-ravaged, had with American assistance regained their footing and become economic competitors (though still "Allies"), and second by the successes of so-called Third World peoples in their efforts to gain freedom from colonization by European nations. The success of Ghana and other African nations in achieving liberation became a source of pride and provided examples that motivated the U.S. movement for civil rights (even as that movement provided motivation and other resources for the liberation movements in Africa and elsewhere). During this historical maelstrom, yet another powerful challenger appeared on the world's stage: the large and increasingly powerful communist Soviet Union. Animated by its own ideology promoting the global expansion of socialism and communism as liberation from the oppressions of capitalism, the Soviet Union entered into conflict with America and other Western, anticommunist nations. Southeast Asia, Vietnam in particular, became a battleground on which, it was determined, America would stop the successful spread of communism before it ended up on the shores of America.

By the mid 1960s, the civil rights movement, spearheaded by the National Association for the Advancement of Colored People (NAACP), the associated NAACP Legal Defense Fund, the National Urban League, and other organizations (e.g., the Brotherhood of Sleeping Car Porters and Maids headed by H. Philip Randolph and, in the South, the Southern Christian Leadership Council), brought forth deeply critical reviews of American life by measuring reality with the yardstick of the nation's highest principles. The result was the exposure, yet again, of the enormous and brutal gaps between the principles of justice and the realities of injustice lived daily by those who were the victims of racism, ethnocentrism, and sexism. Furthermore, among those engaging in the review and exposé were persons who began to take fuller note of the realities of power in America: the ability to order one's life and the lives of others, particularly through the public and private institutions—and their supporting laws and norms—that make up this nation's economic and political system, its social and cultural infrastructure, and its educational institutions. Increasingly, these persons turned their attention to questions of how power was put to use perpetrating injustices, by whom, and on what terms they legitimated their actions with the support of key institutions of law and learning. Again, the contradiction inscribed in the nation at its founding was confirmed: for all of the rhetoric celebrating the "essential equality of Man," power in America was gained and exercised along the lines of racial (and ethnic) groups for the benefit of a particular race, to the detriment of other races.

Since race seemed a "natural" feature of human life that would not disappear, then perhaps racial conflict was unlikely to be eradicated by the achievement of a "beloved community" in which racial distinctions would supposedly wither away and be of no consequence once racial segregation was eliminated and everyone had been taught to tolerate (if not always love) everyone "without regard for race, creed, color, or national origin." Such sentiments were shared by many in the civil rights movement. Others, however, argued forcefully that it behooved Black folk to organize on the basis of an appropriation and appreciation of their racial heritage and identity in an effort to achieve and exercise power in their own behalf according to an agenda fashioned in accord with their needs, interests, and desires as a people. From these persons the call went forth across the land (and beyond) for African Americans to organize to achieve Black Power!

As noted, the ideas and ideals guiding the civil rights movement had been heavily influenced by the political philosophy of liberalism and further enhanced by heavy doses of religious and secular humanism. All of this was exemplified in a political philosophy that opted for a strategy of moral suasion backed by the non-violent massive passive resistance so eloquently and passionately articulated and demonstrated by Martin Luther King, Jr. The emergence, then, of the call for Black Power from an increasingly militant "youth wing" of the movement—the Student Nonviolent Coordinating Committee (SNCC, or "Snick," as it came to be called)—was particularly disturbing for King and others, especially white supporters. A decisive turning point was reached when SNCC—for several years a multiracial organization—asked all white members to leave the organization and to aid the struggle by working in their own communities, through organizations of white people. Their leaving, some in the organization argued, would clear the way for SNCC, composed entirely of Black members and thereby independent of the influence of white people, to come together more effectively to consolidate an agenda for achieving Black power and better facilitate efforts to achieve and exercise this power in the interests of Black people. Many of the members of the organization had come to regard this step as crucial to achieving self-clarification and building sufficient confidence to effectively organize the struggle by Black people to achieve freedom, independence, and self-reliance.

During this same period (the late 1960s), the call to independence and self-reliance was being forcefully articulated by Malcolm X. Many young Black people in and around the civil rights movement, as well as many not actively engaged in movement activities but animated nonetheless by its historic struggles, were growing tired of the gradualism of King and the mainline civil rights organizations. These "young radicals" became especially critical of the petitioning and pleading on the part of Black leaders when trying to convince white folk to grant them rights that were already guaranteed by the Constitution and the Bill of Rights. There was no gradualism advocated in Malcolm X's approach: he called for "Freedom now!" and, following the injunctions of his teacher, Elijah Muhammad, spiritual leader of the National of Islam, he enjoined Black people to "Do for self!"

Malcolm X drew on a number of valuable resources to broaden his sense of the plight of Black people in America and the type of resources they might tap for guidance in "doing for self." Among the resources were his enormously penetrating critical reflections on America and the civil rights and Black Power movements, his religion—Islam—and critical reflections on his experiences during trips to Africa. One of his contributions to Black politics was his realization that the struggle of Blacks in America was directly linked to the struggles for independence in Africa and in other Third World nations.

Many of the young people in SNCC and other organizations of Black folk listened to Malcolm and followed his intellectual and practical leads. The Black Power movement, then, had very deliberately found common cause with movements for liberation of colonized and oppressed peoples in Africa and other places in the Third World, and in doing so brought an international dimension to the struggles of Black folk in America that had not been visible during the civil rights movement focused around the efforts of Martin Luther King, Jr. The Black Power movement thus became much more than a political movement seeking civil and political rights in America. It encompassed, as well, a number of other cultural agendas and organizational forms. There were the Black arts movement and other promotions of Black cultural nationalism that deeply affected contemporary music, poetry, art, literature, and dance. Curricula and disciplines in educational institutions at all levels were deeply affected and new academic disciplines such as Black Studies programs appeared. Further, the Black Power movement spawned nationalist political and economic community-building organizations and movements (e.g., the creation or reinvigoration of local, state, and national political organizations) that helped elect Black candidates to political office in numbers matched only during the period of Reconstruction following the Civil War a century earlier. The influence of the movement was also seen in the formation of international political, cultural, and economic organizations and movements (as seen in various Pan-African endeavors). Still, there is an even more potent legacy of the movement. With the advantage of hindsight, we can now identify the Black Power movement, or the collection of organizations, persons, movements, agendas, and so on, that have in common a commitment to the idea of organizing efforts on behalf of Black people on the basis of a shared heritage and identity as people of African descent, as a defining historical antecedent to what is now referred to as "the politics of identity, difference, and recognition."[2]

THE POLITICS OF DIVERSITY

In this mode of politics, identity and difference are defined in racial or ethnic (or gender) terms and require for their full authentication that others recognize and validate this identity-constituting difference on the terms that members of the racial or ethnic group (at least those defining the group's identity) require. And it is recognition on these terms that secures the group's status and the status of its members in the body politic. This recognition secures as well the group's rights and privileges, including the right of self-definition, which flow in significant part from the group's identity.

The politics of difference, identity, and recognition that seek to make a virtue of racial and ethnic (as well as gender and sexual-orientation) differences is a serious challenge to the rationalizing and legitimating ideas and ideals that have defined the project of *e pluribus unum,* devoted, as it is, to the assimilation, integration, and social bonding of individuals who are without defining and constraining affective ties to natal communities. This project has been legitimated by a philosophy of democratic liberalism that requires a commitment to universal principles of political organization and law, secured by the authority of a singular form of reason and applied impartially and equally to "essentially identical" individuals without regard to morally irrelevant attributes of race, creed, or color. However, the fact that the politics of difference, identity, and recognition has motivated so many groups beyond African Americans— groups that now, via this form of politics, are posing their own challenges even to African American political projects—is a matter of even greater importance. And not just in the United States. Throughout the world—in Canada, the former nation-state of Yugoslavia, the former Soviet Union, across the continents of Africa and Latin America, in Great Britain, France, Germany, and so on—political struggles centering on valorizations of racial and/or ethnic identities are reshaping political landscapes and having global impacts. In light of the situation in the former Yugoslavia in particular, as the killing, oppression, and displacements of "ethnic cleansing" continue as part of a program of ethnic fascism, we cannot but be troubled by the dangerous possibilities of a politics of difference, identity, and recognition gone mad. And it is irresponsible of us to denounce and dismiss those who raise alarms (as does Arthur Schlesinger, Jr., in his book *The Disuniting of America,* in which he worries about what he sees as an overemphasis on what makes persons and groups different at the expense of what commonalities unite us) as reactionary conservatives and not consider seriously and carefully their concerns. For in reality, all of us, to the extent that we care about ourselves, our "people," and our nation, are conservators.

Still, what is it we would conserve? Our particular group and the institutional means by which its cultural life is perpetuated? And, to what ends? Group reproduction at the expense of justice and stability in the nation as a whole? For what reasons? And where there are conflicts in and among the answers to these and other important questions, and thus conflicts in and among the projects persons and groups engage in to realize and live out their answers, how, and on what and whose terms, are the conflicts to be resolved? In order for a society to be stable and enjoy peace, justice, and harmony over any extended period of time, there must be a consensus shared by its members that rests on deep commitments of studied acceptance and loyalty regarding the means— that is, the principles of justice and order, their justifications and applications—by which an ordered and stable social life is achieved.

The situation in America as well as in other nations is complicated by a confluence of factors that make it difficult to achieve such a consensus. As noted, the civil rights and antiwar movements helped to expose the centuries-old hypocrisies that disguised the linkages among racism, capitalist exploitation, and a general lack of social justice even as an officially racially divided nation proclaimed itself leader of the "free world." This exposure helped spawn the politics of difference, identity, and recognition. With its emergence in a variety of forms, this politics has generated a great deal of skepticism regarding the viability of liberal individualism as the key to the formation of a peaceful and just nation in which racial, ethnic, gender, and sexual-orientation identities (as well as religious orientations and other private concerns) have no publicly and legally sanctioned importance in terms of influencing just distributions of rewards, responsibilities, and sanctions.

There are other important and complicating factors as well. During this same period in America's history, and influenced by similar developments, a significant number of persons in the nation's schools, colleges, and universities contributed to the skepticism. For example, some examined aspects of the political philosophy of liberalism and, in many cases, found it inadequate to the task of giving what many thought to be necessary, due to the importance of race, ethnicity, gender, or sexual orientation, to the formation and maintenance of healthy personal and social identities. That is, we are not, these critics asserted, simply individuals bereft of important affective ties to significant others that could be formative of the very persons we are and give our lives meaning and direction. From this perspective, the idea of the person—the individual— at the heart of liberalism is thought to be impoverished and much too "thin" to meet the requirements of communities.

Other skeptics argued along another vein that it is not possible to provide a satisfactory account of the kind of human reason required by liberalism, that is, reason as a universally identical capacity exercised in an equally identical and singular fashion and producer of universally valid singular results when directed at questions regarding what is *the* right and *the* good for social or individual life. Such questions, it is argued, are always particular to members of a particular community with a particular history and agenda for the future; the answers are likewise particular, however similar (but never quite identical) to the answers of people in other communities. The effort to produce an account of the one true form of universalizing rationality for questions of right and good living, the argument continues, a quest that has consumed the efforts of major thinkers off and on for well over two thousand years, has not and cannot succeed. By this account, neither reason nor God has ordained American (or Western) liberal democratic capitalism as the form of social life best suited to the human species; nor does America's history represent the apex of human evolution to which all other peoples should look to as the guiding star for their own historical development.

Rather, our accomplishments are much more modest, and our prospects for success just as modest.

This skepticism has contributed to a palpable absence of consensus, a loss of confidence in America's guiding public philosophy, and in reason as the final authoritative tribunal for settling questions of the right and the good. Recent challenging and historic developments, if not attended to properly, could threaten social unity: the politics of difference, identity, and recognition, the challenges of an increasingly competitive globalized economy, political realignments of nation-states as the once-colonized struggle to transform political independence into economic and cultural self-reliance, the fragmentation of older nation-states into several new nation-states along ethnic-nationalist lines of long lineage, and the effects of massive global population shifts. Indeed, America continues to attract millions as the fabled land of stability and opportunity, resulting in seismic demographic changes: more than a million new immigrants a year are entering the country. If the present rate of immigration continues for another half-century, by the year 2050 people who trace their origins to western Europe will be a numerical minority in the United States. African Americans, once the nation's largest minority group, will be outnumbered by Hispanics.[3]

The current championing of multiculturalism is, then, in many ways both a result of and an influence on the increasing racial and ethnic diversification of American life. And to the extent that multiculturalism involves the promotion and legitimation of an approach to cultural meanings that recognizes that the cultures of various racial and ethnic groups have historical as well as contemporary insights and continue to provide the makers, consumers, and bearers of these cultures with resources vital to well-being, then it serves to intensify the politics of difference, identity, and recognition. This is especially the case when proponents of multiculturalism argue that in a nation of diverse cultural groups it is important that knowledge and appreciation of the cultural heritage and achievements of groups other than one's own be cultivated in the nation's young people as part of their educational preparation to inherit this nation and decide its future. Neither knowledge nor the resulting appreciation, it is argued, can come by way of the monoculturalism that for so very long has set the educational agenda and shaped the curricula of America's educational institutions. No longer can the educational system be guided by the cultural values of liberal humanism. Liberal humanism can no longer serve the needs of democratic pluralism by espousing a highly selective historical narrative that situates the defining values of progressive, high-Western civilization at the top of a hierarchy of value-embodying, race-defined civilizations. In today's unsettled and emotionally charged historical situation, the orienting and unifying meanings and symbols that made *e pluribus unum* the guiding project in a racialized American experiment in nation building can no longer be taken for granted, either as satisfying for all who would be "American" or as salient for a project in nation making. Even cursory surveys of our national situation and of situations in several nations already noted cannot but lead one to the conclusion that the politics of difference, identity, and recognition is likely to be a driving force in social life for several decades to come.

AFRICAN AMERICA AND IDENTITY

For African Americans this is a particularly challenging situation. A significant minority among us have been major contributors to the emergence and development of the politics of difference, identity, and recognition by virtue of our contributions to (and the benefits we have drawn from) various dimensions of the Black Power movement. Similar movements involving women, Hispanics, gays, and lesbians have followed in the wake of the movement, often drawing substantial conceptual, ideological, and strategic resources from its legacies. Black folk have frequently participated in the formation of influential multiracial and multiethnic coalitions devoted to progressive struggles often waged around terms of identity and recognition. Still, there is a great deal more intellectual and practical complexity in the body politic today brought on by increasing racial, ethnic, and cultural diversity and increased group competition. In terms of complexity, it is no longer easy or appropriate (and never was, quite frankly) to frame the struggles of black folk in the much too simplistic terms of the black race (us) versus the white race (them). Now we have been joined by other "peoples of color" who have been victims of oppression at the hands of "whites:" by women— white, black, and of color—who have suffered several forms of oppression *as women*; by gays and lesbians, who are waging a struggle to be freed from the invidious confinements and distortions of their lives and senses of themselves by norms and practices of heterosexual or celibate "normalcy;" and by other groups organized, for example, on the basis of age or impaired physical abilities. All are sharing in giving definition to the politics of difference, identity, and recognition. Though once enslaved and continually oppressed in a racialized America for over three centuries, African Americans can no longer lay claim to a privileged status and demand a special moral sanctity for their struggle. Hence, it is both unbecoming and unproductive to compete with any other group for the status of "most victimized," and all that might come with that dubious status in the way of sympathies, pity, or resources and rewards. There has been more than enough of this debilitating competition between black and Jewish persons and organizations over the years. Too often this has involved the shameful retreat to the necrophilic tactic of comparing counts of those who died in the death camps versus those who died in the slave ships and on the breaking grounds, on the assumption that retributive justice requires a privileged victim and that this status can best be won by laying claim to a holocaust strewn with the most bodies.

For African Americans who would engage in the politics of difference, identity, and recognition, this is a time for serious stock-taking and reconsideration. If the description of the historical situation I have offered is even moderately close to being accurate, then we seem compelled as a group, yet again, to achieve greater practical unity and coordinated action in this precarious period of heightened competition among racial and ethnic groups. But group solidarity on what grounds? And to what ends? Neither widespread unity on the basis of who we take ourselves to be in our shared identities as persons of African descent nor unity on the basis of a shared agenda and strategy is at hand or immediately forthcoming. It has never been the case that *simply* being black or claiming African descent has been enough to produce racial unity through shared identity. Not even the experience of slavery and its aftermath were enough, in themselves, to produce either shared identity or political unity. Rather, with a great deal of deliberate effort, widely (though not universally) shared identities, varying across times and spaces but still sufficient to underwrite Black communal life, political mobilization, and struggle in varied forms and in particular localities, have been forged out of shared and similar experiences. This communal life, until rather recently, has provided the nurturance necessary for survival and well-being during the brutal circumstances of enslavement and under conditions of institutionalized indignities that continue to define, more or less, the life of oppression and discrimination generally experienced by people of African descent. But the increasing social diversity and complexity in America being played out in the debate and efforts regarding multiculturalism present the challenge of once again having to work out what it means to be African and American in the late twentieth century.

The matters of personal and social identity are difficult to specify in a settled manner and are always charged with a host of complex and sometimes conflicting meanings and implications. Since identity is always a matter of interpretations of meanings that are both socially imposed and more or less self-constituted (for example, the meaning of being "Negro" or African in America, or of the supposed uniquely defining "racial" and/or cultural features of African peoples), identity is always socially and historically conditioned and variable. Some factors, to name a few, are: class (e.g., levels of education, occupation, and income levels), religious affiliation or the absence of such, other organizational affiliations, locales (the neighborhood, city or rural area, state, region in which one lives) and their demographic configurations, and physical ability and makeup and the ways these are perceived and valued, personally and by others. It has never been the case that all Black folk, by virtue of being "Black"—biologically, socially, or culturally—have shared a singularly defined sense of themselves. African peoples have always been diverse in our similarity, similar in our diversity.

Nineteenth- and early twentieth-century proponents of racial typology claimed that there were a variety of immutable races, each of which was determined by a distinct and inheritable biological morphology. In addition, however, it was also thought that race-defining biological factors also determined the cultural and moral developments of a given race. Such thinking has shaped much of our orientation to racial groups over the years and continues to play a powerful role in our identifying, thinking and talking about, and interaction with persons and groups racially and ethnically different from us. This influence is still felt in our frequent search for a singular, enduring, and defining identity shared by all members of a race, and is biologically determined.

During the 1950s and 1960s, the hold of biological racial-typology thinking was loosened by more critical scientific work in genetics, evolutionary biology, comparative cultural anthropology, and other disciplines, which made clear the error in thinking that there were fixed, causal linkages between biological factors and cultural factors in determining racial groups: biology does not determine culture; nor, therefore, does it provide fixed grounds for a singular shared identity. With this loosening of the hold of "race" as a term referring to fixed biological types, "ethnicity" emerged as the concept employed in the social sciences, in particular, to characterize diverse groups of peoples less in terms of hereditary biological characteristics and more in terms of cultural distinctiveness and common descent. In other words, the ethnic group was considered primarily as "a transgenerational vehicle for the transmission of an authentically rooted culture."[4] "Culture," then, came to play an increasingly significant role in defining different groups of people, though biologically based factors still play an important role in group differentiation. Nevertheless, the shift from biology to culture as the major factor in defining different groups has not eliminated intergroup (or even intragroup) conflict as groups compete for resources of various kinds, and in doing so stake out in ethnic terms their claims to power and precedence.[5]

In this regard, there are those African Americans (and others) who make the very serious mistake of thinking that a shared identity as a basis for political unity in social struggle is to be found in a supposedly primordial and shared commonality based upon either inheritable biological traits or on a presumed *cultural* unity thought to be provided by diverse African peoples sharing some distinct and invariant set of uniquely distinguishing cultural traits and practices. And indeed, African peoples throughout the African continent and the African diaspora do have many things in common— cultural and experiential, but we are also different in many ways. A lineage that stretches back to the African continent as a land of origin is part of what we have in common. But depending on each of our family situations in terms of descent, our lineages stretch in many directions, including various places in Europe. Still, a major aspect of our individual histories has involved our having been continuously racialized—that is, defined biologically and culturally as a distinct race—and forced to live our lives, to greater or lesser extents, within the boundaries of racialized social worlds. African peoples, over time, have had similar experiences of enslavement, transport and dispersal, and colonization, though even these experiences, tied to diverse locations and circumstances, have differed in terms of the ways in which victims faced the situation and struggled for survival and independence. Consequently, we have created and sustained, with continuous revision, relatively distinct cultures as racialized peoples, yet cultures that are, at the same time, different from one another in various ways.

How we form, revise, maintain, or overthrow imposed identities are always matters of importance, particularly in a nation such as ours, which has long been structured by racialized oppression and social hierarchies heavily defined by white supremacy. To assist us in reviewing and revising our identities and life agendas, we have available to us the centuries-old traditions that have been bequeathed to us by generations of "race women" and "race men," that is, those persons who devoted their lives to the crucial work of fashioning meanings into articulate configurations to provide mobilizing and rehabilitative identity formations in and through which Black folks might fashion flourishing lives.[6] Still, as we turn to these resources once again to consider who we are and who we might become, Africa does not await us as a ready-made reservoir of final meanings to which we can turn for components out of which to construct identities and agendas for the present and future. As noted thinker Stuart Hall has observed, the meanings of "Africa" for all of the peoples of that very large continent, as well as for those of us of African descent in the diaspora, are not fixed in some primordial state but are the result of a series of discontinuous changes spanning several centuries. Thus "there can . . . be no simple 'return' or 'recovery' of the ancestral past which is not re-experienced through the categories of the present: no base for creative enunciation in a simple reproduction of traditional forms which are not transformed by the technologies and the identities of the present."[7] The truth of this is clearly evident in our concern to articulate identities appropriate for African Americans, that is, for persons of African descent in America—the great majority of whom have never visited, let alone lived on, the African continent. Further, we are also deeply connected, in many ways, to America as our national home. Thus we are compelled to weigh the relative significance of being African, in some important New World sense, and American.

Today it is virtually impossible to sustain the wishful fiction of a permanent and collective "one *true* racialized self" shared by all Black folk. Rather, study of the efforts of those who came before us will show unequivocally that we, as a group and as individuals, are never finished products, but are always becoming. "Far from being grounded in a mere 'recovery' of the past, which is waiting to be found, and which, when found, will secure our sense of ourselves into eternity, identities are the names we give to the different ways we are positioned by, and position ourselves within, the narratives of the past."[8] We are constantly redefining ourselves as our situations change, and we do so creatively with likewise changing narrations of our identity-shaping histories. And as these narrations are formed to a significant degree out of our involvement in social worlds we share with cultural others, we make use of repertoires of meanings and practices that, in many cases, were not available to previous generations of Black folk. So it will be, hopefully, with those Black folks who follow us.

Which is why new, critical narrations of our histories are so very crucial, why the battles to insure that these histories are included in the curricula of educational institutions in which young people of African descent are schooled are so crucial, and why there must be institutions in and through which Black people can see to the culture creation that ensures the remaking of African peoples as we prepare for possible futures. Thus we have a major stake in the battle to set aside the long-standing agenda of Euro-American-focused monoculturalism that would "make of many, one" through an assimilative project that takes seriously only the norms and identities of a modernity that was at war with its own founding traditions. In suffering "the illusion that they had no illusions,"[9] the makers of this modernity took pains to jettison traditional allegiances and identities in favor of an identity, constructed anew with the resources of reason alone, that regarded the entire globe as its private dominion in which to pursue a progressive future of unlimited possibilities.

Still, as we noted at the outset of this discussion, many—though not all—of the architects of modernity, in spite of their commitments to reason-sanctioned universality and equality (as ideals if not as concrete facts, for most of them realized that all persons were not *in fact* equal), continued to believe in qualitative differences among racial groups. The racialized injustices that continue to exist, based as they are on liberalism and modernity, demand our countering efforts and our vigilance. At the same time, however, we must continue to contribute to efforts to understand the challenges and opportunities presented by America's unprecedented demographic and cultural diversification fueled and sanctioned by the democratic impulses of the politics of difference, identity, and recognition. We must be intimately involved in the search to find "the ties that bind" those with welcomed differences into a united nation of diverse ones—individuals as well as groups—without the injustices of dehumanizing hierarchies predicated on any supposed superiority of race, ethnicity, or gender.

Education can be—must be—a major factor in achieving such an end, for schooling at all levels continues to be a major mechanism of socialization in America. Colleges and universities in particular are the principal institutions in which much of the critical reflection and reinterpretation must continue; followed by the passing on of these knowledges to students to discover ways to transform the potential for social fragmentation inherent in emphasizing racial/ethnic cultural differences into a wealth of diverse resources for vital national life. And these efforts must not be unduly constrained by norms for research, scholarship, and pedagogy that are conceived as having no connection to "politics," that is, connection to the work of achieving a stable and just pluralist-democratic society. Rather, these must be decidedly self-conscious efforts devoted to the formation of frameworks for local, national, and international political life that promote democratic inclusion through critical recognition and appreciation for the cultural practices and legacies of all who comprise our body politic. Racial/ethnic segregation and isolation must be ended by constructing a rejuvenated democratic pluralism that integrates into a united whole the diversity of persons and peoples who take important facets of their complex and changing identities, as well as of their life commitments and agendas, from cultural communities in which racial, ethnic, gender, and sexual commitments, among others, play defining, positive roles that these persons do not wish—and should not be required—to relinquish totally.

What is needed is the refashioning of monocultural education into a venture devoted to these ends, a venture that should involve our clarifying and cultivating a host of reorientations and new practices in knowledge production and teaching, as well as the recognition and incorporation into the curriculum of heretofore unrecognized cultural legacies of various peoples. A central concern should be the development of forms of knowledge and of teaching that facilitate the translation of local knowledges and their interconnections of particular cultural groups so as to allow them to be shared by other cultural groups. This sharing must become a major factor in the continuous process of nation building that no longer requires all persons to assimilate to the dominating cultural legacies and agendas of a particular race.

To this effort, African Americans have much to contribute through the resources of a number of traditions and forms of literature, history, philosophy, art, dance, music, religion and theology, social science, and contributions to the natural sciences, politics, and medicine. African and African American Studies programs are principal resources for the study of these contributions. In each case serious study provides opportunities in knowledge recovery, knowledge production, knowledge validation, and knowledge mediation, all of which are of major importance to a politics of identity, mobilization, and recognition that serves Black folk seeking guidance from norms of validity and truthfulness. A great deal of effort in modern Black Studies, guided by notions of "Afrocentricity" in particular, has been devoted to clarifying and articulating historically informed and settled knowledges and values to secure for African-descended peoples a sense of themselves appropriate to the present and future. Thus it is that such efforts have been a major impetus for and contributor to attempts to diversify curricula and pedagogic practices in educational institutions. As a consequence, however, those involved in these efforts have been called upon to defend their work by opponents who charge them with politicizing the curriculum and utilizing a critique based upon race, ethnicity, gender, and sexual orientation.

But in the education and socialization (the two are virtually identical) of members of any society, all that is passed on as officially recognized knowledge is also political in that such knowledge is crucial to ensuring the continuation of the social order within and to which individual and social identities are crucial. Relative to the goal of ensuring social order, a distinction must be made between what passes for "correct" knowledge and competing articulations deemed "incorrect." The candidates for knowledge are numerous and varied. But not all of what is available will be appropriate to survival and well-being. Judgments will have to be made in selecting what is good for social well-being while discarding what is bad. Thus much of the highly publicized hewing and crying about "political correctness" directed at proponents of multiculturalism is dishonest as well as misguided. Dishonest, because many of the persons who attack so-called political correctness are themselves advocating, at the very same time, a form of political life that they deem correct, even though as it pertains to colleges and universities it has nothing to do with bringing about the enrichment of institutional life through the incorporation of the legacies and agendas of excluded cultural groups. And misguided for implying that political correctness is bad, pure and simple.

The issue is not the presence or absence of political correctness. Rather, the crucial and difficult issues surrounding the bases of correctness for the American body politic, given its unparalleled diversity, are: which collection of values and norms we shall utilize, certified and conveyed through what forms of knowledge, and drawing on and validating the resources of what cultures. How should we integrate important elements from the life agendas of many different cultural groups in the agendas that shape the overall historical development of this nation and shape the ways in which we conduct our lives in our various locales and social settings? Among the cultural resources creatively fashioned out of life-and-death struggles and in struggles against efforts to deny and crush our humanity, people of African descent have much to offer that might be of value in the continuation of the American experiment. We will have to take stock of many of these resources, reviewing and possibly revising them as we continue to revise our senses of ourselves as folk of African descent. Since we never revise all aspects of ourselves at once, there is always some continuity between the past and the present that continues into the future. Such continuities are seen in our music, speech, art, dance, and other practices with very long histories that are shared in varying degrees and forms with other African-descended peoples. But we innovate, as well. We always have, and do so by drawing from the world's storehouse of human achievement according to agendas and imperatives that are both self- and other-imposed. How striking an example in the masterful accomplishments of jazz artist Rufus Harley, whose instrument of choice is the bagpipes! How striking an example is jazz itself, a varied art form whose lineage of African descent is beyond question, within which artists of various races and ethnicities perform with instruments drawn from around the world, and who play in time signatures and rhythmic forms that tell much about African peoples and our presences in the New World.

To continue our traditions in important ways even as we change them in other ways is the responsibility of every group and individual who intends to survive in the face of challenges. Today, this is a compelling responsibility for African Americans, one that has been intensified by the unprecedented complexities of racial and ethnic diversity in America. The key is to make of this diversity less a competitive threat and more an opportunity to learn, share, and grow as we revise and sustain the American experiment, this truly historic venture.

4

Whose Rights Shall We Promote?

An Interview with Robert Dawidoff

Dean Harris: The argument you make in *Created Equal*, coauthored with Michael Nava, cannot get any simpler and compact, yet still accurate, than this statement: "The rights of American citizens are not dependent on whether those Americans are popular, but arise by virtue of their citizenship. Correspondingly, any attempt to restrict the free exercise of those rights because of a popular prejudice cannot withstand the searching scrutiny required by the courts and the equal protection clause." Could you enumerate some of the key arguments of your book?

Robert Dawidoff: Well I think the thing you need to start with in the quotation is that the question of rights seems to always shift from the idea that rights just exist to rights that in some way are granted or recognized, and therefore can be defended, endowed, or removed. And so that quote, and I agree that is at the core of our argument, is a statement that imagines equal protection of the law and rights as they ought to be. The arguments in support of that statement are a key strategy of the book, but a strategy that causes us much trouble because it doesn't really fit with what most people think about these things. We argue a certain view of constitutional interpretation—a historical view—and then try to show how that view pertains to lesbian and gay rights. We then show that what stands in the way of equal protection of the law is prejudice, and that that is a prejudice that is hard to sustain given our constitutional frame of reference. Lastly, we try to encourage the reader to start thinking in those terms about an issue that people tend not think about in those terms.

DH: What I took away from reading the book was a more crystallized argument for the protection of gay rights. Previous to reading the book, I supported the protection of the rights of gays, but if someone had asked me to support my stance, I wouldn't have been able to do it as well as I think I can now.

RD: The thing that is interesting about your comment is the broader question it brings up. In the book we do argue for the rights of gays, but on the other hand we have kept other individuals and groups in mind also. We wrote the book with a passion that comes from the fact that we are both gay men writing for an audience that needs to be shown certain things, but with the ultimate purpose of setting gay rights in the context of other kinds of rights. Hence, in the future I might encounter a situation that beckons me to think more clearly and rationally about the rights of some people I like as little as some people like me, and I could rely on this book for guidance. So I hope that if people find our book helpful it will be because it applies not only to gay rights, but to all rights, and about the way such issues can be argued. Of course, we don't know who will be that next group of people. I think, though, that in the book we were sufficiently careful not to argue for any one kind of right. That is to say, I don't think you can get an argument for pedophilia out of this book.

DH: In what way is the struggle for gay rights not a radical movement but a thoroughly conservative one?

RD: Well, it is and it isn't. It is radical in the sense that we are repeating the revolutionary arguments made by the nation's founders over two centuries ago. It is also radical in that we are applying traditional notions of rights and law to a people who have never been covered by those notions. Certainly Jefferson was not for gay rights, because the question didn't even exist then. The notion that "sexual orientation" constitutes a proper category deciding citizenship is pretty bizarre. That notion just hasn't been around for very long.

On the other hand, our argument is a truly conservative one in that this issue is an ordinary civic issue. What we are appealing to in the book are old-fashioned arguments and old-fashioned virtues. I think that the book is quite sincere in saying that we Americans cannot have morally serious lives if we are not given access to the responsibilities of the only common life we all have—civic life. That is a pretty basic and traditional idea in this country. In addition, the vision of America that we aspire to in the book is a very old-fashioned one. Not old-fashioned in a patriotic way, but rather in line with a more Jeffersonian notion that the particular quality of this regime is the degree to which it delivers on its promise of individual freedom.

DH: You talk about your frustration with having to spend so much time arguing against extraneous and irrelevant issues with little or no time dedicated to the truly decisive issues. In the section on media coverage and balance you write, "The consequence of this distorted view of balance is that gays are continually required to battle hate simply to address issues of justice and equity." What do you consider the irrelevant issues and the relevant issues?

RD: There are certainly many more irrelevant issues than relevant ones. The relevant issues are actually fairly austere and dramatic, but stand upon a simple standard of equal protection. Among the irrelevant arguments are morality. It is certainly true that the founders and the founding system assumed a great deal about morality, and certainly assumed a thriving Christian nation. I am all for taking morality seriously, but I'm not too keen on instituting Christian theocracy. I am all for the golden rule and turning the other cheek, but I don't see those Christian morals as necessarily public. Although it is inconvenient for all of us to have to struggle with the implications of that, I do not believe morality should be an issue concerning gay rights.

Sexual conduct is not a relevant issue in deciding citizenship. Sexual practices, unless they violate other people's rights or laws, are beside the point. I don't see how who you love intersects with your right to equal protection of the law. It's interesting that nobody makes that case. You don't hear people argue the case that the protection clause does not cover gays and lesbians because the love relationships they form are same-sex unions. What they say is, it's unnatural, or frowned upon by God. On the other side of the argument, I don't think it is wise for gays and lesbians to tangle in the particulars of Leviticus because that just doesn't have particular relevance to the Constitution.

It is irrelevant to argue stereotypes about a life that most people don't know much about. Certainly my lifestyle as a resident of West Hollywood and that of someone living in Claremont, for example, are different. Claremont life is a couple's life, which isn't the case in West Hollywood because there is such a large population of singles. But lifestyle isn't an issue, no matter its normalcy or marginality. I mean, during the struggle for Black civil rights I don't think anyone argued that African American lifestyle should be a hindrance to the granting of rights. The argument was made then as it is now about the inferiority of the group. It is interesting that I don't hear the argument, as we heard during the civil rights campaign and the similar struggle for women's rights, that we gays are incapable of exercising the franchise. Rather, like anti-Catholicism, anti-Mormonism, and anti-Semitism, it seems to be about the reticence to accept people as fellow citizens because they are different, or practice some secret rite or ritual.

DH: Let's talk about a key gripe anti-gay-rights people have: the so called granting to gays of "special rights." You make the interesting observation that the fact that gripe exists shows just how much these people view gays and lesbians as out of the ordinary, abnormal. Later you add that actually, gays want an end to their "special status."

RD: Well it is demonstrably true that we don't benefit from any special rights, but rather that we suffer from being relegated to a special status. Our book does not advocate anything approaching special rights. Special rights connotes rights that another group doesn't enjoy. In a sense, we aren't even arguing for equal rights but rather equal access. We gays and lesbians are really not willing to spend the whole of our lives trying to get everything for gays that heterosexuals currently enjoy. It would be a waste of time. But, it is absolutely unacceptable that equal rights be denied us. And it is insulting to us, as it should be to you, that *equal* rights are responded to as if they were *special*.

You know, the hardest part to deal with in that argument is that it's hard to know just what to say to the person who holds that position. What is so special about employment equality? Employers are not allowed to discriminate against a person on the basis of age, sex, religious affiliation, or race. Why is it so hard to agree to add sexual orientation to that list? People seem to think we are such monsters for making that demand. It would be instructive to those people to switch the argument around and consider what the reality of that law says about middle-aged, Christian, white, heterosexual males. Why does this country even require such equal access laws?

Now, it could be argued that in a sense affirmative action is a special right. But it is a special right with the understanding of making up for past injustices and curing a system of injustices. It may turn out that in the future special measures will be necessary in order to secure and protect gay people in their enjoyment of constitutionally mandated equal rights. But at this moment very little of what we and other people are talking about can reasonably be identified as special. And we certainly aren't talking about affirmative action in the book. I personally have mixed feelings about any sort of affirmative action for lesbians and gays. What happens when you take an identity that is so private, personal, and cannot be seen, such as sexual orientation, and turn it into an identity that must be cultivated and sought after? I mean, with few exceptions, companies with affirmative action policies typically don't have a hard time telling an African American from a white person. When it comes to gays, however, I think the whole issue gets a bit trickier.

DH: In the chapter entitled "The Ick Factor" you argue that the gay struggle is not about sex. Elsewhere you write, "Homosexuality is not exclusively about sex any more than heterosexuality is." Explain what you mean by that. And, how do you deal with someone who is hung up on sex and sees gay rights in only those terms?

RD: People always talk about homosexuality as if it's about sex. How did homosexuality become just about sex? African Americans often talk about the fact that when whites discuss race they are always talking about Blacks. As if white people cannot be considered to be a racial group nor have a race problem themselves. It's as if the history of America were not a history of white people acting on the basis of race. It's the same thing with gays and lesbians. The use solely of sexuality to define and encompass the gay man has more to do with discrimination than with anything one might call reality. It just isn't true that our lives are only about sex.

Speaking of irrelevant issues and sex, we argue in the book that the issue of promiscuity is not an issue of citizenship. Now, there does seem to be a tendency—and I think a very healthy tendency—among gays who are coming out to cut through many of the moralistic restrictions concerning sexuality that are publicly imposed, although not privately observed, in American life. Once you begin to realize how bogus, how dishonest and hypocritical the issue of sexuality is in one's own life—for instance married men who participate simultaneously in a gay relationship—it's hard to take all that moralism seriously. I mean, the Catholic church has always been a place where gay men congregated. You'd never know it, though, because the topic is so taboo among the hierarchy. (One issue of interest to me is the same-sex monastic tradition within that church. How did those men overcome their sexual desire, assuming they did, of course?) The trouble is that we live in a society that has tended for various reasons to be very uneasy with open sexuality. In Latin America it is much easier to be open about one's homo- or bisexuality. Now, that has not led to a corresponding positive treatment of gays and lesbians. But it shows that the sexual attitudes a culture embraces have a great deal to do with the character of discrimination a group may suffer.

Finally, there is the scare of AIDS. There is no question that the accident, and it most assuredly is an accident, that in the United States and parts of Europe HIV and AIDS have been associated with the sexual practices of gay men has meant that our lifestyle has been targeted as somehow synonymous with that virus. But again, not only is that irrelevant, but if our critics would for a minute ignore their own theories about how gay men contracted the virus and instead look at the positive response to the disease, much could be learned. It seems to me that gay men and lesbians—and heterosexuals—have crossed over such incredible barriers of gender, sexual orientation, and hostility to stand with those who are infected, that rather than ignoring the disease and the corresponding response, Americans should see it as a lesson on how to construct community out of conflict, desperation, and chaos.

DH: You make the following comment about John Stuart Mill's essay *The Subjection of Women:* "He also knew how limited the uses of reason might prove against ingrained belief, founded in feeling, supported by religion and custom, and reaffirmed by the rituals of individual and common life." What place has reason had in the discussion over gay civil rights?

RD: We are living in a time when reason lacks proper respect. One of the things in the book that should upset many people is our critique of reason in modern society. Reason is the sine qua non of political argument. We need a populace that values reason and its tools. And, of course, good argument requires opposing sides that are willing to discuss together critical and controversial issues. These values and civic realities are in short supply in this country. We can't have a common polity unless we have people who are willing to think and talk about things together.

In a way, it could be said that what I am getting at is compromise. The reason why we don't include religion in public argument is not because anyone hates religion, but because it is understood that as a public matter, almost by definition religion defies compromise, and, therefore, is an unreasonable basis for public argument. Religion is a little like slavery: It is something about which you cannot compromise in some basic way. Once you decide that your salvation is the most important thing in your life, and to gain that salvation requires particular views and actions on your part, then there really isn't any room for anybody to disagree, however well meaning. The founders of our country knew this. They knew it well. They were not people who were innocent of the world. They had the history of the reformation to instruct them. They were quite understandably nervous about what a polity would do with issues that couldn't be compromised. That's the reason behind the Establishment Clause.

They did, though, have the benefit of a relative moral consensus. It would be nice if we had one now in this country. But a moral consensus that is achieved at the price of individual liberty and equal protection of the law for a group of citizens is an unworkable and unsustainable system.

I think another reason why we were so struck with Mill and rational argument is that we have both been surprised at how hysterical the issues surrounding homosexuality have become. I mean, did you listen to the Senate hearings on gays in the military? Public figures are afraid to discuss this issue. The only public figure who has said anything reasonable about gays and lesbians is Tom Hanks—an actor. When I listen to the discussion over gay rights, I am sorry to say I do not recognize rationality in much of it. There is even a paucity of it within the gay community. I worry, therefore, about the future of political argument when we seem so ready to hold that all rationality is suspect, and therefore, all arguments are the same. What other means do we have to license serious discussion? I'm worried about those people who are participating in the public square and have lost faith in reason and compromise.

Let me also add that, of course, it is easier for you—the generic you—to argue rationally because it is not you whom they are coming to get. That places a greater burden on you to provide us with basic rights so as to create a space wherein discussion can take place about further rights.

DH: One of the key sections of the book for me was the one entitled "The American Roots of Gay Rights." In it you discuss the Constitution, Jefferson and Hamilton, and America's love/hate relationship with freedom. We seem to demand it for ourselves (myself), but believe others (you) incapable of respecting and utilizing freedom responsibly. You quote Randolph: "I love liberty, I hate equality."

RD: That's not the kind of thing people typically understand about themselves. One of the things thinking people have to remember is that liberty is a tremendous responsibility, for which most people most of the time are ill prepared. I don't know about you, but if I am going to be making decisions everyday about all sorts of issues, it's hard to keep liberty and freedom uppermost in my mind. The Founders clearly came from a tradition in which they were determined to have as much political liberty as possible but were very concerned about what the implications of setting the self free would be. I don't see how a sensible person who has any acquaintance with human nature and human behavior, or with themselves, cannot be thinking about that issue. One of the things I worry about concerning freedom in the U.S. is that it is so strongly associated with indulgence, with nationalism, with patriotism, and not with that old notion of freedom as responsibility. I also think that traditions of freedom and responsibility always suggest two things: it can't be just "Control yourself," but rather, there also must be a place for freedom as a belief.

DH: Talk about the fear of sexual freedom and acting in a way that subverts the mainstream: "The movement forces people not only to confront their prejudices but perhaps to face their own fantasies as well. The question of sexual orientation demands an exacting and, for many, extremely uncomfortable self-examination."

RD: You tell me why Sam Nunn is so afraid for all those sailors. One of the implications of gay openness is that one will be a whole lot less likely mistaken about who one is trying to hit upon. What gay men choose to do is love other men, to own up to that feeling, and to say that this feeling is as much, or as little, a basis of one's life as any other passionate feeling.

That there is something about my own sexuality and the possibilities that that fact sets up is very scary, especially here in America. As a gay man I have to listen to people spout off such invective, like how gays eat their own feces. Let me tell you, that thought does not appeal to me. The claim, recently reported in the newspaper, that the average gay man eats the feces of his lover is absurd and insulting. Think about it, what makes someone want or need to say that? It's like someone saying of a 5'11'' tall person, you're pretty short. That statement says more about the speaker's perception of height than anything approaching reality.

DH: I was watching an afternoon talk show recently whose topic was lesbian parents. Some woman asked one of the parents if she would raise the child up in an unbiased manner so that the child would be able to choose his or her sexual orientation. Let's talk about propaganda, recruitment, and bias in the home, media, culture, and so forth. Recently an anti-gay-rights activist has been calling for "no promo homo" in the media. Who is recruiting whom and how? Is the issue properly promo homo, or promo hetero?

RD: Heterosexual culture can be defined as the recruitment of men and women for heterosexual practices, a recruitment that makes sense from the sexual majority's point of view. It may indeed make sense for a culture to support its families and its biological future by preferring childbearing families, straight or gay. It is less clear to me that the connection between the majority sexual orientation and the multibillion dollar commercial system that exists to serve and enforce it is a good or moral thing. But all you have to do to see how the recruitment really works is to spend a day living normally but as if you were not heterosexual. Do everything you normally do with a consciousness of your interest in the same sex. You will see how much of your life has to be lived while you get the message that your sexual orientation and the moral and personal life you hope to realize are not prized by your culture. You will also see how heterosexual culture excludes and demonizes lesbians and gay men all the time. I know it sounds corny, but spend a day gay like me and you will see how the cultural environment recruits us and wants to change us or shame and disable us.

By the way, the natural environment does not do this. I think almost every lesbian or gay man I know or have read about has had to deal with the way in which the society tries to recruit us to go against our nature and punishes us if we won't or can't. The best way to find out about this is to read lesbian and gay literature, which abounds with the stories of the real recruited, of lesbians and gay men drafted into the boot camps of straightness. Probably the reason that recruitment is such a powerful scare word among homophobes is that the sexual majority is conditioned to thinking that being in the sexual minority is a bad and unnatural thing, so any encounter with gays raises the fear that one's own children will be different; connected to this is the common aspect of the rhetoric of oppression. The oppressor commonly attributes his own methods to the target of his hatred. This is nothing new—as we show in our book—and it continues to thrive.

DH: Why is the religious right so vociferous and damning about homosexuality?

RD: Well, you know, they're just using us to get to you. They would not be putting so much effort into this if they were merely trying to get rid of us. I'm the hook: It's you they want! It is, really! Do you think they would make all this fuss about a bunch of queers? Anyone interested in these issues has to ask him- or herself, why do these people get so upset? What are they after? Is it your experience in life that when people get so hysterical that they must turn people into demons, that they do so because they are after those demons? Or, rather, is it because they see those people symbolically? I'm quite sure it is the latter. And what is it that we symbolize to these people? Moral disorder, obviously. Now, you would have to be an idiot not to notice that we live in the midst of moral chaos. We clearly do. The question is, what makes you decide to focus on a certain group and make them the symbol of decay? Why not guns? I'm sorry, but we gays are not a moral problem. Guns are. Of course, the other side of the conflict is money, which sets up the following provocative equation: gays symbolize moral decay; the church is fighting moral decay; therefore, send money so that the religious right, especially rich televangelists, can fight against gays and lesbians and therefore snuff out moral decay.

DH: You discuss the crucible of coming out and how that process creates an "unshakable core of certainty of self." Being a heterosexual white male, and therefore avoiding many of the crucibles other minorities are forced to negotiate, I wonder what it is like to have such a self? I'm not asking what it's like to come out, but is the structure upon which your identity is built different in some way from mine because yours was created through fire?

RD: I love that sentence, but if you push me too hard on it, I'll have to admit that it is an ideal. It is not the case that any present group of people can be said to have that. At the very least, though, I can say that for any person who goes through the process of recognizing his or her homosexuality, that identity becomes something, and if you can stick with it, it really is something. In order to be, do, and choose gay—and you do have to choose it, it's there, but you have to choose to make the most of it—you will for forced to go through a series of unpopular and unconventional experiences which may cultivate in you a particular strength. But as I said, I wouldn't say that about myself in particular. And one does have to be wary of the kind of discourse that claims that I, or a group, have access to authenticity and you don't. I know too many gay men and lesbians to allow me to say that as a group we tend to be more confident or better than another. But, the recognition and subsequent expression you go through means that the choice you make is something to stand up for.

The ideas behind that statement are actually rather difficult for me to verbalize. There is a difference between what we go through and what people of color go through. Consider family. Many gays, especially when they first come out, have a real tough time with their family. The students that come to me and say, "Well, my family doesn't approve"—you always respond with, "Well, just give them time; they're your family, they love you." Part of you is swearing at them while the other is pleading for their acceptance. You do both. You swear at them under your breath, and you try to be patient with them. And in the meantime I can be a surrogate family to them, and they can be a surrogate family to me. Most of us do eventually get back with our families. But I'll tell you, for the majority of people I know, the real people in our lives are the gays and/or lesbians that we are close to. Each of us had to make an effort to find others based upon what we knew about ourselves. That means that they don't *have* to take you in, unlike family. One really learns about family and community within those groups.

DH: One of the arguments Iris Young makes in her book has to do with violence, or the fear of, as a type of oppression. When gay lives are seen as less valuable and a threat to the mainstream, it is easier to accept the fact of violence against gays. Even the Vatican holds that it is not unjust to discriminate against gays.

RD: Oh, certainly. I mean look how many books have gay serial killers. Now, maybe you aren't a great fan of that genre, nor am I, but let me tell you, there are many fictional serial killers who are gay. Even today, if you want to write a book and make a shortcut to perversion, use a gay protagonist.

Look at the statistics and see who is getting beat up. It is a common occurrence here in West Hollywood for a gay man to get chased down by a carload of men who subsequently catch him and beat him. Remember that huge sailor who beat to death his gay shipmate? He said in his defense that it is immoral to be gay. These guys were shipmates! Think of it, getting beaten to death. No gun was involved, no knife was involved. Beat to death, and he brings up morality? And the guy really got off with less than he should have. Why? Because it is okay to do violence to gays.

In most places in this country, a gay man or lesbian cannot assume protection will be voluntarily extended to him or her by the local police force. I'm pretty sure I would get it here in West Hollywood. But it's sad to realize that I can only get protection here because I live in an area that is populated by a large percentage of gays. That is not the case in 99 % of the cities and towns in this country. Let's say, for example, that I am on my way to school driving through La Verne and stop off to get gas. And let's say I give you, the attendant, an extra look because you are good looking. What's the harm? You're pleasant to look at. Not only could I get beat up for that, but it is probably enough to excuse the violence in the minds of many.

Maybe it doesn't happen anymore, but there is a point in every "sissy" kid's life, or tomboy's life, when they find out they are different. What is the typical reaction from his or her peers? It's violence. And it's probably doubly difficult for women because they are violated for being female and because they have separated themselves from men. Most people I know have been beat or know of someone who has been beaten, or even killed. We are plain frightened. In some places I have been afraid for my physical security. Isn't that crazy? It really shouldn't be that way. I could understand that feeling if I were in Vietnam in 1965. But here? Look around West Hollywood and see how many gays have these huge muscular physiques. It's armor. Nothing more.

DH: Why should gay rights matter to America?

RD: Gay rights must matter to America because until lesbians and gay men enjoy equal protection of the laws and individual freedom to live their private lives, the freedoms other Americans enjoy are not rights but privileges. The history of liberty is the history of the extension of freedom and equality on the rational basis of natural rights philosophy. Once raised, the issue of gay rights is unavoidable because the enemies of equal rights for lesbians and gay men are in effect the enemies of individual freedom and equal protection of the laws as organizing principles of society. They claim a different principle, their religious understandings or their personal view of what is natural and normal. Americans need to champion the rights of others not just for some abstract reason but because the rights of each depend on the rights of all. If equal rights is to be a privilege, then who is to receive that privilege, and on what basis, and by whose decision, and with whose consent? The simple reason for America to care about gay rights is that to care about gay rights is to care about everyone's equal rights in the only way we know how. Missiles can protect the country, but freedom depends on civic vigilance. The only way you can protect your own equal rights is to recognize that you enjoy them because you are like everyone else, even if you are in the sexual majority and the rights at stake are those of a sexual minority. We are all alike when it comes to equal protection of the laws, and we are all different when it comes to individual freedom. That is the truth of which gay rights is the current litmus test. In the past it has been other struggles, and in the future it will be other struggles. But for now, it is gay rights that define the struggle for equal protection of the laws and individual freedom in the United States. That is why they matter to America.

5

Five Faces of Oppression

Iris Marion Young

> Someone who does not see a pane of glass does not know that he does not see it.
> Someone who, being placed differently, does see it, does not know the other
> does not see it.
>
> When our will finds expression outside ourselves in actions performed by
> others, we do not waste our time and our power of attention in examining whether
> they have consented to this. This is true for all of us. Our attention, given en-
> tirely to the success of the undertaking, is not claimed by them as long as they
> are docile . . . .
>
> Rape is a terrible caricature of love from which consent is absent. After rape,
> oppression is the second horror of human existence. It is a terrible caricature of
> obedience.
>
> —Simone Weil

Many people in the United States would not choose the term "oppression" to name
injustice in our society. For contemporary emancipatory social movements—socialists, radical feminists, American Indian activists, Black activists, gay and lesbian activists—oppression is a central category of political discourse. Political dialogue that
utilizes oppression as a central category involves adopting a general mode of analyz-
ing and evaluating social structures and practices, which is incompatible with the language of liberal individualism that dominates political discourse in the United States.

A major political project for those of us who identify with at least one of these
emancipatory movements must be to persuade people that the language of oppression
makes sense of much of our social experience. We are ill prepared for this task, however, because we as a society have not generated an acceptable working definition of
oppression. While we find the term used often in the diverse philosophical and theoretical literature spawned by radical social movements in the United States, we find
little direct discussion of the meaning of the concept as used by these movements.

In this chapter I offer an account of oppression as I understand its use by new social
movements in the United States since the 1960s. I will begin by reflecting on the

conditions of the groups said by these movements to be oppressed: among others, women, Blacks, Chicanos, Puerto Ricans and other Spanish-speaking Americans, American Indians, Jews, lesbians, gay men, Arabs, Asians, old people, working-class people, and the physically and mentally disabled. I aim to systematize the meaning of the concept of oppression as used by these diverse political movements and to provide argument and illustrations to clarify the wrongs oppression names.

Obviously the groups just named are not oppressed to the same extent or in the same ways. In the most general sense, all oppressed people suffer some inhibition of their ability to develop and exercise their capacity and to express their needs, thoughts, and feelings. In that abstract sense all oppressed people face a common condition. Beyond that, in any more specific sense, it is not possible to define a *single* set of criteria that describe the condition of oppression of the groups mentioned. Consequently, attempts by theorists and activists to discover a common description or the essential causes behind the oppression of all these groups have frequently led to fruitless disputes about whose oppression is more fundamental or more grave. The contexts in which members of these groups use the term oppression to describe the injustices of their situation suggest that oppression names in fact a family of concepts and conditions, which I shall divide into five categories: exploitation, marginalization, powerlessness, cultural imperialism, and violence.

In this chapter I will elucidate each of these forms of oppression. But first we must understand how limited our present view of oppression is and how that view must be broadened so as to include oppression as a *structural* concept.

OPPRESSION AS A STRUCTURAL CONCEPT

One reason why many people would not use the term oppression to describe injustice in our society is that they do not understand the term in the same way as do new social movements. In its traditional usage, oppression means the exercise of tyranny by a ruling group. Thus many Americans would agree with radicals in applying the term oppression to the situation of Black South Africans under apartheid. Oppression also traditionally carries a strong connotation of conquest and colonial domination. The Hebrews were oppressed in Egypt, and many uses of the term oppression in the West invoke this paradigm.

Dominant political discourse typically uses the term oppression to describe societies other than our own. Within this anticommunist rhetoric both tyrannical and colonialist implications of the term appear. For the anticommunist, communism denotes precisely the exercise of brutal tyranny over a whole people by a few rulers, and the will to conquer the world, bringing hitherto independent peoples under that tyranny. In dominant political discourse, it is not legitimate to use the term oppression to describe American society, because oppression is the evil perpetrated by others in other countries.

New Left social movements of the 1960s and 1970s, however, shifted the meaning of oppression. In this new usage, oppression designates the disadvantage and injustice some people suffer not because a tyrannical power coerces them, but because of the everyday practices of a well-intentioned liberal society. In this New Left usage, the tyranny of a ruling group over another, as in South Africa, must certainly be called oppressive. But oppression also refers to systemic constraints on groups that are not necessarily the result of the intentions of a tyrant. Oppression in this sense is *structural* rather than the result of the personal choices of, or policies put forward by, individuals. Its causes are embedded in unquestioned norms, habits, and symbols, in the assumptions underlying institutional rules and the collective consequences of following those rules. Oppression names, as Marilyn Frye puts it, "an enclosing structure of forces and barriers which tends to the immobilization and reduction of a group or category of people."[1] In this structural sense, oppression refers to the vast and deep injustices some groups suffer as a consequence of, for example, the frequently unconscious assumptions and reactions of well-meaning people in circumstances of ordinary interaction, or media and cultural stereotypes, or structural features of bureaucratic hierarchies and market mechanisms—in short, the normal *processes* of everyday life. Therefore, it is essential to remember that we cannot eliminate structural oppression by simply getting rid of those that wield power, by creating new laws, or by simply modifying behavior or attitudes because oppressions are systematically reproduced in major economic, political, and cultural institutions.

This systemic character of oppression implies that an oppressed group need not have a correlate oppressing group. While structural oppression involves relations among groups, these relations do not always fit the paradigm of conscious and intentional oppression of one group by another. Michel Foucault suggests that to understand the meaning and operation of power in modern society, we must look beyond the model of power as "sovereignty," a relation between ruler and subject, and instead analyze the exercise of power as the effect of often liberal and "humane" practices of education, medicine, bureaucratic administration, production and distribution of consumer goods, and so on.[2] The conscious and unconscious actions of many individuals daily contribute to maintaining and reproducing oppression. Such people are usually just doing their jobs or living their lives and do not understand themselves as agents of oppression.

I am not suggesting that within a system of oppression individual persons do not intentionally harm others in oppressed groups. The raped woman, the beaten Black youth, the locked-out worker, and the gay man harassed on the street are all victims of intentional actions by identifiable agents. Nor am I denying that specific groups are beneficiaries of the oppression of other groups and thus have an interest in the continuation of that oppression. Indeed, for every oppressed group there is a group that is privileged in relation to that group.

In accordance with ordinary political usage, I suggest that oppression is a condition of groups. Thus before exploring the meaning of oppression, we must examine the concept of a social group.

THE CONCEPT OF A SOCIAL GROUP

In the way that I will be using the term, oppression refers to structural phenomena that immobilize or diminish a group. But what is a group? Deciding this is an important task, for some groups may make claims to reparations, special benefits, or equal rights as a consequence of past or present oppression. The question then is, Do we wish to grant equal standing to all groups? Our ordinary discourse differentiates people according to social groups, such as women and men, age groups, racial and ethnic groups, religious groups, and so on. Social groups of this sort are not simply collections of individuals, for such groups are more fundamentally intertwined with the identities of the people described as belonging to them. They are a specific kind of collectivity, with specific consequences for how people understand one another and themselves.

A social group is a collective of persons differentiated from at least one other group by cultural forms, practices, or way of life. Members of a group have a specific *affinity* with one another because of their similar experience or way of life, which prompts them to associate with one another more than with those not identified with the group or to associate with them differently. Groups are an expression of social relations, that is, a group exists only in relation to at least one other group. (For a group to exist, another group must also exist or be created, so that each can differentiate itself from the other.) Group identification arises, then, in the encounter and interaction between social collectivities that experience some differences in their way of life and forms of association, even if they also regard themselves as belonging to the same society.

So, for example, as long as they associated solely among themselves, a Native American tribe thought of itself only as "the people." Upon encountering other tribes, though, an awareness of difference was created; the others were named as a group, and the first group came to see themselves as a group. But social groups do not arise only from an encounter between different societies. Social processes also differentiate groups within a single society. The sexual division of labor, for example, has created social groups of women and men in all known societies. Members of each gender have a certain affinity with others in their group because of what they do or experience, and differentiate themselves from the other gender even when members of each gender consider that they have much in common with members of the other gender. Members of socioeconomic classes often find they have an affinity for others of their own class. This is so because members of a class often come from similar backgrounds; cultivate similar tastes, attitudes, and politics, and socialize with similar types of people.

Political philosophy typically has no place for a specific concept of the social group. When philosophers and political theorists discuss groups, they tend to conceive them either on the model of aggregates or on the model of associations, both of which are methodologically *individualist* concepts that ignore the idea of group affinity or "throwness" as constitutive of social groups. To arrive at a specific concept of the social group, then, it will be useful to contrast social groups with both aggregates and associations.

An aggregate is any classification of persons according to some attribute. Persons can be aggregated according to any number of attributes—eye color, the make of car they drive, the street they live on. Some people interpret the groups that have emotional and social salience in our society as aggregates, as arbitrary classifications of persons according to such attributes as skin color, genitals, or age. George Sher, for example, treats social groups as aggregates, and uses the arbitrariness of aggregate classification as a reason not to give special attention to groups. "There are really as many groups as there are combinations of people and if we are going to ascribe claims to equal treatment to racial, sexual, and other groups with high visibility, it will be mere favoritism not to ascribe similar claims to these other groups as well."[3]

But "highly visible" social groups such as Blacks or women are different from aggregates, or mere combinations of people. A social group is defined not primarily by a set of shared attributes but by a sense of identity. What defines Black Americans as a social group is not primarily their skin color; some persons whose skin color is fairly light, for example, identify themselves as Black. Though sometimes physical attributes are a necessary condition for classifying oneself or others as belonging to a certain social group, it is identification with a certain social status, the common history that social status produces, and self-identification that defines the group as a group.

Social groups are not entities that exist apart from individuals (each requires the other), but neither are they merely arbitrary classifications of individuals according to attributes that are external to or accidental to their identities. An individual's own identity is partially constituted by group meanings in terms of the cultural forms, social situation, and history that group members know as theirs because these meanings have been forced upon them, or forged by them, or both. The heritage of activism that Martin Luther King, Jr., has left to African Americans as a group in their struggle for equality and self-determination is felt just as much by many young African Americans as an individual and personal inheritance.

A second model typically used to conceive of social groups is that of associations. By an association I mean a formally organized institution, such as a club, corporation, political party, church, college, or union. Unlike the aggregate model of groups, the association model recognizes that groups are defined by specific practices and forms of association. Nevertheless, it shares a problem with the aggregate model. The aggregate model conceives the individual as prior to the collective, because it reduces the social group to a mere set of attributes attached to individuals. The association model also implicitly conceives the individual as ontologically prior to the collective, as making up, or constituting, groups.

This contract model of social relations is appropriate for conceiving associations, but not groups. In a contract model individuals constitute associations; individuals come together as *already formed* persons and set the association up by establishing rules, positions, and offices. The relationship of individuals to associations is usually voluntary, though even when it is not, the individual has nevertheless usually entered the association. The person is prior to the association also in that the person's identity and sense of self are usually regarded as prior to and relatively independent of association membership.

On the other hand, as mentioned above, groups do constitute individuals. A person's particular sense of history, affinity, and separateness, even the person's mode of reasoning, evaluating, and expressing feeling, are constituted partly by her or his group affinities. This does not mean that persons have no individual styles or are unable to transcend or reject a group identity. Nor does it preclude persons from having many aspects that are independent of these group identities.

As I pointed out earlier, the social ontology underlying many contemporary theories of justice is methodologically individualist or atomist. It presumes that the individual is prior to the social. This individualist social ontology usually goes together with a normative conception of the self as independent; the authentic self is autonomous, unified, free, and self-made, standing apart from history and affiliations, choosing its life plan entirely for itself.

One of the main contributions of poststructuralist philosophy has been to expose as illusory this view of a unified self-making subjectivity: a view that posits the subject/individual as an autonomous origin or an underlying substance to which attributes of gender, nationality, family role, intellectual disposition, and so on might attach. Conceiving the subject in this fashion implies conceiving consciousness as outside of and prior to language and the context of the social interaction that the subject enters.

A more powerful account of social groups that avoids the problems inherent in both the aggregate and association models of social groups and recognizes the strengths of poststructuralism is that of group affinity. A person joins an association, and even if membership in it fundamentally affects one's life, one does not take that membership to define one's very identity in the way, for example, that being Navaho might. Group affinity, on the other hand, has the character of what Martin Heidegger (1962) calls "thrownness": one finds oneself as a member of a group that one experiences as *always already having been*. (Our identities are defined in relation to how others identify us, and they do so in terms of groups that are always already associated with specific attributes, stereotypes, and norms.)[4]

From the thrownness of group affinity it does not follow that one cannot leave groups and enter new ones. Many women become lesbian after first identifying as heterosexual. Anyone who lives long enough becomes old. These cases exemplify thrownness precisely because such changes in group affinity are experienced as transformations in one's identity. Nor does it follow from the thrownness of group affinity that one cannot define the meaning of group identity for oneself; those who identify with a group can redefine the meaning and norms of group identity. Indeed, oppressed groups have sought to confront their oppression by engaging in just such redefinition. The present point is that one first finds a group identity as given, and then proceeds to take it up in a certain way.

Groups, I have said, exist only in relation to other groups. A group may be identified by outsiders without those so identified having any specific consciousness of themselves as a group. Sometimes a group comes to exist only because one group excludes and labels a category of persons, and those labeled come to understand themselves as group members only slowly, on the basis of their shared oppression. In Vichy France, for example, Jews who had been so assimilated that they had no specifically Jewish identity were marked as Jews by others and given a specific social status by them. These people "discovered" themselves as Jews, and then formed a group identity and affinity with one another. A person's group identities may be for the most part only a background or horizon to his or her life, becoming salient only in specific interactive contexts.

In addition, although social processes of affinity and differentiation produce groups, they do not give groups a substantive *essence*. There is no common nature that members of a group share. As aspects of a process, moreover, groups are fluid; they come into being and may fade away. For example, homosexual practices have existed in many societies and historical periods. Yet gay men and lesbians have been identified as specific groups, and so identified themselves, only in the twentieth century.[5]

And finally, arising from social relations and processes, group differences usually cut across one another. Especially in a large, complex, and highly differentiated society, social groups are not themselves homogeneous, but mirror in their own differentiations many of the other groups in the wider society. In American society today, for example, Blacks are not a simple, unified group with a common life. Like other racial and ethnic groups, they are differentiated by age, gender, class, sexuality, region, and nationality, any of which in a given context may become a salient group identity.

Assuming an aggregate model of groups, some people think that social groups are invidious fictions that essentialize what others believe to be merely arbitrary attributes. From this point of view, problems of prejudice, stereotyping, discrimination, and exclusion exist because some people mistakenly believe that group identification makes a difference in the capacities, temperament, or virtues of group members. This individualist conception of persons and their relation to one another tends to identify oppression with group identification. Oppression, in this view, is something that happens to people when they are classified in groups. Because others identify them as a group, they are excluded and despised. Eliminating oppression thus requires eliminating groups. People should be treated as individuals, not as members of groups, and allowed to form their lives freely without stereotypes or group norms.

This book takes issue with that position. While I agree that individuals should be free to pursue life plans in their own way, it is foolish to deny the reality of groups. Despite the modern myth of a decline of parochial attachments and ascribed identities, in modern society group differentiation remains endemic. As both markets and social administration increase the web of social interdependency on a world scale, and as more people encounter one another as strangers in cities and states, people retain and renew ethnic, locale, age, sex, and occupational group identifications and form new ones in the processes of encounter. Even when they belong to oppressed groups, people's group identifications are often important to them, and they often feel a special affinity for others in their group. I believe that group differentiation is both an inevitable and a desirable aspect of modern social processes. Social justice requires not the melting away of differences but institutions that promote reproduction of and respect for group differences without oppression.

THE FACES OF OPPRESSION

The concept of oppression has been current among radicals since the 1960s, partly in reaction to Marxist attempts to reduce the injustices of racism and sexism, for example, to the effects of class domination or bourgeois ideology. Racism, sexism, ageism, and homophobia, some social movements asserted, are distinct forms of oppression with their own dynamics apart from the dynamics of class, even though they may interact with class oppression. From often heated discussions among socialists, feminists, and antiracism activists in the last ten years, a consensus is emerging that many different groups must be said to be oppressed in our society and that no single form of oppression can be assigned causal or moral primacy. The same discussion has also led to the recognition that group differences cut across individual lives in a multiplicity of ways that can entail privilege and oppression for the same person in different respects. Only a complex account of the concept of oppression can adequately capture these insights.

Accordingly, I offer below an explication of five faces of oppression as a useful set of categories and distinctions that I believe is comprehensive, in the sense that it covers all the groups said by New Left social movements to be oppressed and all the ways they claim or are said to be oppressed. I derive the five faces of oppression from reflection on the condition of these groups. Because different factors or combinations of factors constitute the oppression of different groups, making their oppression irreducible, I believe it is not possible to give one essential definition of oppression. The five categories articulated in this chapter, however, are adequate to describe the oppression of any group as well as its similarities with and differences from the oppression of other groups.

Exploitation

To understand this first "face" we must first begin with Karl Marx. The central function of Marx's theory of exploitation is to explain how class structure can exist in the absence of legally and normatively sanctioned class distinctions. In precapitalist societies, domination is overt and accomplished through directly political means. In both slave society and feudal society, the right to appropriate the product of the labor of others partly defines class privilege, and these societies legitimate class distinctions with ideologies of natural superiority and inferiority.

Capitalist society, on the other hand, removes traditional juridically enforced class distinctions and promotes a belief in the legal freedom of persons. Workers freely contract with employers and receive a wage; no formal mechanisms of law or custom force them to work for that employer or any employer. Thus the mystery of capitalism arises: When everyone is formally free, how can there be class domination? Why do class distinctions persist between the wealthy, who own the means of production, and the mass of people, who work for them? The theory of exploitation answers this question.

Profit, the basis of capitalist power and wealth, is a mystery if we assume that in the market goods are bought and sold at their values. Marx's labor theory of value dispels this mystery. Every commodity's value, he says, is a function of the labor time necessary for its production. Labor power is the one commodity that in the process of being consumed produces new value. (Labor, purchased with wages, is consumed in the production of a commodity.) Profit, then, comes from the difference between the value of the labor performed (a commodity's selling price minus all costs but labor) and the value of the capacity to labor, which the capitalist purchases with wages. Profit is possible only because the owner of capital appropriates any realized surplus value.

C. B. Macpherson reconstructs this theory of exploitation in a more explicitly normative form.[6] The injustice of capitalist society consists in the fact that some people exercise their capacities under the control, according to the purposes, and for the benefit of, other people. Through private ownership of the means of production and through markets that allocate labor and the ability to buy goods, capitalism systematically transfers the powers of some persons to others, thereby augmenting the power of the latter. In this process of the transfer of powers, according to Macpherson, the capitalist class acquires and maintains an ability to extract benefits from workers. Not only are powers transferred from capitalists, but also the powers of workers diminish by more than the amount of transfer, because workers suffer material deprivation and a loss of control, and hence are deprived of important elements of self-respect. Justice, then, requires eliminating the institutional forms that enable and enforce this process of transference and replacing them with institutional forms that enable all to develop and use their capacities in a way that does not inhibit, but rather can enhance, similar development and use in others.

The central insight expressed in the concept of exploitation, then, is that this oppression occurs through a steady process of the transfer of the results of one social group to benefit another. The injustice of class division does not consist solely in the distributive fact that some people have great wealth while most people have little. Exploitation enacts a structural and hierarchical relation between social groups as well. Social rules about what work is, who does what for whom, how work is compensated, and the social process by which the results of work are appropriated operate to enact relations of power and inequality. These relations are produced and reproduced through a systematic process in which the energies of the have-nots are continuously expended to maintain and augment the power, status, and wealth of the haves.

Many writers have cogently argued that the Marxist concept of exploitation is too narrow to encompass all forms of domination and oppression. In particular, the Marxist concept of class leaves important phenomena of sexual and racial oppression unexplained. Does this mean that sexual and racial oppression are nonexploitative, and that we should reserve wholly distinct categories for these oppressions? Or can the concept of exploitation be broadened to include other ways in which the labor and energy expenditure of one group benefits another and reproduces a relation of domination between them?

Gender Exploitation

Feminists have had little difficulty showing that women's oppression consists partly in a systematic and unreciprocated transfer of powers from women to men. Women's oppression consists not merely in an inequality of status, power, and wealth resulting from men excluding them from privileged activities. The freedom, power, status, and self-realization of men is possible precisely because women work for them. Gender exploitation has two aspects: transfer of the fruits of material labor to men, and transfer of nurturing and sexual energies to men.

Christine Delphy considers the first aspect when she describes marriage as a class relation in which women's labor benefits men without comparable remuneration.[7] She makes it clear that the exploitation consists not in the sort of work that women do in the home, for this might include various kinds of tasks, but in the fact that they perform tasks for someone on whom they are dependent. Thus, for example, in most systems of agricultural production in the world, men take to market the goods women have produced, and more often than not men receive the status and often the entire income from this labor.

Ann Ferguson identifies the second form of transference of women's energies to men.[8] Women provide men and children with emotional care and provide men with sexual satisfaction, and as a group receive relatively little of either from men. Due to gender socialization, we women tend to be more attentive to interactive dynamics than men, better at providing empathy and support for people's feelings, and more effective at smoothing over interactive tensions. Both men and women look to women as nurturers of their personal lives, and women frequently complain that when they look to men for emotional support they do not receive it. The norms of heterosexuality, moreover, are oriented around male pleasure, and consequently many women receive little satisfaction from their sexual interaction with men.

Most feminist theories of gender exploitation have concentrated on the family and its patriarchal structure. Recently, however, feminists have begun to explore relations of gender exploitation enacted in the contemporary workplace and through the state. Carol Brown argues that as men have removed themselves from responsibility for children, many women have become dependent on the state for subsistence as they continue to bear near total responsibility for child rearing.[9] This has created a new system of exploitation of women's domestic labor mediated by state institutions. She calls this system public patriarchy.

In twentieth-century capitalist economies, the workplaces that women have been entering in increasing numbers serve as another important site of gender exploitation.

David Alexander argues that typically feminine jobs involve gender-based tasks requiring sexual labor, nurturing, caring for others' bodies, or smoothing over workplace tensions.[10] In these ways women's energies are expended in jobs that enhance the status of, please, or comfort others—usually men; these gender-based labors of waitresses, clerical workers, nurses, and other caretakers often go unnoticed and undercompensated.

To summarize, women are exploited in the Marxist sense to the degree that they are wage workers. Some have argued that women's domestic labor also represents a form of capitalist class exploitation insofar as it is labor covered by the wages a family receives. As a group, however, women undergo specific forms of gender exploitation in which their energies and power are expended, often unnoticed and unacknowledged, usually to benefit men by releasing them for more important and creative work, enhancing their status or the environment around them, or providing them with sexual or emotional service.

Racial Exploitation

Race is a structure of oppression at least as basic as class or gender. Are there, then, racially specific forms of exploitation? There is no doubt that racialized groups in the United States, especially Blacks and Latinos, are oppressed through capitalist superexploitation resulting from a segmented labor market that tends to reserve skilled, high-paying, and unionized jobs for whites.

Is it possible to conceptualize a form of exploitation that is racially specific on analogy with the gender-specific forms just discussed? I suggest that the category of menial labor might supply a means for such conceptualization. In its derivation "menial" designates the labor of servants. Wherever racism exists, there also exists the assumption, culturally or juridically enforced, that members of the oppressed racial groups are or ought to be servants of those in the privileged group. In most white racist societies this means that many white people have dark- or yellow-skinned domestic servants, and in the United States today there remains significant racial structuring of private household service. But in the United States today much service labor has gone public: anyone who goes to a good hotel or a good restaurant can have servants. Servants often attend the daily—and nightly—activities of business executives, government officials, and other high-status professionals. In our society there remains strong cultural pressure to fill servant jobs—bellhop, porter, chambermaid, busboy, and so on—with Black and Latino workers. These jobs entail a transfer of energies whereby the servers enhance the status of the served.

Menial labor usually refers not only to service, however, but also to any servile, unskilled, low-paying work lacking in autonomy in which a person is subject to taking orders from many people. Menial work tends to be auxiliary work, instrumental to the work of others, where those who are served receive primary recognition for doing the job. Laborers on a construction site, for example, are at the beck and call of welders, electricians, carpenters, and other skilled workers, who receive recognition for the job done. In the United States explicit racial discrimination once reserved menial work for Blacks, Chicanos, American Indians, and Chinese, and menial work still tends to be linked to Black and Latino workers. I offer this category of menial labor as a form of racially specific exploitation, as a provisional category in need of exploration.

The injustice of exploitation is most frequently understood on a distributive model. For example, though he does not offer an explicit definition of the concept, Bruce Ackerman seems to mean by exploitation a seriously unequal *distribution* of wealth, income, and other resources that is group based and structurally persistent.[11] John Roemer's definition of exploitation is narrower and more rigorous: "An agent is exploited when the amount of labor embodied in *any* bundle of goods he could receive, in a feasible distribution of society's net product, is less than the labor he expended."[12] This definition, too, turns the conceptual focus from institutional relations and processes to distributive outcomes.

Jeffrey Reiman argues that such a distributive understanding of exploitation reduces the injustice of class processes to a function of the inequality of the productive assets classes own. This misses, according to Reiman, the relationship of force between capitalists and workers, the fact that the unequal exchange in question occurs within coercive structures that give workers few options.[13] The injustice of exploitation consists in social processes that bring about a transfer of energies from one group to another to produce unequal distributions and in the way in which social institutions enable a few to accumulate while they constrain many more. The injustices of exploitation cannot be eliminated by redistribution of goods, for as long as institutionalized practices and structural relations remain unaltered, the process of transfer will recreate an unequal distribution of benefits. Bringing about justice where there is exploitation requires reorganization of institutions and practices of decision making, alteration of the division of labor, and similar measures of institutional, structural, and cultural change.

Marginalization

Increasingly in the United States racial oppression occurs in the form of marginalization rather than exploitation. Marginals are people the system of labor cannot or will not use. Not only in Third World capitalist countries, but also in most Western capitalist societies, there is a growing underclass of people permanently confined to lives of social marginality, most of whom are racially marked—Blacks or Indians in Latin America, and Blacks, East Indians, Eastern Europeans, or North Africans in Europe.

Marginalization is by no means the fate only of racially marked groups, however. In the United States a shamefully large proportion of the population is marginal: old people and, increasingly, people who are not very old but get laid off from their jobs and cannot find new work; young people, especially Black or Latino, who cannot find first or second jobs; many single mothers and their children; other people involuntarily unemployed; many mentally and physically disabled people; and Native Americans, especially those on reservations.

Marginalization is perhaps the most dangerous form of oppression. Via marginalization a whole category of people is expelled from useful participation in social life and thus potentially subjected to severe material deprivation and even extermination. The material deprivation marginalization often causes is certainly unjust, especially in a society where others have plenty. Contemporary advanced capitalist societies have in principle acknowledged the injustice of material deprivation caused by marginalization and have taken some steps to address it by providing welfare payments and services. The continuance of this welfare state is by no means assured, and in most welfare state societies, especially the United States, welfare redistributions do not eliminate large-scale suffering and deprivation.

Material deprivation, which can be addressed by redistributive social policies, is not, however, the extent of the harm caused by marginalization. Two categories of injustice beyond material deprivation are associated with marginality in advanced capitalist societies. First, the provision of welfare itself produces new injustice by depriving those dependent on it of rights and freedoms that others have. And second, even when material deprivation is somewhat mitigated by the welfare state, marginalization is unjust because it blocks the opportunity to exercise capacities in socially defined and recognized ways.

Liberalism has traditionally asserted the right of equal citizenship to all rational autonomous agents. Early bourgeois liberalism therefore explicitly excluded from citizenship all those whose reason was questionable or not fully developed and all those not independent. Thus poor people, women, the mad and the feebleminded, and children were explicitly excluded from citizenship, and many of these were housed in institutions modeled on the modern prison: poorhouses, insane asylums, schools.

Today the exclusion of dependent persons from equal citizenship rights is only barely hidden beneath the veneer of institutionalized care. Because they depend on bureaucratic institutions for support or services, the old, the poor, and the mentally or physically disabled are subject to patronizing, punitive, demeaning, and arbitrary treatment by the policies and people associated with welfare bureaucracies. Being a dependent in our society implies being legitimately subject to the often arbitrary and invasive authority of social service providers and other public and private administrators, who enforce rules with which the marginal must comply and otherwise exercise power over the conditions of their lives. In meeting needs of the marginalized, often with the aid of social scientific disciplines, welfare agencies also construct the needs themselves. Medical and social service professionals know what is good for those they serve, and the marginals and dependents themselves do not have the right to claim to know what is good for them. Dependency in our society thus implies, as it has in all liberal societies, a sufficient warrant to suspend basic rights to privacy, respect, and individual choice.

Although dependency produces conditions of injustice in our society, dependency in itself need not necessarily be oppressive. One cannot imagine a society in which an individual would not at some time need to be dependent on others: children, sick people, women recovering from childbirth, old people who have become frail, depressed or otherwise emotionally needy persons have the moral right to depend on others for subsistence and support.

An important contribution of feminist moral theory has been to question the deeply held assumption that a person must be autonomous and independent to claim and be granted moral agency and full citizenship. Feminists have exposed this assumption as inappropriately individualistic and derived from a specifically male experience of social relations that values competition and solitary achievement over cooperation and dependency. Female experience of social relations, arising both from women's traditional domestic care responsibilities and from the kinds of paid work that many women do, tends to recognize dependence as a basic and lifelong human condition. Whereas according to the autonomy model a just society would as much as possible give people the opportunity to be independent, the feminist model envisions justice as according respect and participation in decision making to those who are dependent as well as to those who are independent. Dependency should not be a reason to be deprived of choice and respect, and much of the oppression many marginals experience would be lessened if a less individualistic model of rights prevailed.

Marginalization, then, does not cease to be oppressive when one has shelter and food. Many old people, for example, have sufficient means to live comfortably but remain oppressed in their marginal status. Even if marginals were provided a comfortable material life within institutions that respected their freedom and dignity, injustices of marginality would remain in the form of uselessness (the elderly are deemed too slow, too feeble, or too static to do meaningful work), boredom (a society that revolves around youth ignores the cultural needs of the elderly), and lack of self-respect. Most of our society's productive and recognized activities take place in contexts of organized social cooperation. Social structures and processes that close persons out of participation in such social cooperation are unjust. Thus, while marginalization definitely entails serious issues of distributive justice, it also involves the deprivation of cultural, practical, and institutionalized conditions for exercising capacities in a context of recognition and interaction.

Powerlessness

As I have indicated, the Marxist idea of class is important because it helps reveal the structure of exploitation: that some people gain power and wealth because they profit from the labor of others. For this reason I reject the claim some make that a traditional model of class exploitation fails to capture the structure of contemporary society. It remains the case that the labor of most people (even professionals) in society augments the power of relatively few. Despite their differences from nonprofessional workers, most professional workers are still not members of the capitalist class. Professional labor either involves exploitative transfers to capitalists or supplies important conditions for such transfers. Professional workers are in an ambiguous class position because they also benefit from the exploitation of nonprofessional workers.

While it is false to claim that a division between capitalist and working classes no longer describes our society, it is also false to say that class relations have remained unaltered since the nineteenth century. An adequate conception of oppression cannot ignore the experience of social division reflected in the colloquial distinction between the middle class and the working class, a division structured by the social division of labor between professionals and nonprofessionals. By social division of labor I mean, who works for whom, who does not work, and how the content of work defines one's institutional position relative to others. Professionals are privileged in relation to nonprofessionals by virtue of their position in the division of labor and the *status* it carries. In addition to being exploited, nonprofessionals suffer another form of oppression that I call powerlessness.

In the United States, as in other advanced capitalist countries, most workplaces are not organized democratically, direct participation in public policy decisions is rare, and policy implementation is for the most part hierarchical—rules being imposed upon bureaucrats and citizens. Thus most people in these societies do not regularly participate in making decisions that affect the conditions of their lives and actions. In this sense, most people lack significant power. At the same time, domination in modern society is enacted through the widely dispersed powers of many agents mediating the decisions of others. To that extent many people have some power in relation to others, yet lack the ultimate power to decide policies or results. The powerless are those who lack authority or power even in this mediated sense, those over whom power is exercised without their exercising it; the powerless are situated so that they must take orders and rarely have the right to give them. Powerlessness also designates a position in the division of labor and the concomitant social position that allows persons little opportunity to develop and exercise skills. The powerless have little or no work autonomy, exercise little creativity or judgment in their work, have no technical expertise or authority, express themselves awkwardly, especially in public or bureaucratic settings, and do not command respect.

This powerless status is perhaps best described negatively: the powerless lack the authority, status, and sense of self that professionals and the capitalist class tend to have. The status privilege of professionals has three aspects, the lack of which produces the oppression under which nonprofessionals suffer.

First, acquiring and practicing a profession has an expansive, progressive character. Being professional usually requires a college education and the acquisition of a specialized knowledge that entails working with symbols and concepts. Professionals experience progress first in acquiring the expertise, and second in the course of professional advancement and rise in status. The life of the nonprofessional by comparison is powerless in the sense that it lacks this orientation toward the progressive development of capacities and avenues for recognition.

Second, while many professionals have supervisors and cannot directly influence many decisions or the actions of many people, most nevertheless have considerable day-to-day work autonomy. Professionals usually have some authority over others—either over workers they supervise, auxiliaries, or clients. Nonprofessionals, on the other hand, lack autonomy, and in both their working and their consumer/client lives often stand under the authority of professionals.

Though based on a division of labor between mental and manual work, the distinction between "middle class" and "working class" designates a division not only in working life but also in nearly all aspects of social life. Professionals and nonprofessionals belong to different cultures in the United States. The two groups tend to live in segregated neighborhoods or even different towns—a process itself mediated by planners, zoning officials, and real estate people. (Neighborhoods are typically designed and constructed to appeal to a specific class rather than a cross-section of classes.) The groups tend to have different tastes in food, decor, clothes, music, and vacations, and often different health and educational needs. Members of each group socialize for the most part with others in the same status group. While there is some intergroup mobility between generations, for the most part the children of professionals become professionals and the children of nonprofessionals do not.

Thus, third, the privileges of the professional extend beyond the workplace to a whole way of life. I call this way of life "respectability." To treat people with respect is to be prepared to listen to what they have to say or to do what they request because they have some authority, expertise, or influence. The norms of respectability in our society are associated specifically with professional culture. Professional dress, speech, tastes, and demeanor all connote respectability. Generally professionals expect and receive respect from others. In restaurants, banks, hotels, real estate offices, and many other such public places as well as in the media, professionals typically receive more respectful treatment than nonprofessionals. For this reason nonprofessionals seeking a loan or a job or trying to buy a house or a car, will often try to look "professional" and "respectable" in those settings.

The privilege of this professional respectability appears starkly in the dynamics of racism and sexism. In daily interchange women and men of color must prove their respectability. At first they are often not treated by strangers with respectful distance or deference. Yet, when it is revealed that this woman or that Puerto Rican man is a college teacher or a business executive, she or he is often treated more respectfully. Working-class white men, on the other hand, are often treated with respect until their working-class status is revealed.

I have discussed several injustices associated with powerlessness: inhibition in the development of one's capacities, lack of decision-making power in one's working life, and exposure to disrespectful treatment because of the status one occupies. These injustices have distributional consequences, but are more fundamentally matters of the division of labor. The oppression of powerlessness brings into question the division of labor basic to all industrial societies: the social division between those who plan and those who execute.

Cultural Imperialism

Exploitation, marginalization, and powerlessness all refer to relations of power and oppression that occur by virtue of the social division of labor. These three categories refer to structural and institutional relations that demarcate people's material lives, including but not restricted to the resources they have access to and the concrete opportunities they have or do not have to develop and exercise their capacities. These kinds of oppression are a matter of concrete power in relation to others—a matter of who benefits from whom and who is dispensable.

Recent theorists of movements of group liberation, notably feminist and Black liberation theorists, have also given prominence to a rather different form of oppression, which, following María Lugones and and Elizabeth Spelman, I shall call cultural imperialism.[14] To experience cultural imperialism means to experience how the dominant meanings of a society render the particular perspective of one's own group invisible at the same time as they stereotype one's group and mark it as the Other.

Cultural imperialism involves the universalization of a dominant group's experience and culture and its establishment as the norm. Some groups have exclusive or primary access to what Nancy Fraser calls the means of interpretation and communication in a society.[15] As a consequence, the dominant cultural products of the society, that is, those products most widely disseminated, express the experience, values, goals, and achievements of these groups. Often without noticing they do so, the dominant groups project their own experience as representative of humanity as such. We can see this in this nation's ongoing struggle to export human rights to China. Cultural products also express the dominant group's perspective on and interpretation of events and elements in the society, including other groups in the society—insofar as they attain cultural status at all.

An encounter with other groups, however, can challenge the dominant group's claim to universality. The dominant group reinforces its position by bringing other groups under the measure of its dominant norms. Consequently, the difference of women from men, American Indians or Africans from Europeans, Jews from Christians, homosexuals from heterosexuals, and workers from professionals becomes reconstructed largely as deviance and inferiority. Since only the dominant group's cultural expressions receive wide dissemination, their cultural expressions become the normal, or the universal, and thereby the unremarkable. Given the normality of its own cultural expressions and identity, the dominant group characterizes and constructs the differences that some groups exhibit as lack and negation. These groups become marked as Other.

The culturally dominated undergo a paradoxical oppression in that they are both marked by stereotypes and at the same time rendered invisible. As remarkable and deviant beings, the culturally imperialized are stamped with an essence. The stereotypes (a product of ascribed essences) confine them to a nature that is often attached in some way to their bodies and thus cannot easily be denied. These stereotypes so permeate the society that they are not noticed as contestable. Just as everyone knows that the earth goes around the sun, so everyone knows that gay people are promiscuous, that Native Americans are alcoholics, and that women are good with children. White males, on the other hand, insofar as they escape group marking, can be individuals. They can be—anything.

Those living under cultural imperialism find themselves defined and positioned from the outside by a network of dominant meanings they experience as arising from elsewhere, and proclaimed by those with whom they do not identify and who do not identify with them. This creates for the culturally oppressed the experience that W. E. B. DuBois called "double consciousness"—"this sense of always looking at one's self through the eyes of others, of measuring one's soul by the tape of a world that looks on in amused contempt and pity."[16] Double consciousness is a confused consciousness arising from a conflict between how an individual perceives him- or herself and the devalued, objectified, stereotyped conception that is internalized by the individual. While the subject desires recognition as a human, capable of activity, full of hope and possibility, she receives from the dominant culture only the judgment that she is different, marked, or inferior.

The group defined by the dominant culture as deviant, as a stereotyped Other, *is* culturally different from the dominant group because the actual status of Otherness creates specific experiences not shared by the dominant group, and because culturally oppressed groups are often socially segregated and occupy specific positions in the social division of labor. Members of such groups express their specific group experiences and interpretations of the world to one another, developing and perpetuating their own culture. Double consciousness, then occurs because one finds one's being defined by two cultures: a dominant culture and a subordinate one. Because individuals can affirm and recognize one another as sharing similar experiences and perspectives on social life, persons in culturally imperialized groups can often maintain a sense of positive subjectivity. Hence, oppressed groups will often segregate themselves from others as a means of developing and strengthening their individual and group identity.

Cultural imperialism involves the paradox of experiencing oneself as invisible at the same time that one is marked as different. The invisibility comes about when dominant groups fail to recognize the perspective embodied in their cultural expressions as one perspective among many. These dominant cultural expressions often simply have little place for the experience of other groups, at most only mentioning or referring to them in stereotyped or marginalized ways. This, then, is the injustice of cultural imperialism: the oppressed group's own experience and interpretation of social life finds little expression that touches the dominant culture, while that same culture imposes on the oppressed group its experience and interpretation of social life. In chapter 7 María Lugones and Joshua Price take up an extended account of cultural imperialism.

Violence

Finally, many groups suffer the oppression of systematic violence. Members of some groups live with the knowledge that they must fear random, unprovoked attacks on their persons or property that have no motive but to damage, humiliate, or destroy the person. In American society, women, Blacks, Asians, Arabs, gay men, and lesbians live under such threats of violence, and in at least some regions, Jews, Puerto Ricans, Chicanos, and other Spanish-speaking Americans must fear such violence as well. Physical violence against these groups is shockingly frequent. Rape crisis center networks estimate that more than one-third of all American women experience an attempted or successful sexual assault in their lifetimes. Manning Marable catalogues a large number of incidents of racist violence and terror against Blacks in the United States between 1980 and 1982.[17] He cites dozens of incidents of the severe beating, killing, or rape of Blacks by on-duty police officers who were acquitted of any wrongdoing. In 1981, moreover, there were at least five hundred documented cases of random white teenage violence against Blacks. Violence against gay men and lesbians is not only common but has been increasing in the last ten years. While the frequency of physical attack on members of these and other racially or sexually marked groups is very disturbing, I also include in this category less severe incidents of harassment, intimidation, or ridicule simply for the purpose of degrading, humiliating, or stigmatizing group members.

Given the frequency of such violence in our society, why are theories of justice usually silent about it? I think the reason is that theorists do not typically take such incidents of violence and harassment as matters of social injustice. No moral theorist would deny that such acts are very wrong. But unless all immoralities are injustices, they might wonder, why should such acts he interpreted as symptoms of social injustice? Acts of violence or petty harassment are committed by particular individuals, often extremists, deviants, or the mentally unsound. How, then, can they be said to involve the sorts of *institutional* issues I have said are properly the subject of justice?

What makes violence a face of oppression and a social injustice is less the particular acts themselves, though these are often utterly horrible, than the social context surrounding them, which makes them possible and even acceptable. What makes violence a phenomenon of social injustice and not merely an individual moral wrong is its systemic character, its existence as a social practice, its legitimacy, and its irrationality.

Violence is systemic because it is directed at members of a group simply because they are members of that group. Any woman, for example, has a reason to fear rape. Regardless of what a Black man has done to escape the oppressions of marginality or powerlessness, he lives knowing he is subject to attack or harassment. The oppression of violence consists not only in direct victimization, but in the daily knowledge shared by all members of oppressed groups that they are *liable* to violation, solely on account of their group identity. Just living under such a threat of attack on oneself or one's family or friends deprives the oppressed of freedom and dignity and needlessly expends their energy.

Violence is a social practice. It is a social given that everyone knows happens and will happen again. It is always at the horizon of social imagination, even for those who do not perpetrate it. According to the prevailing social logic, some circumstances make such violence more "called for" than others. The idea of rape will occur to many men who pick up a hitchhiking woman; the idea of hounding or teasing a gay man on their dorm floor will occur to many straight male college students. Often several persons inflict the violence together, especially in all-male groupings. Sometimes violators set out looking for people to beat up, rape, or taunt. This rule-bound, social, and often premeditated character makes violence against groups a social practice.

Group violence approaches legitimacy, moreover, in the sense that it is tolerated. Often third parties find it unsurprising because it happens frequently and lies as a constant possibility at the horizon of the social imagination. Even when they are caught, those who perpetrate acts of group-directed violence or harassment often receive light or no punishment. (Consider the historically light sentences convicted rapists serve.) To that extent, society renders their acts acceptable.

An important aspect of random, systemic violence is its irrationality. Xenophobic violence differs from the violence of states or ruling-class repression. Repressive violence has a rational, albeit evil, motive: rulers use it as a coercive tool to maintain their power. Many accounts of racist, sexist, or homophobic violence attempt to explain the motivation behind the violence as the desire to maintain group privilege or domination. I do not doubt that fear of violence often functions to keep oppressed groups subordinate, but I do not think xenophobic violence is rationally motivated in the way that, for example, violence against strikers is.

On the contrary, I think it is more accurate to say that the violation of rape, beating, killing, and harassment of women, people of color, gays, and other marked groups is motivated by fear or hatred of those groups. Sometimes the motive may be a simple will to power, to victimize those marked as vulnerable by the very social fact that they are subject to violence: that is, "You are a victim, therefore you must be treated as such; hence, I will also victimize you." If so, this motive is secondary in the sense that it depends on a social practice of group violence. Violence-causing fear or hatred of the other at least partly involves insecurities on the part of the violators; its irrationality suggests that unconscious processes are at work.

Violence is a form of injustice that a distributive understanding of justice seems ill equipped to capture. This may be why contemporary discussions of justice rarely mention it. I have argued that group-directed violence is institutionalized and systemic. To the degree that institutions and social practices encourage, tolerate, or enable the perpetration of violence against members of specific groups, those institutions and practices are unjust and should be reformed. Such reform may require the redistribution of resources or positions, but in large part can come only through a change in cultural images, stereotypes, and the mundane reproduction of relations of dominance and aversion in the gestures of everyday life.

APPLYING THE CRITERIA

Social theories that construct oppression as a unified phenomenon usually either leave out groups that even the theorists think are oppressed or leave out important ways in which groups are oppressed. Black liberation theorists and feminist theorists have argued persuasively, for example, that Marxism's reduction of all oppressions to class oppression leaves out much about the specific oppression of Blacks and women. By pluralizing the category of oppression in the way explained in this chapter, social theory can avoid the exclusive and oversimplifying effects of such reductionism.

I have avoided pluralizing the category in the way some others have done, constructing an account of separate systems of oppression for each oppressed group: racism, sexism, classism, heterosexism, ageism, and so on. There is a double problem with considering each group's oppression a unified and distinct structure or system. On the one hand, this way of conceiving oppression fails to accommodate the similarities and overlap in the oppressions of different groups. On the other hand, it falsely represents the situation of all group members as the same.

I have arrived at the five faces of oppression—exploitation, marginalization, powerlessness, cultural imperialism, and violence—as the best way to avoid such exclusions and reductions. They function as criteria for determining whether individuals and groups are oppressed rather than as a full theory of oppression. I believe that these criteria are objective. They provide a means of refuting some people's belief that their group is oppressed when it is not as well as a means of persuading others that a group is oppressed when they doubt it. Each criterion can be operationalized; each can be applied through the assessment of observable behavior, status relationships, distributions, texts, and other cultural artifacts. I have no illusions that such assessments can be value neutral. But these criteria can nevertheless serve as means of evaluating claims that a group is oppressed or adjudicating disputes about whether or how a group is oppressed.

The presence of any of these five conditions is sufficient for calling a group oppressed. But different group oppressions exhibit different combinations of these forms, as do different individuals in the groups. Nearly all, if not all, groups said by contemporary social movements to be oppressed suffer cultural imperialism. The other oppressions they experience vary. Working-class people are exploited and powerless, for example, but if employed and white do not experience marginalization. Gay men, on the other hand, are not qua gay exploited or powerless, but they experience severe cultural imperialism and violence. Similarly, Jews and Arabs as groups are victims of cultural imperialism and violence, though many members of these groups also suffer exploitation or powerlessness. Old people are oppressed by marginalization and cultural imperialism, and this is also true of physically and mentally disabled people. As a group women are subject to gender-based exploitation, powerlessness, cultural imperialism, and violence. Racism in the United States condemns many Blacks and Latinos to marginalization and puts many more at risk, even though many members of these groups escape that condition; members of these groups often suffer all five forms of oppression.

6

Contemporary Chicano Struggles

Isidro Ortiz and Paula Timmerman

In 1992 the Latino population in the United States was about 22.1 million, or about 8.8 percent of the total population. Chicanos constitute the largest group in the Latino population.[1] In 1992 they comprised 63.6 percent of the Latino population and 5.6 percent of the total United States population, numbering approximately 14,062,000.

The Chicano population includes descendants of the Mexicans who were incorporated into the United States after the Treaty of Guadalupe Hidalgo and numerous individuals who have entered this country as immigrants, both legally and illegally. An "invisible minority" throughout much of their history, Chicanos have increasingly become the recipients of journalistic and scholarly attention as their numbers and those of other groups in the Latino population have increased dramatically.

As political scientist John A. Garcia recently observed, the themes of Chicano isolationism, separatism, and balkanism are reflected in much of the burgeoning literature on Chicanos and multiculturalism, in particular journalistic and popular writings.[2] Stated somewhat differently, implicit in the literature are two notions: first, that Chicanos are struggling to isolate or separate themselves from the United States, and second, that Chicanos desire the fragmentation of American society as suggested by the rejection of many Chicanos of coercive cultural assimilation and their insistence on the affirmation of cultural diversity in the United States.

That Chicanos are struggling to isolate themselves or separate from the United States or desire the fragmentation of American society is far from the case. As argued by numerous authors, Chicanos are engaged in a variety of struggles; however, the activism is aimed at structures of oppression that serve to obstruct integration on the basis of equality characterized by authentic cultural pluralism. Moreover, although they have been and continue to be extremely diverse, Chicanos, according to recent surveys, share positive orientations toward American institutions and the United States that are inconsistent with isolationism, separatism, or balkanism.

In this chapter we provide an overview of the struggles by Chicanos against various forms of oppression. We do not pretend to offer a comprehensive delineation of the struggles. Such a task requires a larger context than this chapter provides. Rather, we elaborate our argument by focusing on some of the more prominent ongoing cases of activism against forms of oppression. In documenting the activism and its specific targets and objectives, we challenge the theories of Chicano isolationism, separatism, and balkanization found in the literature on Chicanos and multiculturalism.

CONTEMPORARY CHICANO STRUGGLES

In chapter 5 Iris Marion Young identified five forms of oppression a group such as Chicanos may suffer from. They are cultural imperialism, exploitation, marginalization, powerlessness, and violence. These forms of oppression serve as the targets of much recent and ongoing Chicano collective action.

Struggles Against Cultural Imperialism

According to Young, cultural imperialism "involves the universalization of a dominant group's experience and culture, and its establishment as the norm." By projecting only their experiences the members of dominant group empower themselves while excluding and silencing the experiences and interpretations of social life by other groups. The dominant group imposes its interpretation of "other" social groups as being outside the norm. They are perceived as different and deviant, confined by stereotypical perceptions and rendered invisible. Young states, "Those living under cultural imperialism find themselves defined from the outside, positioned, placed, by a network of dominant meanings they experience as arising from elsewhere, from those with whom they do not identify and who do not identify with them."[3]

Cultural imperialism has been and continues to be the target of Chicano scholars who favor the development of authentic cultural pluralism in the United States. Their struggles have involved and included the articulation and advocacy of new conceptions of citizenship, the institutional prerequisites for cultural pluralism, and theoretical and instrumental changes needed to achieve authentic cultural pluralism and full social participation of Chicanos in American society.

In the United States, anthropologist Renato Rosaldo has argued that on a daily basis Chicanos confront the ideology that everyone must be the same, that is, like white people. Like other groups, they have been taught that "the price of full rights is assimilation" and that "a single national culture and a single language is preferable."[4] This official ideology has been enforced by society through various mechanisms, in particular the schools. During the first part of the twentieth century, for example, the public schools undertook extensive Americanization campaigns within the Chicano population. Today, the English-only movement perpetuates this ideology in its campaign to make English the official language of the United States.

In opposition to this ideology, Chicano scholars have affirmed and continue to affirm *cultural citizenship*. Cultural citizenship "is being able to maintain one's own culture while exerting one's full rights as full human beings."[5] Pioneering the development and examination of this concept have been at least a dozen Chicano and Puerto Rican scholars who have developed the concept over the past five to six years. Some have joined together to form the Cultural Citizenship working group under the auspices of the Inter-University Program for Latino Research. Coordinated by Rosaldo of Stanford University and Puerto Rican scholar Rina Benmayer, a researcher at the Center for Puerto Rican Studies at Hunter College of the City University of New York, the group is attempting to "determine how individuals and communities react to poverty and oppressive situations and resist and empower themselves differently."[6]

Mario Barrera has offered a proposal that would facilitate cultural citizenship for at least some Chicanos and promote the achievement of authentic cultural pluralism. In *Beyond Aztlan: Ethnic Autonomy in Comparative Perspective,* Barrera calls for regional autonomy, drawing upon the experiences of other countries around the world with multiple ethnic and racial groups within their boundaries. According to Barrera, the achievement of "a real rather than illusionary cultural pluralism in the United States" requires a set of supportive institutions that do not exist in this country. Regional autonomy "provides precisely that type of framework—one that alters cultural diversity and self-determination without penalties" for Chicanos. In Barrera's view, regional autonomy "is clearly a kind of in-between solution to ethnic and nationalist demands, poised between separation and secession on the one hand and assimilation without choice on the other."[7] Southern California, southern Texas, and northern New Mexico are potential sites for implementation of this proposal because of the high concentrations of Chicanos in those areas.

Barrera recognizes that "the present climate of opinion" in the United States makes a regional autonomy solution to American ethnic and racial problems "impossible in the short run." Thus he offers a sequential strategy that would "lead" in the direction of regional autonomy "by a series of small steps." The first step is opposition to the English-only movement, which, according to Barrera, "is a continuation of a long American tradition of ethnocentrism, Anglo-conformity, and cultural intolerance," and we might add, cultural imperialism. The second step is the development of a promulticulturalism movement that would have official, legal recognition of the United States as a multicultural, multilingual country as its objective. This movement, according to Barrera, "could begin by aiming for such recognition at the statewide level, with the eventual goal of having such a provision adopted as an amendment to the United States Constitution." The final step is "to educate people to the fact that such ethnic autonomy is not threatening to the territorial integrity of the United States, and that it already exists and functions well in a number of countries." In the absence of the ultimate development of ethnic autonomy, Chicanos will continue to face the very restricted choices of assimilating or suffering the consequences.[8]

Barrera's call for ethnic autonomy takes into consideration demographic trends that portend significant changes for Chicanos and other groups. Nowhere else have the demographic trends been more conspicuous than in California, the state with the largest population of Chicanos and other Latinos in the United States. In this state the Chicano/Latino population is growing rapidly. During the next twenty years, Chicanos and other Latinos will become the largest plurality in the state's population. Moreover, according to recent demographic projections, in the year 2040 Chicanos and other Latinos will become the majority of the state's population. Accompanying these demographic transformations, of course, is and will be a change in the status of the state's Anglo population. Sometime during the this decade, the white population will cease to be the largest racial group in California.

These transformations raise a number of important questions, according to David E. Hayes-Bautista of the Chicano Studies Center at the University of California, Los Angeles. What will be the short term and long term affect on society and its inhabitants when non-whites become a majority? What will happen when whites are no longer in the majority? Will we still be working and living within a political economy that is globally competitive, politically stable, and viable over the long term? According to Hayes-Bautista and colleagues, answers to these questions "can be obtained by an understanding of the dynamics of the rapidly growing Latino population and stable Anglo group." Thus, they have undertaken the task of illuminating the attitudes and behavior of Chicanos and other Latinos in California. Their objective "is to change the public discourse on Latinos by offering a different perspective on Latino attitudes and behavior," a perspective that will facilitate planning for the next century in California. More specifically, they offer a "simple, but radical, paradigm shift for the development of social policy in a Latino-dominant population." According to these scholars, Chicanos and other Latinos have been viewed as conforming to the urban underclass model. However, "the urban underclass model with its emphasis on low labor force participation, high welfare dependency, high family disintegration and a tangle of health pathology does not describe" the attitudes or behavior of Chicanos and other Latinos in California. Rather, Chicanos and other Latinos "should be viewed as an invigorating force within California society rather than a problem population. Latinos' behavior and attitudes should be recognized as reinforcing societal commitment to family, dedication to the work ethic, renewed desire for the education of its children, and the renewal of some of the basic ideals of citizenship and participation." Latinos need to be seen as "investment opportunities." The time has arrived "to begin thinking of investing in the validation and empowerment of Latino dreams and visions that fuel such exemplary behavior." In short, efforts must be taken to "maximize Latino engagement" in the state.[9]

In order to maximize Latino engagement, Hayes-Bautista and his colleagues have also suggested policy actions. Their prescriptions in the area of education exemplify the integrationist thrust of their proposals. In order to maximize the social engagement of Chicanos and other Latinos in the area of education, California must, according to Hayes-Bautista and his colleagues, construct more schools, develop a special initiative that would capitalize on the interest of the parents of immigrant children in the education of their offspring, validate and empower the Latino intellectual tradition by strengthening ethnic studies programs, and develop and implement a multicultural curriculum in the schools. The latter, they argue, is indispensable in and to a multicultural society. As they note, "The success of a multicultural society will require that its members have a fluency in the various intellectual traditions embodied in its populations. The school curriculum needs to reflect the cultural diversity in which literature, history, art, language and science is addressed in schools. All children need a multicultural education to be successful in a multicultural society."[10]

Hayes-Bautista and his colleagues recognize that their suggestions "may seem overly ambitious and perhaps unrealistic in these days of extremely tight state and local budgets." However, in their view, investment in the Latino population is imperative. Activism on the part of Anglos supportive of a multicultural society is also imperative in California. According to Hayes-Bautista and his colleagues, "It is now time for Anglos who support multiculturalism to join the public debate. A fruitful coalition could result from those Anglos joining Latino advocacy groups to forge a new social image of a multicultural California as a desirable and valuable state of affairs. If multiculturalism can be defined in terms of strength rather than remediation, then perhaps it would not appear as threatening."[11]

Struggles Against Exploitation

Young refers to the process of exploitation as the structural relationship between social groups whereby the labor, energy expenditure, and results of one group serve to benefit another. Young not only stresses the unequal distributive function of the ability of such groups to attain access to goods and services, but also emphasizes the lack of options experienced by these groups in regard to the makeup of organizations, the practice of decision making, and the structure of the division of labor. The subsequent relationship of domination experienced by exploited labor groups establishes and perpetuates an unreciprocated transfer of powers and inequality of freedom, status, wealth, and self-realization.

Exploitation has been a consistent phenomenon in the history of Chicanos. By no means has it been accepted passively. Today Chicanos remain engaged in resistance against exploitation and a struggle to achieve economic parity. Resistance to exploitation has been particularly evident in California and Texas. In California such resistance is illustrated by the Justice for Janitors campaign of the Service Employees International Union. This campaign emerged in response to the deunionization of janitorial workers in Los Angeles—the preponderance of whom were Chicanos. In the early 1980s, Chicanos joined with other Latinos in an intensive effort to unionize janitorial workers. When finally organized, their earnings rose to approximately $12.00 per hour. "By 1983, however, a number of non-union cleaning companies hiring undocumented workers as well as non-English speaking legal immigrants had emerged, forcing unions to roll back wage demands."[12] Consequently, by 1988 membership in unions had decreased from 6,000 to 2,500; moreover, wages and benefits declined to $4.00 per hour.

The Justice for Janitors campaign has successfully struggled to reverse this trend. By the end of 1989, approximately 50 percent of the janitorial workers in buildings in downtown Los Angeles had been organized again. During the summer of 1990, the union also achieved the organization of workers of an international cleaning company with extensive operations in Century City. As a result of the union's efforts, hourly wages have increased from $5.00 to $6.50 per hour; the newly unionized workers are also receiving health insurance and other benefits.

The union's campaign has encountered resistance from employers and law enforcement authorities. However, the workers have refused to be daunted by the resistance to their struggle. For example, during the 1990 campaign in Century City, approximately 60 janitors and their supporters required medical treatment, and another 89 were either hit or arrested in a confrontation between 400 members of the union and 150 police officers after a march by the striking janitors and their supporters. After the confrontation, the union filed a lawsuit against the city of Los Angeles, former police chief Daryl F. Gates, and the Police Department. The result was a settlement in which the Los Angeles City Council in September 1993 agreed to pay $2.35 million to the union. The settlement inspired the workers, one of whom declared after the victory: "It is so satisfying to feel my voice for justice has been heard."[13]

In Texas, Chicana workers are in the forefront of struggle against exploitation through their participation in Fuerza Unida. All are organizations of seamstresses "who are fighting, in different ways, to keep their jobs, with decent working conditions, and with retraining and fair compensation when the jobs have already gone." Fuerza Unida is an organization of 1,150 seamstresses who were laid off when the Levi Strauss Company moved production from its San Antonio plant to Costa Rica in 1990 without providing retraining opportunities for the seamstresses. In response, the seamstresses joined together and initiated an ongoing boycott of Levi Strauss products and two lawsuits. In November 1990, moreover, Fuerza Unida organized hunger strikes at the Levi Strauss national headquarters in San Francisco and company offices in San Antonio. As a result of these actions, Fuerza Unida garnered support for its boycott from a diverse array of organizations and elected officials. Through intense bargaining, extensive picketing, and the mobilization of community support, in 1992 the group won retraining for many of the seamstresses. In order to provide additional support for the seamstresses, Fuerza Unida organized and currently operates a cooperative that produces Astro-Tots, a toy that the organization is seeking to market commercially.[14]

Exploitation has been a consistent part of the economic experience of Chicano farmworkers also. Throughout this century they have engaged in strikes and repeatedly struggled to organize viable unions. The most successful struggles occurred in the late 1960s under the leadership of Cesar Chavez and the United Farm Workers (UFW). Chavez initiated the organization of farmworkers in 1962 after a successful stint as director of the Community Service Organization, an organization based on the tradition of community organizing developed by Saul Alinsky. Envisioning the struggle by farmworkers as an integral part of the civil rights movement, Chavez "appealed to the religious identity of his people, depicting their nonviolent efforts as a sacred struggle against the forces of oppression."[15]

With the support of a vast array of groups across the country, in 1965 the UFW organized a successful consumer boycott of grapes that resulted in contracts with major grape growers in 1970. During the 1980s, Chavez and the UFW focused on the lettuce industry, where the growers and Teamsters Union had signed contracts disadvantageous to workers. Although the UFW waged a non-violent struggle in protest, violence ensued, resulting in Chavez being jailed, UFW members murdered, and the strengthening of a coalition between growers, the Teamsters, and the Republican administration. Membership in the union also plummeted.

Despite the intense resistance of growers and the Teamsters Union, Chavez and the UFW ultimately succeeded in improving the wages of farmworkers. They were also instrumental in the enactment of the California Agricultural Labor Relations Act of 1975. This act granted farmworkers in California the right to select unions to represent them in bargaining with their employers. By the early 1980s, however, Chavez and the UFW had experienced several setbacks. After the advent of a Republican administration in California, vigorous enforcement of the Agricultural Labor Relations Act failed to occur. Consequently, organizing of farmworkers became extremely difficult, resulting in a general decline in working conditions and wages.

Dismayed but undaunted, Chavez and the UFW launched a new grape boycott in 1984 appealing to consumers by drawing attention to the extensive use of pesticides on grapes and the pesticide poisoning of farmworkers. By the beginning of this decade, Chavez and the UFW had succeeded greatly in raising the consciousness of consumers to the plight of farmworkers throughout the country. Chavez died unexpectedly in Arizona in April of 1993, but his death "stimulated dramatic new interest in the UFW's drive to organize and protect U.S. agricultural laborers." In the aftermath of Chavez's death, the UFW's membership has increased by about 3,000 to approximately 25,000. The union's grape boycott has also experienced a revival. It is receiving support in the form of volunteers and funding from labor unions. Moreover, consumers—Chicano and non-Chicano—have been endorsing the boycott and refraining from purchasing grapes as well as protesting the serving of grapes at organizational functions.[16]

Underlying the continuation of the UFW's struggle is the perception that exploitation of farmworkers persists in California and elsewhere. As Arturo Rodriguez, Chavez's successor, recently noted when asked whether change in the conditions found by farmworkers had occurred since the 1960s and 1970s:

Not enough. There's still a tremendous amount of exploitation that takes place. As consumers, how can we sit down at the table and enjoy meals day after day without really thinking about the people who go out and pick those fruits and vegetables. It's an injustice and disgrace when you think about how much wealth this country has and yet the people who are responsible for feeding us oftentimes live in poverty, and are exploited to the degree where the women, to provide the basics to their children have to suffer sexual harassment.[17]

Low-income Chicanos have been victims of class exploitation in the form of environmental racism. From the mideighties to the present, Chicanos have engaged in resistance against environmental racism. Through their struggles, they have contributed to the development of the environmental justice movement in the United States. A multiethnic and multiclass social movement, the environmental justice movement addresses "issues that affect humans, flora, fauna and the physical environment, locally, nationally and internationally." The movement builds upon the recognition that injustices have "occurred in the past that stem from racism and discrimination. Such practices have put communities of color at risk." It seeks "remedies for the past injustices and to promote fairness in future environmental actions."[18]

The Mothers of East Los Angeles (MELA) has been, and remains, the most prominent and successful of Chicano groups struggling against environmental racism. MELA is a loosely knit group of over 400 Mexican American women. The group emerged in response to the proposed construction of a 1,700-inmate prison in 1985 in East Los Angeles. In March 1985 California Governor George Deukmejian proposed to locate the prison in East Los Angeles, which already served as a repository for prisons, hazardous industries, and other undesirable facilities. The proposed prison was to be located within a mile of a major barrio, Boyle Heights, and within two miles of thirty-four schools. In response to the proposal, California Assemblywoman Gloria Molina informed a small group of Chicana parishioners of the proposed construction and requested they help to mobilize the residents of East Los Angeles against the prison. The women formed MELA and launched a massive campaign against the prison.

MELA has also organized against several other projects. In 1987, for example, MELA focused on a toxic waste incinerator proposed for Vernon, a small city adjacent to East Los Angeles. The construction of the incinerator threatened to further decimate the air quality in the area. In its battle against the project, MELA collaborated with a diverse array of groups, including Greenpeace, the National Resources Defense Council, the Environmental Policy Institute, the Citizens Clearinghouse and Hazardous Waste, the national Toxics Campaign, and the Western Center on Law and Poverty. These groups afforded MELA technical assistance, expert testimony, and lobbying, research, and legal assistance.

In conjunction with its allies, MELA targeted the agencies responsible for awarding a permit for the incinerator project. They mobilized more than 500 residents to attend a 1987 hearing of the Department of Health Services (DHS) on the project. They also mobilized opposition in other public forums, questioning the DHS's decision that allowed California Treatment Services (CTS) to advance the project without the preparation of an environmental impact report. Moreover, MELA and its allies joined with the City of Los Angeles in a lawsuit demanding a review of the decision. As a result of the struggle by MELA and its allies, California Assemblywoman Lucille Roybal-Allard launched a successful initiative to change California law and require environmental impact reports for all toxic waste incinerators.

While it fought the incinerator project, MELA continued struggling against the proposed construction of the prison. In September 1992, it won a major victory when

California Governor Pete Wilson decided to abandon the project in the face of MELA's continuing opposition. MELA has also involved itself in a dispute in Kettleman City, California, between a local group, El Pueblo para el Aire y Agua Limpio (People of Clean Air and Water) and a company that proposed the siting of a hazardous waste incinerator in Kettleman City. With the support of MELA and other environmental groups, El Pueblo recently succeeded in preventing construction of the proposed incinerator.

Struggles Against Marginalization

According to Young, "Marginalization is perhaps the most dangerous form of oppression. A whole category of people is expelled from useful participation in social life and thus potentially subjected to severe material deprivation and even extermination . . . . It also involves the deprivation of cultural, practical, and institutionalized conditions for exercising capacities in a context of recognition and interaction."[19] During the latter part of the nineteenth century and the first half of this century, Chicanos experienced extreme marginalization. Contrary to the traditional description of Chicanos as a sleeping giant, they did not passively accept the marginalization. They made repeated efforts to overcome their socioeconomic and political marginality. The struggles continue today.

In the late 1960s and early 1970s, Chicano students demanded the establishment of Chicano Studies departments and programs in institutions of higher education across the Southwest. In the wake of vigorous struggles for such programs, colleges and universities launched programmatic and curricular initiatives and recruited and hired more Chicanos. Thus in California, for example, by 1990 Chicano Studies departments and programs existed on at least forty-one college and university campuses. As a result of the establishment of these departments and programs, Chicanos won the opportunity to take courses focusing on the history, heritage, and experiences of Chicanos in the United States. Moreover, a body of scholarship by Chicanos emerged and grew rapidly.

During the 1980s, however, many Chicano Studies programs and departments found it difficult to sustain the momentum of earlier years in the context of a conservative political climate and fiscal retrenchment. Many departments remained static or languished. On many university and college campuses, the units often remained on the fringe of institutional life, struggling with inadequate resources and a lack of academic legitimacy.

During the 1990s, however, the movement for Chicano Studies has regained momentum with the emergence of a new generation of Chicano student activists who, like their counterparts in the 1960s, see the elaboration of Chicano Studies departments and programs and the incorporation of Chicano Studies courses into the traditional curriculum as vital to their personal development and the development of the Chicano population. Like their predecessors, moreover, they have turned to direct action to achieve their goals. During the spring of 1993, Chicano students staged protests at institutions of higher education ranging from Williams College in Massachusetts to San Jose State University in California. Almost invariably, the students demanded the establishment or expansion of Chicano Studies programs, departments, and courses and/or the hiring of Chicano/Latino faculty.

The struggle for Chicano Studies has been especially intense at the University of California, Los Angeles (UCLA). At UCLA a Chicano Studies program was established in 1973. From 1974 to 1987, however, the program remained marginal in the university; its marginality was even acknowledged by the university's Academic Senate. From 1974 to 1987, the senate reported that the Chicano Studies program was experiencing difficulty and recommended the provision of additional faculty and other types of university support in order to strengthen the program. The recommendation, however, was not accepted by the university administration.

During the 1987–88 academic year, an Academic Senate committee recommended the disestablishment of the program and the suspension of the Chicano Studies major. The recommendation was not implemented at that time. However, the program continued to operate with inadequate resources, and in February of 1990 the Chicano Studies major was suspended by the university.

In response, the Chicano student organization *Movimiento Estudiantil Chicano de Aztlán* (MECHA) instituted a campaign to develop support for the program among the Chicano community in Los Angeles. In April 1990 the organization held a demonstration in support of an autonomous Chicana/o Studies department and demanded that UCLA Chancellor Charles Young meet with community leaders. Although the meeting did not occur, the community leaders formed the United Community and Labor Alliance in support of establishing an autonomous department.

On January 15, 1992, a faculty proposal for a Chicana/o Studies Department was submitted with 12 junior and senior level faculty signatures and the support of the majority of Chicano/Latino professors at the university. Several months later, an Academic Senate committee and several departments endorsed the creation of a Chicano Studies department. Chancellor Young finally made a decision on the request at the end of April. He chose to maintain the major in its existing interdepartmental form and eschew the creation of an autonomous department.

In response, a group of students called Conscious Students of Color organized a sit-in at the UCLA Faculty Center over the future of the Chicana/o Studies library and the Chicano/a Studies department. In the ensuing confrontation with police, 99 protesters were arrested. MECHA responded by organizing a rally attended by over 1000 people demanding the establishment of the department and the release of the arrested students. In the face of the Chancellor's continuing refusal, another rally was held on May 21: this time nearly 2000 people rallied in support of the department. Four days later, students and a group of Chicano faculty began a hunger strike. The strikers pledged to continue their strike until a Chicana/o Studies department was created and the charges against the student protesters dropped. Their fourteen-day hunger strike concluded in a decision by the chancellor to create the Cesar Chavez Center for Interdisciplinary Studies. This center does not have departmental status, however. It will, though, be an autonomous unit with authority to hire faculty and develop curriculum.

As Buss has noted, "Virtually all modern social change movements that include both men and women, such as the civil rights movement and the new left, have marginalized their female members."[20] The movements for Chicano Studies and Women's Studies were not exceptions when it came to Chicanas. As de la Torre and Pesquera have noted:

The Chicano movement and the "second wave" of the women's movement which emerged during the 1960s called into question social and ideological patterns that justified systems of racial and gender inequality. Both movements used political action and ideological critiques as weapons in the struggle against oppression. These movements gave birth to Chicano Studies and Women's Studies programs, which developed new conceptual frameworks to analyze Chicanos and women. In theory, the particular circumstances of Chicanas should have found expression in Chicano and feminist discourses, but they did not . . . . The politics and theoretical formulations of these movements . . . denied, subsumed or neglected the "triple oppression" status of Chicanas.[21]

Thus in the early 1970s a struggle for Chicana Studies emerged in the wake of the marginalization of Chicanas in the field of Chicano Studies and Women's Studies, as well as traditional disciplines. The first step in this struggle was the development by Chicanas of "alternative avenues, 'safe spaces' to develop intellectually and continue their trajectory of political dissent." The creation of these spaces was facilitated by the "emergence of a small but critical mass of Chicanas" in institutions of higher education "who persisted in posing Chicana questions."[22]

Given their existence within Chicano Studies, Chicana academics and scholars focused on their efforts within Chicano Studies programs and the National Association of Chicano Studies (NACS). In 1982 at the University of California, Berkeley, several Chicanas organized Mujeres en Marcha in opposition to the male domination within Chicano Studies departments and the NACS. Subsequently, at the annual meetings of the association, the women organized and presented an unprecedented panel on sexual politics. The following year, about a dozen Chicanas in attendance at the NACS meeting joined together to form the Chicana Caucus. They demanded that the next NACS conference focus on gender and proposed "Voces de la Mujer" (Voices of the Women) as the conference theme. Through these actions, they sought to "institutionalize" the discussion of gender politics at NACS meetings through the Chicana Caucus and the yearly plenary. In 1983 other Chicanas institutionalized a separate safe space for the development of Chicano Studies by creating Mujeres Activas en Letras en Cambio Social (MALCS). MALCS is "dedicated to the documentation, analysis, and interpretation of the Chicana/Latina experience in the United States."[23]

In 1984, as a result of the work of the Chicana Caucus, "Voces de la Chicana" became the theme of the first Chicana Plenary at the annual NACS conference. Participants also succeeded in having the proceedings of the conference published under the title *Chicana Voices: Intersections of Race, Class and Gender.*

The members of MALCS and other Chicana scholars currently are "inviting main-stream feminists to reflect on their own convergence with male hegemonic practices that oust minority scholars (in this case women of color) or silence them as speaking subjects in theoretical discourses or race, class and gender oppression."[24] Moreover, they have criticized and continue to criticize Chicano scholarship. According to one Chicana scholar, Chicana Studies scholars have "successfully deconstructed Chicano movement discourses that privilege the Chicano male subject and draw on cultural male symbols (Che, Pancho Villa, brave Aztec figures on sexy calendars) as illustrations of groups resistance to domination." They have illuminated the "uncomfortable convergence between alternative nationalist and mainstream hegemonic discourses of culture, which foreground patriarchy." Chicanas are also "infusing largely unexplored class themes with new forms of identity that have until now been absent from Chicano/a cultural production."[25]

Struggles Against Powerlessness

As set forth by Young, the concept of powerlessness refers to a group "that do[es] not regularly participate in making decisions that affect the conditions of their lives and actions." It also "designates a position in the division of labor and the concomitant social position that allows persons little opportunity to develop and exercise skills."[26]

Historically, Chicanos have fought against powerlessness. During the 1960s, the Chicano power movement emerged as a response to this condition. Efforts to em-power Chicanos include efforts to promote voter registration and participation, institution building, leadership development, and coalition formation among Chicanos themselves and between Chicanos and other groups.

The efforts to increase voter registration and participation are spearheaded by the Southwest Voter Registration and Education Project (SWVREP). Formed in 1974 by the late Willie Velasquez, SWVREP set out to achieve two goals: gaining respect for the Latino vote, and the election of a base of Chicano and Latino officials as a foundation for the political empowerment of Chicanos. By 1990, SWVREP had been instrumental in the registration of approximately five million Latinos. To achieve this goal, SWVREP conducted extensive voter registration campaigns across the Southwest where the political participation of Chicanos and other Latinos was negligible.

To achieve its second objective, SWVREP joined with the Mexican American Legal Defense and Education Fund to successfully challenge electoral discrimination against Mexican Americans. In particular, it focused on the practice of gerrymandering, which historically has had the effect of dilution of the Latino vote. The result has been the dismantling of discriminatory election systems and the election of hundreds of Chicanos to public office.

Currently, SWVREP, under the leadership of Andy Hernandez, is emphasizing community political development and the development of mechanisms of political accountability. To achieve these ends, the project is conducting leadership training and establishing a new network of locally controlled and operated voter registration drives. The project's leadership training sessions brings together seventeen regional planning councils consisting of elected officials and community leaders in the seventeen regions into which SWVREP has divided the five states of the Southwest. At the two- and three-day seminars, Latino officials are updated about the issues that have traditionally concerned Latinos—education, housing and health, and issues such as U.S. foreign policy and municipal finance. Members of the councils also direct the development of voter registration campaigns, thereby enabling local Chicano leaders to take "ownership" of local voter registration projects.

The Southwest Voter Registration and Education Project's registration campaigns seek to capitalize on the rapid growth of the Chicano population. Projections for population growth in the next century predict that Chicanos will exert considerable clout in the electoral arena. Non-citizenship on the part of large numbers of individuals of Mexican descent remains a major obstacle to the empowerment of Chicanos, however. According to Harry Pachon of the Tomas Rivera Center, "Noncitizenship . . . is the reason why one-third of all adult Hispanics in the United States in 1980 were unable to vote and shape the social and economic policies that affected their lives."[27] Cognizant of the urgency of citizenship to the empowerment of Chicanos and other Latinos, several groups have undertaken naturalization campaigns. The National Association of Latino Elected and Appointed Officials (NALEO) has been, and remains, in the forefront of these efforts. Comprised of elected and appointed officials of Chicano and other Latino descent, the organization has illuminated the factors underlying low naturalization rights among Latinos, conducted education activities aimed at increasing understanding of and participation in the naturalization process on the part of Chicanos and other Latinos, and investigated and reported patterns of political participation of immigrants and the attitudes of Chicanos regarding immigrants and proposed immigration policy proposals. In September 1993, NALEO reported the findings of its survey of the attitudes of Latinos in California regarding restrictive immigration policy proposals set forth by California governor Pete Wilson. In its report *The Unheard Voice of One Out of Every Four Californians: What Do Latinos Think about Anti-Immigrant Rhetoric?* NALEO reported: "Latino residents of California overwhelmingly oppose Governor Wilson's program to curb illegal immigration. A large majority feel that he is promoting anti-immigrant hatred by the way he is framing the issue. Most Latinos think that the debate over illegal immigration is creating a climate that will facilitate discrimination and racism against all Latinos and which could lead to the type of violence that many countries in Europe are experiencing."[28]

In contrast to the efforts of SWVREP and NALEO, other Chicanos have been pursuing empowerment of Chicanos through the application of the theory of community organizing developed by the late Saul Alinsky and his Industrial Areas Foundation. In the forefront of these efforts has been Ernesto Cortes, a professional organizer trained by Alinsky and his successor Ed Chambers. During the 1970s Cortes was instrumental in the creation of organizations such as the Communities Organized for Public Services (COPS) in San Antonio, Texas; the United Neighborhood Organization (UNO) in Los Angeles; the El Paso Interreligious Sponsoring Organization (EPISO) in El Paso; and other organizations throughout the Southwest. Constituting a vibrant part of the citizen empowerment movement of the 1970s and 1980s, these organizations by the beginning of this decade had "definitely enhanced the empowerment of local residents and balanced the influence of other forces in the communities where they were created and operated."[29]

Struggles Against Violence

Violence may be defined as the exercise of physical force for the purpose of violating, damaging, or abusing members of a group. Young includes in this form of oppression "random unprovoked attacks" on the persons or property of a group. She also includes "less severe forms of harassment, intimidation, or ridicule simply for the purpose of degrading, humiliating, or stigmatizing group members." According to Young, "The oppression of violence consists not only in direct victimization, but in the daily knowledge shared by all members of oppressed groups that they are liable to violation, solely on account of their group identity. Just living under such a threat of attack on oneself or family or friends deprives the oppressed of freedom and dignity, and needlessly expends their energy."[30]

Historically, Chicanos and other Latinos have been stereotyped as violent people. Chicanos and other Latinos have frequently been the victims of violence, however. They continue to suffer the oppression of violence at the hands of private individuals and law enforcement authorities. According to the U.S. Department of Justice, from 1979 to 1986 Chicanos and other Latinos "suffered an average each year of 439,000 violent crimes (rapes, robberies and assaults) and 830,000 person thefts. During the period from 1979–86 Chicanos and other Latinos experienced higher rates of victimization from violent crime than did non-Latinos. For every 1,000 Latinos age 12 or older, there were 11 robberies and 12 aggravated assaults; in contrast from every 1,000 non-Latinos there were 6 robberies and 10 aggravated assaults."[31] Excluding rape injuries and those victims in which the presence of injury was not ascertained, there were 23,750 serious injuries and 105,986 minor injuries suffered by Chicanos and other Latinos as a result of violent attacks.

In the early seventies, the U.S. Commission on Civil Rights noted that "Mexican American citizens are subject to unduly harsh treatment by law enforcement officers" in the form of physical and verbal abuse.[32] Two decades later Chicanos and other Latinos continue to experience harsh treatment at the hands of local law enforcement authorities, in particular at the hands of immigration officers. From May 5, 1988, to May 4, 1989, according to the American Friends Service Committee Immigration Law Enforcement Project (ILEMP), there were at least 380 cases of human and civil rights violations committed by immigration law enforcement officers in five regions studied by the ILEMP: San Diego, California; the Rio Grande Valley of Texas; El Paso, Texas; Tucson, Arizona; and southern Florida. The 380 incidents in these areas involved a minimum of 814 direct victims. The incidents included 55 cases of physical abuse and 11 cases of shootings ending in death or serious injury.

Physical abuse by immigration law enforcement officials making an arrest was the most frequently occurring abuse in the five areas. The types of abuse experienced by Chicanos and other Latinos at the hands of immigration officials included: "tightening handcuffs so that victims' wrists were injured; kicking victims during pat searches; striking victims with a variety of instruments and pushing victims against a series of objects." As a result of these abuses, unarmed Latinos experienced injuries ranging from bruises to fractures.[33]

Latinos were also subjected to inappropriate use of firearms that often resulted in death or serious injury. In most of the incidents, "victims were killed or injured by gun shot wounds to the back as persons . . . attempted to return across the border to Mexico." Improper use of firearms included "firing warning shots or pointing firearms at victims during non-life threatening situations."[34]

Chicanos have not remained passive in the face of the violence. Across the country campaigns are underway against the violence. San Diego is the site of one campaign that reflects the thrust of antiviolence mobilization. Spearheading the campaign is a coalition of Chicano organizations working together as the Raza Rights Coalition (RRC).

In order to deter police abuse, the RRC in 1992 initiated community patrols to monitor police activity. Usually conducted once a week, these patrols involve RRC members forming a caravan of vehicles with cameras and other equipment. During the course of the caravan, the RRC distributes bilingual leaflets outlining its position and demands on the police and immigration issues.

In May 1993, the RRC held its 2nd Tribunal against Police-Migra Terror. The objectives of the tribunal included: illuminating law enforcement abuses, in particular violence against Chicanos; mobilizing Chicanos against the abuses; and providing documentation for presentation to international human rights agencies. The event involved testimony from victims of abuses and witnesses to abuses as well as testimony from representatives from organizations active on the issue of police and immigration misconduct.

When immigrant bashing became common in California during the summer of 1993, the RRC denounced the practice as actions motivated by racism and electoral ambitions. It also initiated a series of actions in order to achieve its goals of securing the elimination of the U.S. Border Patrol, the demilitarization of the border, and the resignation of the San Diego Border Patrol Sector Chief.

In early October, the RRC joined with other Chicano organizations to sponsor a march and rally to protest the immigrant bashing. One of these groups was the American Friends Service Committee U.S.-Mexico Border Project. Directed by internationally recognized human rights activist Roberto Martinez, this group labors to achieve protection for the human rights of immigrant workers by documenting human rights abuses and mobilizing opposition to the abuses. In early 1990, for example, the project supported a march by the Comite Civico Popular Mixteco (CCPM), a statewide organization of Mixtec Indian immigrants from Mexico. The march was conducted to protest an incident that occurred on January 3, 1990, when an immigrant entered a store in Carlsbad, California, to purchase a cup of coffee. He allegedly was handcuffed and taken to the rear of the store, where he was beaten by store employees. After holding the worker for several hours, the store employees bound the worker's arms and legs and covered his head with a paper bag. Before releasing the worker, however, they painted the bag with a face and the words "No mas aqui" (No more of you here).

In 1991 the project also organized a "peace patrol" along the Tijuana River levee at the U.S.-Mexico border. The weekly patrol was initiated in an effort to deter violence against undocumented immigrants. Through these actions the project has brought attention to violence against undocumented workers. Nevertheless, the violence and immigrant bashing continues. Thus, the project continues to focus attention on documenting incidents and sponsoring forums on violence and hate crimes against Mexican immigrants. In conjunction with other organizations, moreover, it protests action that encourages violence against persons of Mexican descent. For example, in March 1993 the project joined with other Chicano organizations to denounce a California State Superior Court decision ruling that California's hate crime law was unconstitutional. The ruling occurred in a case involving an incident in October 1992 when five white men attacked three Mexican workers with a baseball bat.

As anti-immigrant hysteria in California has increased, the project has explored new responses. For example, in October 1993, the project formulated a Mexican shoppers' boycott of businesses in San Diego in order to deter abuses and additional scapegoating of the immigrants. Its boycott project received support from citizens on both sides of the border. Nearly 6,000 fewer vehicles and 20,000 fewer people crossed the U.S.-Mexico border during the weekend of the boycott.

CONCLUSION

In summary, contrary to recent claims that Chicanos are struggling to isolate themselves from or to promote the fragmentation of the United States, Chicanos across the United States are struggling against forms of oppression that historically have impeded their integration on the basis of equality in American society and thwarted authentic cultural pluralism in the United States. Chicano activism against oppression involves men and women from diverse classes. On the whole, it takes the form of conventional forms of political action. Moreover, it often cuts across ethnic and racial lines as Chicanos join with other ethnic and racial groups to achieve their objectives. In addition, Chicanos exhibit a strong attachment to the United States, as revealed by the findings of recent studies of the political attitudes and values of Chicanos and other Latinos. Ultimately, Chicanos may not succeed fully in their struggles against oppression; moreover, the United States may be plagued by polarization and balkanization. The thrust of Chicano activism and orientations make it highly unlikely that such unfortunate developments will have their roots in the Chicano population.

7

Dominant Culture: *El Deseo por un Alma Pobre* (The Desire for an Impoverished Soul)

María Lugones and Joshua Price

CENTRAL CONCEPTS

El proceso de dominación cultural requiere que la población crea que es imposible que más de una cultura informe la estructura social y la estructura de la personalidad a un nivel profundo. The process of cultural domination instills in the members of society the belief that it is impossible for more than one culture to inform the social structure and the structure of personality at a deep level.

It is one thing for a society to be multicultural in the sense of having restaurants that offer "ethnic" foods or places of entertainment where the music, art, and literature of different cultures is showcased. In such a society people may appreciate these differences without being deeply affected by them. It is another thing for a society's institutions, such as its courts, the different organized ways of producing material life, the practices that comprise government, and the institutions of education, to be multicultural. In this latter case, society can be considered multicultural *structurally*. The members of such a society will also be multicultural: their ways of making decisions, perceiving, valuing, and desiring will be deeply and complexly informed by several cultures. Drawing the contrast between *structure* and *ornament* is central to the understanding of cultural domination. Ornamental cultural pluralism not only is compatible with cultural domination, but is its product.

As a first approximation, we can say that a culture is dominant when it significantly or solely informs the institutional structure of the society, and when the processes through which it came to inform itself involve the reduction of other cultures to ornaments.

The reduction of culture to ornament is both a process of interpretation and of cultural erasure. As the dominant culture interprets non-dominant cultural ways as socially pointless, it robs them of meaning. But interpretation by the dominant culture has the power to turn interpretation into reality, to turn non-dominant ways into meaningless rituals. When one enacts a non-dominant culture as ritualized and as filtered through the dominant imagination, one's cultural practices have been successfully turned ornamental. It is easy to see that one can, without incompatibility, enact a non-dominant culture as ornamental as one assimilates into a dominant culture. One can also see that a person who enacts *only* a non-dominant culture and enacts it as ornamental is devoid of personhood and agency. This is an unusual and terrifying phenomenon. Only to the extent that one enacts one's non-dominant culture in resistance to erasure and reduction to ornamentation can one be a historical agent, someone who exercises judgment in a non-dominant vein. But the dominant culture will attempt to rob such historical agents of their sense.

As ornamental, non-dominant cultures are necessary to the perpetuation of the dominant culture in two ways. They lend the dominant culture a sense of its own importance and originality. Practitioners within the non-dominant culture who are reduced to ornaments are perceived as persons who use values and norms that are both socially irrelevant and exotic. Their interiority—their exercise of judgment and agency—is cast aside as pointless, meaningless. They are understood as lacking in sense, lacking in judgment. But at the same time as they are judged inferior, their presence is also socially valuable because it highlights the requirement to use a certain set of values, norms, and meanings in order to be accorded full agency, personhood, and interiority; that is, in order to be understood as a full subject. As lacking full personhood, agency, autonomy, and the ability to make judgments, they are justifiably devalued from the dominant culture's standpoint.

From the dominant culture's standpoint, full personhood can be gained only by becoming a practitioner of the dominant culture through assimilation. The process through which the culture that constitutes one's interiority—the structure of one's personality—is turned into an ornament is part of that process of assimilation. When the process is successful, one becomes ornamentally "cultured," the non-dominant culture becomes a superficial affectation, a veneer of difference.

One can easily see, then, that if a culture is dominant, the society will be structurally monocultural. The argument in this chapter draws a connection between a culture being a "dominant culture" and what we will call "monocultural." The connection lies in domination. The argument for this connection provides an understanding of the meaning of "dominant culture."

The dominant culture in a society is not just the mainstream culture, the one that happens to inform the institutions of that society. "Mainstream" does not capture the most important aspects of the meaning of *dominant* culture. The process through which a culture's rules and values come to inform the institutional structure of the society is what marks it as dominant. That process involves the erasure of other cultures and their concomitant reduction to ornaments: it is a process of domination. *El deseo por la monocultura es un deseo de tener un alma pobre.*

Monoculturalism in the United States

In the United States, the culture vying to become the dominant culture is a historically threaded mix of Anglo and European cultures that we will call "Anglo culture" as a problematic shorthand. This name can be thoughtfully challenged, as it tends to reduce all the complexity in one direction. But it is the name Latinos give to this culture because the exclusive and aggressive use of the English language is one of its characteristics.

*Mono*culturalism is the political stance that proposes that the United States is and should be a monocultural society. Monoculturalists could discuss this claim over lunch at an Indian or Mexican restaurant without contradiction, since they do not mind ornamental cultural pluralism. As we said, a society is culturally pluralistic in an ornamental sense when the many cultures are inactive in informing the personality, character, beliefs, and values of workers/citizens and the structure of the economic and political system. Monoculturalism advocates assimilation when it advocates that only one culture inform the civic, economic, and social structure of the United States. Given that when a culture is dominant the society tends to be structurally monocultural, we can begin to see the connection between dominant culture and monoculturalism: monoculturalism is the politics behind a culture's becoming dominant. It is a politics that advances the adoption of certain ways of valuing, perceiving, and acting that make the existence of a dominant culture desirable and that lead people to promote it in everything they do in their daily lives.

The Paradox of Cultural Domination

Cultural domination is undermined by a seemingly unproblematic yet systematic everyday reality of Anglo culture's status as a *culture among many*. Yet the politics of monoculturalism creates the perception that Anglo culture is not a culture. The term "culture" is used within Anglo culture to mark differences from its own conceptions of people and things. Therefore, Anglos *act,* whereas non-Anglos *practice* their culture. This use understands these ways of conceiving people and things as static and practiced ritualistically rather than creatively. Cultures in this understanding are provincial and do not change. When "culture" is used in this way, only non-dominant cultures are declared to be and turned into cultures. In contrast, Anglo culture conceives of itself as expressive of what is universal, and so beyond "culture" in a narrow, provincial sense: it is postcultural, it is not a "culture" at all. From this point of view, cultural domination and erasure appear reasonable, a means to get at what is most truly human. "Culture," then, is a devaluing label that justifies a prohibition against participation in civic life. "Full citizens lack culture and those most culturally endowed lack full citizenship."[1]

There is an impression of down-to-earth common sense built into the perception that Anglo culture expresses the American way of life, the best way of life, and the human way of life. This common sense sometimes openly embraces Western "high culture," but it is often disdainful of intellectual, theoretical critique. This down-to-earth, commonsense character of the universalistic extension of Anglo culture hides from itself its dominating character. It is captured well in the proponent of English-only who says; "If English is good enough for God, it is good enough for me."

So we see that whether Anglo culture is a culture or not is a political issue. Its status as a culture can only be named from a multicultural political position. Thus adherents do not call themselves "monoculturalists." This term names those who "see" what they do and how they act as the reasonable, the unmarked, and the desirable way for all humans to behave, to be a culture, all the while unable or unwilling to perceive their own culture at all. To see their culture as a culture would be to see it as a culture among many. But then, why would that culture rather than other cultures expressed in the society be deserving of institutional status as a dominant culture? Monoculturalists never have to answer this question. At the center of the logic of their position is the unstated claim that theirs is not a culture at all. Given this unstated and unstatable claim, they do not see any need to understand other cultures or to compare them with their own. They use the terms "culture" and "ethnic" pejoratively. They do not perceive the need to compare and to argue about the nitty-gritty of the merits of particular practices, values, and beliefs. Their ignorance of other cultures is not perceived as a handicap since their stance is not comparative. Comparison and evaluation are irrelevant to what they advocate. This explains why monoculturalists get angry when someone uses the term "dominant culture" and indict the use as political rather than descriptive.

Description and Prescription

Monoculturalism, as we have said, involves the claim that the United States both is and ought to be a monocultural society. That is, monoculturalism involves both a description and a prescription. That it slides back and forth from description to prescription is important. Introducing the concept of multiculturalism will clarify the importance of this move from "is" to "ought" and back.

Multiculturalism also slides back and forth between description and prescription as it proposes both the claim that the United States is a multicultural society and that its many cultures *should* inform institutionalized civic, economic, and social life. Multiculturalism is thus a political stance. It rejects the idea that assimilation and cultural destruction should be core elements of civic, economic, and social life as it rejects an ornamental view of culture. It involves a prescription and description of reality and a blurring of the line between them: "We are here to stay!" is one way of stating the description that shows its prescriptive character. It is an injunction and a challenge, as well as a statement of one's presence in society as a member of one culture among many.

Our cultural integrity, all that distinguishes us as "us," in this willfully polyglot America, is nothing less than the historic and the collective affirmation of our own self, today, in public and open visibility. It is our distinctive "us" culture, the beautiful, the "get into it/down and up to go on and on" music of our beautiful, Black, and Third World, beleaguered, widely despised, stubbornly continuing lives. It is that music that we have eked out, devised, improvised, sanctified, and moved to, to keep our spirit intact, to bless and hold the spirit of us, as peoples, strong and holy as all life itself—life that we will not now, life that we have never, simply, or in any other way, let go.[2]

Multiculturalism sees that there is more than one culture, evaluates that there should be more than one culture, and argues that there should be more than one culture where it counts, rather than merely ornamentally. Then it exhibits that there already is more than one culture where it counts when it enters political contestation, political struggle against monoculturalism. It can exhibit more than one culture because of the nature of its challenge to monoculturalism. Oppositionally and defiantly, the cultures assert themselves as counting, as not relegated to the private or to ornament, but as exercised politically in fashioning a society that is structurally multicultural. The society's many cultures enter the political terrain asserting and protesting that they exist, demanding to exist, to flourish, and to inform the important threads of life. The claim that all our cultures ought to exist is advanced from the very position of existing.

The struggle against monoculturalism reveals monoculturalism's slide from description to prescription—there is and there ought to be only one culture—as a mechanism of cultural erasure: "There is one culture" is revealed as "We'll make it be one culture." This is then revealed as the rule: "Let there be one culture." As we will see later in this chapter, this collective will that there be only one culture is backed by certain needs and attitudes that are logically connected to it: the need for certainty, the valuing of agreement or commonality, and finding simplicity pleasing or fitting.

Monoculturalism and multiculturalism both contain a blur between description and prescription, but the logic of the blur is different in each case. The description that there is only one culture is not so much a description of what is, but rather evidence of a project to make it the case. Monoculturalism's project is to bring reality in line with its assertions. It asserts that there is but one culture, discounting all evidence to the contrary by not seeing anything as counterevidence as it simultaneously attempts to destroy all counterevidence. Multiculturalism also proposes to alter reality, and not merely describe it. But multiculturalism, as it enters politics, evidences and validates its own descriptions. Non-ornamental multicultural reality becomes visible in political defiance.

Though one may think that a project of elimination presupposes and requires the existence of the object to be eliminated, that is not the case when it comes to the logic of monoculturalism. As Marilyn Frye argues in her description of this logic in the related case of erasure of women from the domain of persons; "A project of annihilation can be seen to *presuppose* the nonexistence of the objects being eliminated. One begins with a firmly held view [that the object does not exist] and adopts as one's project the alteration of the world to bring it into accord with that view." Concrete evidence that the world is otherwise removed rather than acknowledged as evidence. "Erasure of fact and destruction of concrete objects does not demonstrate recognition of the fact or object; it is on the contrary, direct manifestation of the belief that those are not the facts and the belief that no such individual objects exist."[3]

This practice of eliminating counterevidence has a history in the context of European expansion and imperialism. Mary Louise Pratt has noted this logic at work in nineteenth-century travel writing by Europeans about Africa. She has observed that this genre of writing

is a configuration which, in (mis)recognition of what was materially underway or in anticipation of what was to come, verbally depopulates landscapes. Indigenous peoples are relocated in separate manners-and-customs chapters as if in textual homelands or reservations, where they are pulled out of time to be preserved, contained, studied, admired, detested, pitied, mourned. Meanwhile, the now-empty landscape is personified as the metaphorical "face of the country"—a more tractable face that returns the European's gaze, echoes his words, and accepts his caress.

Pratt notes that exploration writing was not merely a misrecognition of what the explorers found, but it was specifically a prescriptive gaze upon a future that they were working toward. "In scanning prospects in the spatial sense—as landscape panoramas—this eye [of the explorer/writer] knows itself to be looking at prospects in the temporal sense—as possibilities for the future, resources to be developed, landscapes to be peopled or repeopled by Europeans."[4]

So, through this sliding from description to prescription and back, one can work toward annihilating other cultures without ever perceiving that there actually are other cultures. Confronted with evidence of another culture, one proceeds to erase the evidence rather than acknowledge it as evidence. Success in erasure confirms the belief that there was no such thing.

In contradistinction, multiculturalism blurs description and prescription as it evidences and affirms the existence of many cultures. It exhibits reality *as* multicultural through political struggle. Monoculturalism can attempt to destroy the evidence and therefore achieve a reality that is monocultural. But it cannot exhibit reality as monocultural as it attempts to erase other cultures. During the struggle between monoculturalism and multiculturalism, monoculturalism is caught in the act: the act of erasure.

That is why the logics are different. The logic of multicultural blurring of description and prescription disrupts the logic of monoculturalism: it inserts its evidence incontrovertibly. Of course, the success of monoculturalism can save its own logic. Erasure of cultures does press toward making society monocultural. But as we emphasize, in the moment of struggle, the disruption of this logic is achieved. Monoculturalists can continue to declare the defiant cultures non-existent, but the meaning of this declaration has been disrupted.

So we can see that the claim that the U.S. is a multicultural society is a complex and political claim. The description of society as multicultural is made from certain reference points. Other reference points obscure its multicultural qualities and lead one to perceive the society as monocultural. We are arguing that one point of reference is to be preferred because it uncovers a process of domination that is morally abhorrent. The prescription is also made from this reference point, since it is only as one perceives society as multicultural that one can understand the desirability of enriching rather than diminishing society in this respect. Hence, one comes to value all cultures, restitching the institutional fabric of the society and its members' characters, personalities, life plans, and activities.

Method

In the rest of the paper we will argue for the related claims that many cultures do exist and are actively practiced in the U.S., that these cultures should inform the institutional fabric of society, and that Anglo culture is a dominating culture that is striving to erase the variegated nature of cultural life in this country. We will argue using two very different methods. On the one hand, we will appeal to our own cultural experiences—descriptions from location. And on the other, we will unpack the attitudes that back monoculturalism and multiculturalism and that shape the daily contestation between the two.

The first method involves us in open defiance as proponents of multiculturalism. We will describe our own experience of living with others in the United States and we will do so located in the particularities of our own cultures. Our descriptions will exhibit society as multicultural. As we speak politically, we exhibit the cultures not as ornamental, but as contesting for institutional recognition. Our portraits of interpersonal life in the United States from our locations also exhibit and disclose domination at close range: as felt, lived, and exercised as parts of our lives.

We use description from location for two reasons. First, because we believe that when one takes oneself to be simply a citizen, a human being, an American, or a faceless author without qualification, one ceases to see domination. But U.S. society looks different from different positions within it. As our descriptions will show, focusing on the vantage points that each of us brings to the writing of this piece will illuminate the details of cultural domination. Second, we have also encountered many people who are fond of saying that color does not matter, that they treat all people the same. They say that they do not see white people, Anglos, Latinos, Blacks, Native Americans, or Asians; they merely see human beings. Although this thought may be appealing to some, it is dangerous because it commits one to monoculturalism. Such a stance erases differences from perception and thus participates actively in the process of cultural domination through cultural leveling and turning difference into ornament. It is central to our argument and central to multiculturalism that cultural, racial, and gender differences count in the construction of perception and the construction of society.

As you read our descriptions, you may wish to consider how you would describe your own location and what insights your location gives you on the claims we make about how Anglo culture dominates public life in the United States. How does where we stand look to you, from your location? How does that location give you perspective on or restrict your ability to evaluate either of our positions? How might you look from our own position? What stance do you strike in the context of the struggle that we see between monoculturalism and multiculturalism?

Our second method in this essay will be to argue that the project of monoculturalism is advanced through the adoption of a particular set of attitudes: seeking agreement or common ground, valuing and seeking simplicity, and striving for certainty as necessary for making decisions and judgments. These attitudes are integral to the monocultural project. When they are adopted into the daily conduct of social and political life, they tend to make Anglo culture a dominant culture.

We will argue that the project of multiculturalism is advanced through a very different and conflicting set of attitudes. Multiculturalism is backed by efforts to seek understanding through attention to conflicting perspectives without reducing them to a common ground, by valuing and seeking complexity, and by having a positive attitude toward uncertainty as one seeks to take positions and make decisions. The adoption of these attitudes in the daily conduct of life promotes structural cultural pluralism.

Once one sees the attitudes of multiculturalism, one can gain a critical perspective on one's previously held beliefs. Through contrasting the logics, one will see the familiar anew: the attitudes to which one may have had an unthoughtful allegiance will be defamiliarized. The attitudes of *mono*culturalism are usually not seen, but when put forth, they seem indisputable, the only reasonable ones to hold. We dispute this perception by exhibiting a coherent but different set of attitudes that are necessary for a society that is culturally pluralistic on a structural level. In so doing we are revealing the fit between political stance, social organization, and the attitudes and structure of personality.

ON LOCATION

In a Latina Voice: María Lugones

I am a U.S. Latina, though I am not U.S.-born. In identifying as a "U.S. Latina," I mean to convey certain attitudes, perceptions, and commitments. The United States is where I live, where I struggle. Latinos—in all our diversity, coincidences, and mutual antagonisms—are the people with whom I identify. Latinos constitute my lens on U.S. society. My ways of thinking and talking and moving are attuned to life in the United States. The United States is where my attention is focused and my problematic has been shaped. As I attempt to convey an experiential understanding of "dominant culture," I understand myself as a committed and active participant in the struggles against cultural domination. Being anchored as a U.S. Latina gives my experiential account a definite political tone. *No hablo sola. Hablo en compañía, un hablar colectivo sincopado, una trama de muchos hilos: nos escuchamos entre nosotros/as con un oído agudo, atento a los sentidos hechos en una colectivad multíplice.*

As I think of describing my experience of culture in this country and as I think of my ways and the ways of others and of the communication among us, the metaphors that occur to me have to do with breathing, and doing so with difficulty. The air around me is thick, more like oil than like air. *Me ahogo, hermana. Dame una palabra para salir a flote.* I move, speak, listen, gesture with difficulty, as if gasping for ease, ease in the presuppositions of understanding and being understood. Much of the time, my words, gestures, and distances are not understood as I mean them. *Una habla y ellos deciden lo que una está diciendo.* Much of the time my words, gestures, movements, and their directions hang in the thickness of the cultural air as if suspiciously nonsensical, even when I have purposefully tailored them to the circumstances. *Yo se lo que dije. ¿Vos me entendiste, no?* My own communication appears to me as more conscious of interlocutors and the context of interlocution than of the communication addressed to me by those who seem to me to be in their element. To me, my own communication seems directed to the particularities of the communicative situation, but it is taken as thrown carelessly by someone not fluent in "the" culture. I am also conscious of degrees of communicative success. I recognize this awareness in others. *Sabes como yo que el comprenderse es un milagro hecho de urgencia, generosidad, voluntad rebelde.* I see it when I am communicating with interlocutors who do not doubt, question, or seem particularly aware of the degrees of difficulty in communication. The ease or unease with which people say, "I know what you mean."

Even though I experience monoculturalism in this country, I don't experience the United States as a monocultural society. I cross paths every day with those who, like me, practice non-dominant cultures in resistance to domination. *Palabras claves extrañando la bienvenida de la conversación cotidiana, la parte que es caricia para adentro, el aguijón para afuera?* I do not even experience Anglo America as monocultural. I experience my own sense of fluency or lack of fluency and my high consciousness of tailoring my expressions to those around me as markers of cultural complexities within Anglo American life. Do you notice those complexities? I am very aware of where I have achieved some degree of fluency and where my lack of competence accentuates my uncertainty. It happens constantly. I see a constant crisscrossing of complexity: different age groups, different genders, different parts of the country, different occupations, and so on. There is no cultural homogeneity. Dominance thus is not reducible to monoculture, since there is no monoculture. Dominance is the thickness of the air. *Yo veo que no se comprenden entre ellos. No se respetan en sus diferencias. Marcan límites y se rehusan a aprender las palabras y modos de los otros Anglos. Pero a mi, cada uno, desde adentro de sus límites, me exigen que les entienda y les responda en su moneda. Y yo, claro, dada mis posibilidades y mi circunstancia, "le hago el try." Pero igualmente presuponen el fracaso en nuestra comunicación. Y, por supuesto, me hechan la culpa a mi?* All of Anglo American culture is pressed on me as the currency that I must understand and handle without any reciprocity from those who see themselves as its most proper practitioners. Most of the time I am assumed to lack that currency even as understanding is demanded of me. I am marked by a deep sort of stupidity, for of course, children are assumed to know more than I. In my case, then, I experience dominance as I negotiate the different assumptions and standards for communication for different people. It is presupposed that Anglo culture is the only appropriate culture. Therefore, it is presupposed that *I* must cross cultural boundaries. Those not fluent in my ways are never aware of any lack in *them*selves. The lack is all mine, even as I exhibit competence, since competence is assumed to be lacking in *me*.

The dichotomy between private life and public life is also imposed on my experience of speech, of gesturing, of moving through space, the feeling of emotions, and so on. The private, the insular, the place of emotion and intimacy, bereft of any political or public importance. The public, the domain of power, of words that count, of encounters among "full" persons whose influence reaches into other people's lives. The private/public split is imposed on me: certain ways for certain places. All dominant cultural ways are appropriate for public spaces. When expressed in public the "other" ones are experienced as out of place. Their place is in the private sphere—only. But we can, I do, experience our ways in public as deeply resistant, obstinately exhibited in defiance, even as the resistance is discounted as a form of nonsense. *La finura de la palabra labrada laboriosamente, hablada con esa mezcla de desafío y mesura que nos ocupa en el acto casi ritual de la protesta cultural pública.* Having no sense in one's tongue and therefore in one's head. Even when resistance is collective and redundantly and emphatically marked as such to oneself and others, it can be denied sense by those who are mono-sensical. Spontaneous public exercise of non-dominant cultures are translated as ignorant, incompetent, rather than as resistant. It is interesting that practitioners of Anglo culture sometimes break into French without any sense of having gone mad. It gives one an indication of their alliances and values. The presupposition is that whatever sense there is to be made is their sense; they are themselves the arbiters of sense. They do not extend themselves toward an uncertainty that would open up to them the possibility of understanding me even when what I say is not in their vein.

Thus, I experience cultural domination as a directly intersubjective communicative relation that occurs within a political institutionalized context that backs it up. As meaning is made and remade intersubjectively, domination is a relation that is lived in everyday interaction. I contest dominant sense in a tense relation with my interlocutors, backed by the presence, perceptions, and words of others whose ways are not dominant. We invoke each other in sense making within a hostile environment. *Invocación que forma un aire, un ambiente, una posibilidad creativa de voces marchando y haciendo ecos: esa, mana, mujer, chica, nena—¿me comprende señora?—si si, estamos en la misma onda. Ecos que no repiten sino transmiten el sentido transformado a su propio gusto, a su propia modalidad.*

As someone of the dominant culture enters the intersubjective situation of meaning creation, meaning is already presupposed, and the mutuality of participation in meaning creation is erased as the non-dominant speaker is erased from competence. *Borrados. Todavía no. Un momentito, que ya marchamos una murga sincopada, que estamos todavía en la historia, haciendo historia.* Meaning is understood ahistorically, as *pre-*

ceding communication, and arising from individual (sole) authorship (a "this is what I mean" that is immediately presented as a "this is what it means").

As I depict this experience of intersubjective encounter, I uncover the politics, the interpersonal politics of communication that reveals domination: an erasure of the subjectivity and creativity of the non-dominant speaker, a non-hearing, an assumption both that s/he won't make sense and that the only sense to be made is carried by the dominant speaker. *Mi papá es sordo y nos entrenamos todos/as a oir y a ser oídos a pesar de la dificultad. El sonido a la vez precioso y terrible porque él no lo puede tener en su oreja con facilidad y una quisiera poder dárselo.*

As I am aggressively ignored in the communicative act, I understand the ignorance as aggressive, as a willful act of dismissal of sense, a willful act of erasure of the possibility of my sense. As I contest, the aggressive dismissal of my cultural resistance testifies to my presence in the scene echoing in the experience of countless others who are listening to each other, opening ourselves up to the intricacies of cross-cultural and multicultural sense.

In an Anglo Voice: Joshua Price

I grew up with people taking care of me, of my material needs, cleaning up for me. I have grown up fluent in the ways of public space in American culture. I speak a recognizable and generally accepted dialect of English: "not understanding" is someone else's problem. I have grown up trusting my instincts, my intelligence, and my perception.

My motility is not particularly contained or restricted. I occupy a lot of space easily and fluidly. My voice is also very loud, often inappropriately loud in public spaces without my knowing it. I can move about in relative freedom, relative freedom from harassment by men or by the police; the air that I breathe I grew up to believe was my own. I do not, in the main, feel particularly restricted—I am confident of my ability to navigate through everyday life, financially and materially secure.

Although Jewish, I understand myself as an almost-insider to Anglo culture in the United States. From Jewish culture to Anglo culture I experience a gap. In my case, that gap is not obliterated; nevertheless, I am of the ways of Anglo people. That I make the transition to Anglo ways is important to mark, since it robs me of a point of resistance. I know what it is to give something up.

I have come to understand, haltingly, that many things in this country were designed for my use and are at my disposal, and that moreover, many things I assume are, are in fact not. In trying to think about how white control is maintained, I have come to see how I am asked in a million different ways, implicitly and explicitly, consciously and unconsciously, by white friends, by other men, by family, and by white strangers to maintain solidarity and loyalty—often in order to break, exclude, violate, exploit, and deny those people who are outside the inner circle. As I have become more conscious, I have begun to realize with a certain horror how often this happens—how constantly and how frequently I knowingly or unknowingly support cultural and political domination.

I participate actively in cultural domination but also experience a pressure to conform to it. That I perceive cultural domination both internally and externally—as active participant and as pressure from the other people to stand in solidarity—provides me with some evidence of how I shift in perspective on my participation. I speak in an Anglo voice, but I feel a need to problematize that voice and the position from which I speak. The intersubjective politics of my position as located in struggle give me a perception of the dominant politics at work around me and within me. I see political engagement as crafting a radical subjectivity that enables me to notice as I shift in and out of these perceptions—so often tightly wound around me—the contradictory loyalties and affections they call upon. In the context of these shifting points of identity—as practitioner operating within the dominant culture and as rebel dedicated to undermining it—I see this writing itself as an exercise in resistance, as an unveiling of how I experience the dominant culture and my own tense participation in it. As I write, I can see myself shifting from transparent practitioner of dominant culture to a person who can listen, see, and think in more than one cultural modality. I can see that tension in myself as I describe my positions "in an Anglo voice." But let me underscore that this shifting back and forth in perception does not happen alone. My perceptions, identity, and ways of thinking and feeling develop in company, intersubjectively, as I change my habits of everyday life, modifying my attention and my focus and questioning who it is that makes sense and who it is that is transgressing.

Erving Goffman has called the way in which social performances are staged in Anglo American society "impression management."[5] In his account, Anglo Americans help and support one another in teams to try to manage the impression that they leave. The team includes some and excludes others. The team itself is often being made up, or remade, as the interaction unfolds. Certain team members are now included, now excluded. I find it helpful to extend his analysis by focusing on the way in which "impression management" upholds Anglo culture itself—in other words, upholds it as dominant.

In my experience white people act like a team. My personal allegiance is exacted. We support each other. We act in solidarity with one another. But we also police ourselves. As a particular social interaction unfolds, we can defer to one another or show respect, or we can also expose each other. If one or another of us gets out of line, we can embarrass, infantilize, sexualize, or trivialize the other—uncovering ignorance. Hence, in Anglo society, the team in charge can close ranks in mutual support as well as maintain hostile relations. This upholds Anglo culture as the dominant culture. It leads us to grab and hang onto what we take to be "center stage."

I am only liminally aware of the attitudes in myself that constitute me as a member of the "impression management" team. I slide in and out of awareness of my complicity in the small ways in which I uphold the fabric of everyday life. It has been impressed upon me through my interaction with people in resistance to monoculturalism.

Struggle with people outside of dominant culture is crucial to my maintaining a critical awareness of how I collaborate in their exclusion.

I see that it is part of my experience that I am deprived of seeing the ways in which I uphold cultural domination—how I occupy space, how I use my voice, how I have lived a life that requires other people in positions of service to me. It is part of my participation in buttressing monoculturalism that I have seen "not understanding" as someone else's problem, so confident of my ability to move through different ambiances not seeing the complex intersubjective and multicultural threads that weave their way through my life. I can also look at my friends and kin unsentimentally and note that they act in racist and dominating ways—just like me.

I see myself colluding with the Anglo shop clerk who sets out not to understand a Latina I am with, and asks me what she wants. I see myself betray her as I explain. I see myself responding to the appeals of whites for understanding, for attention, for conviviality as my eye wavers from the project of undermining racism and undoing domination concretely in everyday life. I tend to keep that project abstract. For a person of the dominant culture, it is easy to waver under pressure, and the pressure is there. Solidarity is already there, and I am asked to maintain it. It is not easy for one person to disrupt it.

The attitude and impression that Anglos, including myself, try to leave is one of competence, control, and understanding. Given the harshness of white Anglo spaces, this control is far from secure. The atmosphere of white competence and Anglo domination, it is important to note, must be *collectively and actively maintained.* It is not self-sustaining.

I am shoveling snow with a woman. I have never done it before, while she on the other hand has shoveled her walk for twenty years. She tries to show me how to accomplish the task, but I insist that I can do it. I am, after all, physically fit, a grown man, and I can make decisions about how to do things, who to listen to. I do it my way. "White men have inherited a position of command and that means that they cannot admit that anything is beyond them, so they must pretend to capabilities they do not possess."[6] I go through hoops, if not to impress, at least to proclaim knowledge and competence that I do not have.

White people often do not feel obligated to hold up a performance in front of people of color or people that are servicing them. I have seen white Anglos walk around in underwear in front of the cleaning lady as if she were not there. We mistreat one another in restaurants, at the auto mechanic's garage, when the only people to witness the behavior are attendants, waiters, and so on. Our relationship to people who are servicing us is akin to indifference; we do not see them as people who deserve our focus or attention. As Porter Millington says in *Drylongso:*

We know whitefolks, but they do not know us, and that's just how the Lord planned that thing. That is a hell of a thing to think about, you know. First you have to understand that it is not in the color but the thinking, how you might say, the attitude. And it's not in *your* attitude, but in the attitudes of all the people that growed you and of the people that you seen and heard about. One big difference between us and the cracker, or the whiteman, or whatever you want to call him is, he don' know that we know this. He don't really think you know a damn thing. But I have got sense enough not to tell that dude anything but what he thinks I think. I know that the man is not going to thank me if I tell him the truth about anything.[7]

Even as I understand it, it is hard to live with that understanding informing my everyday experience. The curious dialectic lies in our preoccupation with giving an impression that we know how to do things and not particularly caring or thinking at all about how we appear. The difference lies, it seems to me, between a preoccupation with trying to leave an impression of competence and power, and trying to learn how you are in fact perceived. I think that trying to learn how you are perceived need not be a further exercise in narcissism.

To write about how I see monoculturalism as it is practiced in myself and in others is not to manifest self-contempt publicly or to mouth the words of others with little understanding. By writing in this way, from these sources, with this ambivalence about my own participation, I am noting the ways in which I have come to understand things about myself and other people, ways that have been motivated by the insights and challenges of those who resist monoculturalism. Developing with clarity the way in which I believe cultural domination is structural and interactional prepares me to transform my practices and helps to give a complex sense to living as a queer man. I also take this writing to be a process of revealing some of the ways monoculturalism works in organizing desires and licensing ways of speaking and occupying space—all attesting to who one is and can be.

Discussion

Our self-descriptions have been attuned to how these descriptions depend upon other people, both within Anglo culture and at points external to Anglo culture. Our identities are not forged by each of us alone. They are built on the interpretations of other people, how they respond to us, and how we appear to them.

Our locations and our experiences are evidence of the falsity of the monocultural attempt to silence the various perspectives and ways of comportment. The monocultural project is one of domination of all parts of life. We strike a stance to resist, to complicate, and to explode the domination of one culture in economic exchange, in the classroom, on the factory floor, in law, on television, in mainstream politics, in most public spaces. In support of the account of the oppressed, we see more clearly the dimensions of the project of cultural annihilation and domination within Anglo culture.

We are not equally prepared for this task. From our different locations, we see different aspects of monocultural domination and its inner mechanisms as well as how we are pressured to respond to or survive in relation to them. We have very different access to the non-ornamental existence of the many cultures and see with different clarity that cultural homogeneity is a political myth. We are also differently positioned in our resistance to monoculturalism. The multiple perspectives we exhibit are not merely evidence of what monoculturalism looks like from the standpoint of people committed to multiculturalism. Our experiential accounts also reveal the possibility of change, and that change occurs through changes in everyday life and in everyday behavior, including changes in our relations with others in our society.

CERTEZA, SIMPLEZA, Y ACUERDO: LAS BASES COGNITIVAS DEL MONOCULTURALISMO/CERTAINTY, SIMPLICITY, AND AGREEMENT: THE COGNITIVE BASES OF MONOCULTURALISM

Introduction

So far we have argued the connection between a culture's dominance and monoculturalism—the political stance that there is and ought to be one culture. We have argued that monoculturalism bridges the gap between is and ought through cultural domination. We have also argued that the process of cultural erasure and domination is a daily affair, carried out by ordinary persons differently located in society in their daily interaction. Anglo culture becomes dominant through daily interactions that privilege it over other cultures. We have also begun to demonstrate that cultural pluralism flourishes in daily interactions that do not privilege Anglo culture.

In this section, we will look more closely at this daily interaction, paying attention to cognitive practices that guide people in their cultural usage. By cognitive practices we mean the attitudes and expectations that constitute our attention as selective, that underlie our perceptions, evaluations, and choice of action. The overriding questions for us, are on the one hand, What guides particular members of society in particular situations of action, decision making, and communication to privilege Anglo culture? What guides them to select an Anglo American understanding of a particular situation? What cognitive practices frame that privilege? And on the other hand, What guides members of society to cross and combine cultures in particular situations of action, decision making, and communication? What cognitive attitudes guide them to perceive cultural complexity and enable them to work with it?

We ask ourselves what guides members of society to engage each other in an Anglo cultural mode in a variety institutional locations: at work, in school, at the doctor's office, in interaction with the police, at government offices, in neighborhood meetings, in church, at home, at parties, in a bus. We have in mind the admitting nurse at a hospital who thinks he/she can only accept information in English. We are thinking of a judiciary system that utilizes the Anglo American legal process as if it were culturally neutral and acts as if legal processes have to be monocultural in their very conception, structure, and procedures. The translator may translate words, but the *process* is still monocultural.

As we will see, certain cognitive practices enable a monocultural political stance and a structurally monocultural society, and others enable a multicultural stance and a multicultural pluralistic society. We remind ourselves here that a structurally monocultural society can and perhaps must be an ornamentally pluralistic society. Seeking certainty, simplicity, and common ground or agreement are cognitive practices that guide people to privilege Anglo culture in the United States. We will see that these cognitive practices turn Anglo culture into a dominant culture and ground monoculturalism.

As we argue, we will describe these cognitive practices. We will show that a reality or society based on these practices makes monoculturalism reasonable and a dominant culture necessary. We will show, too, that these practices require erasure of other cultures and are thus morally objectionable. But we will also show that they are avoidable practices.

To those who are their practitioners, these cognitive practices seem unavoidable. Because monoculturalism is grounded in these cognitive practices, its moral justifiability is tied to the moral quality of the practices. If these cognitive practices were the only ones possible for human beings in the construction of their intersubjectivity, evaluating them morally would be pointless and monoculturalism would be unobjectionable, at least on that count. The rock falling off the side of the mountain onto a passing car is a bad thing, but there is nothing immoral about its falling, as it cannot be helped. To entertain the possibility of evaluating this episode morally is to begin to look at whether the rock could have been prevented from falling and who could and should have done that. So monoculturalism, grounded on these practices, could be morally evaluated only if the practices were avoidable. We understand that many people do not see monoculturalism as objectionable because it is based on cognitive practices that appear to them as the only ones possible.

Our intention is to reveal a culturally pluralist conceptual framework that is grounded upon an alternative set of cognitive practices. As we introduce alternative cognitive practices, we will clarify the culturally pluralist conceptual framework. In unveiling an alternative set of cognitive practices, we will reveal the cognitive practices constitutive of monoculturalism as avoidable. The introduction of this alternative set will also reveal that the cognitive practices that ground monoculturalism are morally bankrupt because they are avoidable and culturally erasing. We believe the alternative practices are more desirable and preferable precisely because they do not erase other cultures.

We will first explain what we mean by the three cognitive practices. We will then show how they work together to provide a scheme by which one way of doing things is reasonable, necessary, and desirable.

Certainty, Simplicity, Agreement

Those who seek certainty have the underlying faith that they can arrive at perceptions or actions that are undoubtedly correct or true. Such persons have the expectation of finding all the facts about a particular matter and of potentially reaching incontrovertible judgments based on those facts. When certainty is achieved and reality is described from the position of certainty, there is no room for disagreement, no room for doubt, no room for reevaluation. This is thought to be a very demanding but achievable ideal. Two views of the same matter cannot be allowed. Therefore, this position requires that a multiplicity of contemporaneous realities be dismissed from possibility before investigation can begin.

The disposition toward certainty is a form of simplification, since it requires that the world of perception and interpretation be sifted through toward simple either/or truths and falsities. This sifting through, this separating of "extraneous," "irrelevant," and "insignificant" material from the central and significant is one of the operations by which certainty is made possible. The dismissal does not problematize the sifting operation itself, thus it makes certainty possible. Those who seek certainty consider evidence and decide what is irrelevant and eliminate it. They mold a complex reality into simple terms: what is clear and pertinent, separated from what is shadowy, contradictory, and extraneous. Certainty is made possible through this exercise in simplification. That things are straightforward is a requirement for seeking certainty. When things are not straightforward, they are "ironed out" and "clarified" or excluded from consideration.

Certainty and simplicity are often discussed in connection with the goal of a common ground or good. In a public discussion in a democracy, many people have the expectation that good arguments will be clear, simple, and understandable. They expect to understand others at all levels. They think of all people as fundamentally the same. If the arguments or perspectives advanced by others in public discussion are complicated or unfamiliar, and thus difficult to understand, they are for that reason discounted. The assumption that all people are the same leads them away from the possibility that two different conceptual worlds are meeting, worlds that include different possibilities and different accounts of reality, one not reducible to the other. Rather, they interpret all conflicts at the level of the individual as motivated by selfishness. They think that the discussion is kept from reaching a common solution due to participants' pursuit of conflicting self-interests. A common ground or a common good is seen as always possible, and as the goal of public discussion because without it there would be "anarchy" in the sense of lawlessness, arbitrary violence, and willful disregard for one another. Nothing important is lost from eliminating conflicting interests because what is central and important is assumed to be what people have in common.

Such a discussion begins with the premise that by the end, the participants will hold things in common. Wherever they begin, the project is to develop or to discover a common ground. This is an injunction to commonality amongst people who may see things differently. To achieve a common ground, people push for compromise. The ability to compromise is valued very highly since it makes achieving a common ground or agreeing upon a common good possible. Compromise entails that people give up their differences rather than live with their differences. Those who favor compromise do not conceive of the possibility of learning from each others' differences. They do not conceive of the possibility of seeking the satisfaction of complex needs and the pursuit of complex interests, some of which they do not share. Compromise, though necessary, is always to be done fairly—no one is unduly pressured or coerced to give up more than anyone else. Searching for a common ground and a common good is tied to simplifying reality: no important irreducible differences are allowed. All differences and conflicts are reducible and reduced toward commonality.

Do these three cognitive practices—certainty, simplicity, and the goal of a common good— really make monoculturalism both reasonable and necessary? We can ask this question in a different way: Will a person who acts in accord with these cognitive practices be open with any depth to other cultures or other ways of seeing things? Is he or she capable of noticing them? Does he or she promote a politics that ensures their existence, or one that contributes to their annihilation?

We begin with the attitude and expectation of certainty. We have argued that this cognitive practice requires that multiple realities go unseen through the lens of one privileged understanding of reality. By multiple realities, we mean the simultaneous enactment of different conceptions of people, different customs, different values, and different understandings of how to relate to each other and fundamental aspects of identity such as gender. The expectation of certainty rejects the possibility of more than one account. Of alternative accounts of reality, of contesting versions or perspectives, of different cultural frameworks, all except one are assumed to be decidedly false or distorted. This judgment is entailed by the cognitive attitude of certainty.

Simplicity means that of these alternative accounts of reality, some will be judged irrelevant or unimportant relative to a particular set of values and beliefs. Some accounts may be judged irrelevant because they are unfamiliar to the person seeking simplicity, in the sense of not being included in the conceptual framework of her or his culture. Sometimes things are not familiar to us but are not conceptually odd, like a plant one has never seen before. But some things cannot be understood without having one's set of possible concepts enlarged or investigating a new set of concepts. The seeker of simplicity rejects out of hand what is unfamiliar in these senses by privileging a familiar conceptual set. To privilege a particular culture requires a willingness to privilege a particular set of concepts, values, and ways of doing things.

Privileging simplification may itself do violence to a particular alternative account, since simplification may be foreign to it. Another culture may be discarded or made orderly if considered unsimple by the seeker of simplicity. It may be remade in the image of the seeker of simplicity's culture.

Finally, in the expectation that the many cultures present will join to develop or discover a common good, we see the fundamental incompatibility with multiculturalism. The search for a common goal insists on political union forged by compromise. But compromise is guided by the love of simplicity and certainty, and thus is not understood as requiring a deep understanding of another's culture. Mis-recognizing other cultures is one thing, but the search for common good promises and requires that even between cultures whose values, attitudes, and expectations are neither reducible to each other nor known to the seeker of agreement, a commonality will be found— must be found. Not having noticed the particularities of another culture, one insists on agreement and a common goal. There is no reduction, but rather an assumption of reducibility exercised through a monosensical understanding of the compromise situation. The complex problems of communication are neither investigated nor resolved, but rather are set aside in an act of simplification in the direction of one culture.

Thus we return to monoculturalism, to the project that there is and ought to be only one culture. First we have seen that these three cognitive practices are inconsistent with understanding another culture with any depth and tolerating its practice. Differences must be made subordinate to the common ground. Erasure is thus necessary. We see, then, that monoculturalism does not have to be a consciously willed project. It is part of the logic of these three cognitive practices, which make other cultures impossible to see. One of the conclusions to be drawn, then, is that these three work together to form not just indifference and misunderstanding but positive violence in political "union." We can see how these cognitive practices are invested in cultural domination.

As Anglos come to political discussion (and to all other intersubjective communication) fluent only in Anglo ways and pressing Anglo ways on others who are fluent in more than one culture, their exercise of these cognitive practices requires that they privilege Anglo culture. These cognitive practices are barriers that make it difficult, if not impossible, to see other cultures in the scene, and they work toward the erasure of other cultures.

Pero para la gente de color, gente de otras culturas, la situación es completemente diferente. People from other cultures, non-Anglos, are used to crossing, to seeing things in more than one way. They cross to places where cultures other than their own shape the ways of doing things. This crossing is done for many different reasons, and in many different ways and directions. Author bell hooks describes her experience:

To be in the margin is to be part of the whole but outside the main body. As black Americans living in a small Kentucky town, the railroad tracks were a daily reminder of our marginality. Across those tracks were paved streets, stores we could not enter, restaurants we could not eat in, and people we could not look directly in the face. Across those tracks was a world we could work in as maids, as janitors, as prostitutes, as long as it was in a service capacity. We could enter that world but we could not live there. We had always to return to the margin, to cross the tracks, to shacks and abandoned houses on the edge of town. There were laws to ensure our return. To not return was to risk being punished. Living as we did—on the edge—we developed a particular way of seeing reality. We looked both from the outside in and the from the inside out. We focused our attention on the center as well as on the margin. We understood both.[8]

As hooks describes it, one develops multiple perspectives by crossing back and forth.

The understanding of cultural crossers is crucial to the possibility of a multicultural society: it makes vivid the possibility of understanding more than one's own desires, life plans, and possibilities or those of one's own people. But this understanding is a fragile one when it is accompanied by exploitation and subordination. It can make the possibilities of those with power seem very attractive. In this atmosphere, one may feel not only the attraction of things on the other side of the fence, but also the attraction of the cognitive practices themselves—certainty, simplicity, and common ground. One may feel that adopting these practices is both a deep giving up of oneself and the promise of coming to see wonderful things: the world simple and graspable *y todo lo necesario para hacer poder hacerse la América.* Success and improvement—a better world in which everyone can live happily and in material comfort—seem achievable because one understands the key to the logic of the American system. A community leader may work hard to adopt, exercise, and teach these cognitive practices so as to fashion a vision of a secure community, a strong community, a safe community, an assimilated community, with home owners and businesses and political clout downtown. These ends sometimes lead practitioners of non-dominant cultures to strive for common ground, for simplicity and certainty. These ends lead people to adopt these practices while failing to recognize that the cognitive practices of Anglo culture follow a logic of domination. Simplicity, certainty, and common ground are practices of erasure, not inclusion. Erasure towards super exploitation or extermination. Coming to adopt these cognitive practices as one's own is the mark of a deep form of assimilation.

We can see the importance of these cognitive practices as the Anglo monoculturalist slides back and forth from description to prescription. The searches for certainty, simplicity, and agreement presuppose the existence of only one culture. Other cultures are not seen. All evidence to the contrary is discounted because the eyes guided by these practices cannot see other cultures except as ornament. Thus the circle is complete: monocultural reality is ensured by a monocultural cognitive framework. A structurally and culturally pluralistic society is unimaginable because it is outside the conceptual domain. So contestation must be taken to the deep level, to the level of practices of cognition.

We have described here the three cognitive practices that ground monoculturalism and have suggested some of the ways in which they are part of the personality structure in dominant culture. We have shown how they are tied to the political stance of monoculturalism by arguing how it is impossible to see other cultures if one has internalized those practices. As we look at the institutions that govern our lives, we see that they also operate with the assumptions embedded in these cognitive practices.

But how otherwise is communication possible? How else can history be told, if it is not simplified in some way? How can the news be related unless condensed? How can one make a judgment in court except with certainty and finality? How can one respond to the needs of the moment, to the needs of a democracy, if the union includes so many languages, experiences, and perspectives? How from this plenitude can one society be forged? Answering these questions in the direction of multiple voices requires alternatives to the cognitive practices of monoculturalism.

INCERTIDUMBRE, COMPLEJIDAD, COMPRENSION ABIERTA: LAS BASES COGNITIVAS DEL MULTICULTURALISMO/UNCERTAINTY, COMPLEXITY, OPEN-ENDED UNDERSTANDING: THE COGNITIVE BASES OF MULTICULTURALISM

This section develops the beginnings of a theory of multiculturalism. It provides the cognitive groundwork toward living together, understanding each other, and engaging in the necessary communication for an organizing of life in society that is attentive to multiple voices, multiple constructions of gender, multiple understandings of what is valuable, multiple conceptions of people and customs, and multiple understandings of how to relate to each other. The groundwork is so far modest: it consists of sketching three cognitive attitudes that predispose one to communication across cultures and to decision making that arises from communication across cultures rather than from cultural erasure. These attitudes or cognitive practices are in conflict with the attitudes of monoculturalism. Adopting them constitutes in itself an act of resistance to life lived in a monocultural mold. The cognitive attitudes we suggest are already practiced by many in resistance to monoculturalism, and they already structure the personalities of many cultural resistors.

As groundwork toward a multicultural society and as central to unity in multicultural struggle, we propose three cognitive practices: living with uncertainty, living with and within complexity, and living with a deep appreciation for conflicting perspectives as a prerequisite for open-ended understanding. Thinking of these cognitive attitudes in connection with a theory of multiculturalism helps us to see the need to develop a theory of complex communication and a theory of complex unity. At this stage, we will merely point to these concepts as we clarify that the stage of the theorizing mirrors the stage of the struggle. At this stage we need to work toward the formation of a complex unity via complex communication among those practitioners of nondominant cultures who face each other, fragmented and separated by the strategies of monoculturalism.

Introducing this set of cognitive practices also serves an important purpose in the argument of this chapter: it demonstrates that the cognitive practices tied to monoculturalism are conceptually avoidable, and thus that monoculturalism is itself avoidable.

Incertidumbre/Uncertainty

Vamos en el carro. I am driving the car. Me dice que hay que doblar en la próxima esquina y que ya viene un pozo a la derecha y que hay una curva estrecha en la próxima cuadra. He says to me that I need to turn at the next corner and that there is a big hole on the right side of the street and that the curve in the next block is really tight. No puede manejar porque es ciego. He can't drive because he is blind. Pero siente el camino, lo tantea. He feels the road. He understands the road in a way totally different from mine.

I am teaching my aerobics class in Spanish in a church basement in a Mexican neighborhood in Chicago. The women speak only Mexican Spanish. They are very unaccustomed to exercise. I describe the steps and moves in a loud voice over the music with little sense of making sense. I throw out several terms that may do the trick—"Formemos una ronda. Un círculo. Tómense las manos para dar vueltas"—as I demonstrate forming a circle. I am uncertain in my communication, so I try everything that occurs to me and I listen to their words, their laughter at mine, the nice concord or discord that we attain as we patiently extend our possibilities.

As one understands that reality is multiple, one comes to expect that fluency in one of these understandings of reality does not guarantee even a basic degree of fluency in other important conceptual frameworks. Thus one becomes epistemically humble; one is not sure one is understanding what one is hearing, nor is one sure that one is being understood. Uncertainty reigns.

Uncertainty in this sense requires humility, curiosity, urgency in communication, and a sense of open-endedness to understanding and being understood. It requires a *lack* of spontaneity in communication as one questions one's own judgment about what one is seeing, thus deferring on-the-spot decisions. It takes time to unravel why people are saying what they are or acting the way they are. Even then, one never feels on unshakable ground. Even if one thinks one understands, one gives uptake and respect to conflicting or even contradictory accounts. One does not give in to the tendency to reduce one account to another nor to erase either. One gives uptake to diversity of expression without searching for a reduction to a standard way. One listens for different languages, to code switching, and to linguistic hybridization. Uncertainty provides a particular atmosphere for communication and decision making. It provides an atmosphere in which one makes time for articulating what is hard to articulate, for naming that which has no name.

Complejidad/Complexity

To give this kind of tacit respect is to attend to the multiplicity of contemporaneous realities, to be open to the possibility of being critical without presupposing that only one view can be correct or assuming the possibility of only one reality or one level of reality. To move in the direction of uncertainty is to cultivate in oneself an appreciation of the complexities involved in daily life. To attend to multiple perspectives is to be aware of the shadowy, the seemingly insignificant, or the apparently irrelevant ways in which people act. It is to wonder at the silence, at the anger, at the humor, without dismissing it.

As one moves in the direction of complexity, one notices the changes people go through from cultural framework to cultural framework, from universe of meaning to universe of meaning, as well as the changes one goes through oneself.

*In some contexts he feels that he is identified as plainly Anglo. Other times, he is
Jewish. Other times he is culturally unmarked. Sometimes all three happen at the same
time in different eyes. To many people he is gay, others read him as straight. As he
notices how he is identified, he also feels his posture change, as well as his use of his
hands, his vocabulary, and his intonation. How he marks himself is an active process.
However, he is marked in ways over which he has no control. It is not the case that
some readings are truer than others.*

One's identity shifts in a deep sense given different understandings. How one identifies others can also be subtle and ongoing. In appreciating complexity, one relin-
quishes the need to separate, classify, straighten, and simplify people, events, or situations. To simplify is to lose the multicultural character; to ignore the many and shifting
identities we inhabit; to mute people and curb their possibilities.

Those who learn to live with uncertainty and with complexity begin by apprentic-
ing themselves to the situations they are in. If to simplify is to mute, then to approach
things in their complexity is to listen distrusting the belief that one understands everything one is hearing. We have argued that one of the operations of simplification is to
separate material deemed irrelevant or insignificant from what is central and significant. As Mitsuye Yamada has written, "We must remember that one of the most insidious ways of keeping women and minorities powerless is to let them only talk about
harmless and inconsequential subjects, or let them speak freely and not listen to them
with serious intent."[9]

Comprension Abierta/Open-Ended Understanding

Spending time sorting out what others are perceiving will lead to a consideration of
conflicting perspectives. As one approaches situations in this way, one does not assume that discussions will end on a common ground, agreement, or consensus. One
does not assume that what is finest about being human is common to us all. Rather, one
takes up situations in all of the multiple, rich, subtle, and difficult to articulate actions,
perspectives, politics, ironies, kinds of anger, and senses of right and wrong. One gives
oneself a lot of time to understand what is transpiring in its complexity. Otherwise, one
is led to seek resolution, consensus, agreements, or plans for action that are simplistic
and closed to further discussion, that reduce complex and layered possibilities. Seeking resolution too quickly indicates a discomfort and impatience with cultural plurality
and tends to erase it.

It might be protested that to live without agreement is to live in conflict. Without a
foundation of agreement, one cannot forge a social pact that avoids chaos and anarchy.
But this is only true if one thinks that living with difference is impossible. Living
among others with a deep appreciation of conflicting perspectives on reality is not only
possible but enriching. Not to do so is either to dismiss other perspectives or to do them
violence.

A common ground cannot be assumed to be necessary without doing violence. Oppression does exist. Some people oppress and others are oppressed. One way that oppression works is that the oppressed are forced to accept unfair deals. Think about signing your land away because you cannot afford a lawyer when you cannot understand the document you are signing; think about picking up after your husband; think about being shot to death at the Attica prison riot for not "obeying" the order to drop to the ground, an order issued in a language you do not understand; think about saying no to rape and being understood to be liking it; think about "your" representative coming to your neighborhood and not having even the beginning of an idea of the values, needs, and ways of the people living there. If someone were to propose that the only way an oppressed person and his or her oppressor could live together would be to create a common good or to stand on common ground, we would worry that the common good or common ground would be in the oppressor's terms. This is one of the ways that oppression works—by coercing agreement. Thus we see the entanglement of violence, coercion, and the common good.

The entanglement of violence and the common good can serve as the epigraph of this section. We have advanced and explained an alternative set of cognitive practices: uncertainty, complexity, and an understanding that does not avoid conflicting perspectives. A logical connection ties them together. We believe these to be a preferable set of practices to the ones that ground monoculturalism. People practiced at living with uncertainty, without a common ground, and with a complicated understanding of the world provide by their example proof that monoculturalism is not inevitable. It is possible to flourish according to a set of cognitive practices different from the three that ground monoculturalism.

CONCLUSION: *UNIDAD COMPLEJA Y SOCIEDAD MULTICULTURAL/*COMPLEX UNITY AND MULTICULTURAL SOCIETY

We have offered an understanding of three cognitive practices that clearly favor the multicultural project. Internalizing them inclines one toward hearing each other, learning about each other, coming to understand what we do not understand, coming to see the borders of our own worlds, and making our worlds larger or getting ourselves from our world to another's world. These are the first ingredients in a theory of complex communication. Such a theory, unlike traditional cultural relativism, has a strong political bent, one that calls for cross-cultural understanding and struggle against cultural erasure. Such politics suggest a need to undermine social fragmentation in favor of a complex unity that understands shifting identities. The unity that results is a transformation of the very concept of unity. Unity must take seriously the complexity of our communities, our cultures, our relationships, and ourselves. Thus, unity in this sense arises out of complex communication: communication that is open to understanding one another as fundamentally different in desires, beliefs, ways of using language, and ways of using one's body. This unity can give rise to complicated knowledge that does not reduce us to being simply images of each other.

The alternative set of cognitive processes forms the basis of a different understanding of the processes of decision making and communication. Decision making cannot be conceived according to the model of homogenous voices at the bargaining table coming to a compromise, nor as the process of reducing different voices to a homogenous voice.

The United States already has many inhabitants who are fluent in more than one culture and adept at crossing cultures. Many in the United States already firmly maintain in their mind more than one understanding of themselves, of others, and of their relations.

Monoculturalism is not the natural order of things. Rather, it is a process of domination through simplification and reduction. It is a suppression of possibilities that are already present in our multicultural society. Cultural domination does not mean society is monolithic. Rather, it means that people outside of the Anglo mainstream are prohibited from expressing themselves in a way other than in a monocultural voice. Monoculturalism is central to the workings of our society, and a central mechanism of oppression.

We have contested monoculturalism and the domination of Anglo culture in a multiplicity of voices, our own included. We have attempted not to flatten our own voices in the contestation. We have dug deeply into domination to reveal its deep structure—the set of cognitive practices that make monoculturalism a conceptual necessity. But these practices are not themselves necessary practices; most of us who are multiculturally fluent experience a fragmenting of ourselves through these practices. These practices become instruments of torture, a torturing of our complexity, a flattening and a reduction of ourselves. They also become a temptation: we become tempted by fragmentation, by simplicity, and by the offerings of simplicity. We become tempted to dwell on our fragmented guises in the mirrors of Anglo eyes.

We live in uncertainty as we seek to see, multiply, and fashion ways of communicating and relating across and within realities. As we fashion procedures for making decisions and institutions that honor the concomitant complexity, we reject reduction and erasure. We have begun to show the ways of complexity at a deep level, in the very ways in which we perceive and conceive. Thus we have taken the contestation against domination to a different terrain, one that questions the structure of cognition. Concentrating on each other's voices, on what we say about ourselves and each other, will itself be transformative. Listening without fear and then responding and thinking deeply about oneself in relation to others can further the transformation toward a complex unity.

8

Korean American Dilemma: Violence, Vengeance, Vision

Edward T. Chang and Angela E. Oh

It has been almost two years since Korean Americans in Los Angeles found themselves painfully bearing witness to the mass destruction visited upon Los Angeles on April 29, 1992. In the Korean American community, the Los Angeles riot is known as *Sa-ee-Gu* (April 29).[1] The toll taken upon the largely immigrant population of Korean Americans was devastating. Approximately 2,280 businesses were destroyed and in excess of $400 million dollars was lost in physical damage.[2]

In the aftermath, community and government leaders began the process of documenting the causes for the explosion, identifying resources that could be brought to bear, and creating programs through which relief could be provided. However, government programs simply were not designed to meet the needs of immigrant Korean business owners whose property had been destroyed. To these Korean American victims, the concept of America as a land of opportunity was little more than a cruel hoax on unwitting immigrants.

The purpose of this chapter is to analyze the way in which the 1992 Los Angeles riots initiated transformation within the Korean American community. This chapter is divided into three parts. The first traces the history of Korean immigration to the United States. The second provides an overview of the Korean American community. And the third considers future prospects for the Korean American community in Los Angeles. The Los Angeles riots of 1992 may well be remembered as a turning point in Korean American history similar to the internment experience of Japanese Americans during World War II. The riots opened the eyes of Korean immigrants to the problems of institutional racism, social and economic injustice, and the fallacy of the American dream.

THE FORGOTTEN GENERATION: 1903-1924

Prior to 1903 Korea was known as a Hermit Kingdom because its doors were closed to "foreign devils." From the early nineteenth century, Western nations displayed ever greater interest in establishing contact with Korea for trade and other purposes. The Korean government responded, however, by rejecting all Western demands for trade, and closed its doors to Westerners.

Migration was also discouraged. Confucian teaching strongly discouraged migration from ancestral lands. Filial sons, in particular, were taught to pay tribute to their ancestors in their homeland. In addition, the Japanese government, which exercised complete control over the Korean government and its people, prohibited Korean immigration to Hawaii because they feared it would jeopardize the welfare of Japanese immigrants in Hawaii. Japanese officials argued against Korean immigration to Hawaii by claiming that "Koreans were lazy, dirty, unskillful, heavy smokers, and did not live orderly lives, making their worth as competition somewhat limited."[3] Due to many internal and external factors, then, it was not easy for Koreans to secure immigration to America (specifically, Hawaii) at the turn of the century.[4]

Things changed, though, for a very short period in the early part of this century. Between 1903 and 1905, more than 7,000 Koreans emigrated to Hawaii to work as sugar plantation laborers.[5] They are a forgotten generation because their struggles and contributions have never been adequately preserved. Only recently have Asian American historians and scholars begun to document the struggle of these first Korean immigrants. It was these early pioneers who set the foundation for the development of the Korean American community. They established the first social, political, and economic institutions, such as *Donghoe* (village council), voluntary associations, women's organizations, churches, and independence movement organizations—all of which continue to thrive today.

Like other Asian pioneers who came during the turn of the century, Korean immigrants saw America as a great land of opportunity. It was "gold mountain" and the "land of paradise." Not surprisingly, most early immigrants were young, single, and male. They were brought to Hawaii as part of a capitalist strategy to diversify the labor force. The plantation owners wanted to bring in Korean workers as a counterbalance to the more numerous Japanese in the hope of avoiding strikes, and thus keep wages low. Korean immigrant workers were often introduced as strike breakers on the plantation. Anti-Japanese sentiments could be exploited by the planters to whip up desire on the part of Korean workers to disrupt organizing efforts initiated by Japanese laborers.[6] In the end, Korean immigrants were nothing more than a tool used to generate maximum profits for the sugar plantation owners. More than 400,000 workers from thirty-three different countries were recruited by the Hawaiian Sugar Plantation Association by the 1930s.[7] Like so many others who arrived on these shores, Korean immigrant laborers suffered from labor exploitation and racial discrimination. They earned less than a dollar a day for ten or more hours of painstaking work under extremely difficult conditions (women earned about two-thirds that rate). Because of harsh working conditions and low wages, many Korean immigrant workers were eager to leave the plantations as soon as their contract expired.

In 1905, Korean immigration came to an abrupt end when the imperial Japanese government prohibited the migration of Korean workers to Hawaii. The Japanese government stopped Korean immigration to Hawaii because they wanted to protect the interests of Japanese American workers in Hawaii, who had waged complaints that their interests were being undermined by the arrival of Korean laborers.[8]

In addition, the Japanese colonial government wanted to limit independence activities by Koreans abroad, especially in Hawaii and the United States. Many Koreans fled to Manchuria and the United States to resist oppression and to organize against Japanese rule. Koreans in Hawaii and on the mainland provided crucial financial support to the independence movement in Manchuria and Korea.[9] Park, Yong-Man established *Kundan* (the military) in Hasting, Nebraska, to train Korean soldiers for armed confrontation against the Japanese military. Syngman Rhee, who later became the first president of the Republic of Korea in 1948, formed the *Dongjihoe* (Comrade Association) and the Korea Commission to lobby against Japan's colonial domination of Korea. Ahn, Chang-Ho was a key figure in forming the Korean National Association (KNA) in an effort to unite the Korean community in the United States.

The early Asian (including Korean) immigrant community was primarily a bachelor society composed of young, single males. Discriminatory laws designed to restrict Asian immigration limited entry to Asian women.[10] For these reasons, gambling, opium, and prostitution thrived in Chinatown.[11] In 1908, however, Japan negotiated a gentleman's agreement with the United States, which allowed entry to the wives of Japanese immigrants. Since Korea was a colony of Japan at that time, Korean immigrants were able to bring their wives over from Korea. Known as "picture brides," more than a thousand of them entered the United States between 1910 and 1920, bringing with them a measure of social stability to the Korean immigrant community.[12] Picture brides worked side by side with their husbands, becoming once again the backbone of the community as they carried on their traditional role in the home.

Not all the women, however, became housewives. Some ran small businesses such as boarding houses for immigrant bachelors. Such supplementary income was essential to a family's economic progress.

THE NEW URBAN IMMIGRANTS

According to the U.S. census, the Korean American population has increased dramatically from 70,000 in 1970 to approximately 800,000 in 1990.[13] These "new urban immigrants" are highly educated, family-oriented, middle-class professionals who reside in large metropolitan areas.[14] In contrast to the earlier immigrants, who were young, single, and male, families with young children make up the core of today's Korean immigrant population. Since the majority of Korean immigrants come from Seoul and are already accustomed to living in a large city, most tend to settle in large cities such

as Los Angeles, New York, and Chicago. Recent Korean immigrants are often por-
trayed as a model minority. According to the model minority image, Korean immigrants are highly motivated, productive, and willing to sacrifice for the future.

The current wave of Korean immigration is a direct result of socioeconomic and
political relations between the United States and South Korea. Since the Korean War,
the United States government—in the name of protecting democracy and freedom—
has provided unconditional support for dictatorship regimes in South Korea. The brutal 1980 massacre of the citizens of Kwangju, torture of political prisoners, and arrests
of students and labor demonstrators are all examples of human and civil rights violations that have been ignored by the U.S. government in an effort to sustain its influence
in the region.[15] In exchange for non-intervention, the South Korean government has
consistently supported the political and economic policies of the United States government.

In addition, it is important to note that South Korea has undergone profound political and social changes. In 1993, the people of South Korea elected the country's first
non-military president, Young-Sam Kim. As a result, South Korea has become more
open and democratic. Not surprisingly, the number of Korean immigrants to the United
States appears to be decreasing. However, it is important to keep in mind that the entry
of working-class and service-class Korean immigrants will likely continue to remain
steady in the future. This is based on the prediction that Korea will not be able to
provide adequate jobs for its rapidly growing population. Although the Korean economy
enjoyed double digit growth during the 1970s and 1980s, the pace of economic growth
is expected to slow as it faces stiffer competition from other industrialized countries,
especially those in Asia.

COMMUNITY IN TRANSITION

Korean Americans represent about 1 percent of the total population of the city and
county of Los Angeles and the state of California. During the past twenty years, the
Korean American community in Los Angeles has grown at a staggering rate. The last
two decades have seen the Korean American population grow by a factor of sixteen,
from 8,900 in 1970, to 60,618 in 1980, to 145,431 in 1990.

The ethnic Korean community in the United States is primarily an immigrant community, with a high percentage being foreign-born. According to the 1990 census, the
proportion of foreign-born Korean Americans was 80 percent. Korean immigrants
face language and cultural barriers, racial prejudice, immigrant bashing, and discrimination. Unlike other Asian immigrants, who tend to settle on either coast, Korean
immigrants are dispersed all over the United States, with high concentrations in California, New York, Illinois, Texas, Colorado, Ohio, and Minnesota.

Los Angeles's Koreatown, bound on the west by Crenshaw Boulevard, on the east
by Hoover Street, on the north by Santa Monica Boulevard, and on the south by Venice
Boulevard, is ten times larger than Chinatown and Little Tokyo combined.[16] Korean

Americans make up about 23 percent of the resident population of Koreatown. Between 1970 and 1990, the Korean American population in Koreatown increased from 1,099 to 23,995, more than a twentyfold increase.[17] Koreatown functions as the center of the cultural, social, and economic activities that affect the daily lives of Korean Americans. Koreans in Los Angeles have formed numerous social, economic, cultural, and political associations and organizations to help them adjust to life in the United States. In southern California the Korean American community supports 150 social organizations, 86 alumni associations, 600 Christian churches, 18 Buddhist temples, 4 television stations, 3 radio stations, and several newspapers.[18]

Following is some additional demographic information about the Korean population in the Los Angeles area:

1. Approximately 65–70 percent of Korean immigrants are observant, church-going Christians.[19]
2. The mean length of residence for Korean Americans is about 10 years.[20]
3. Approximately 45 percent of men and 38 percent of women are U.S. citizens.
4. Koreans living in Los Angeles possess a higher-than-average level of formal education. Sixty-nine percent of male heads of household are college graduates. Among female spouses and women heads of household, 50 percent are college graduates.
5. Sixty-seven percent of Korean American women work outside of the family.
6. The largest occupational category of adult Korean males—40 percent of the total—is the self-employed businessman.

The growth of Korean-owned businesses in the African American community definitely contributed to the conflict between the two communities during the 1980s and 1990s. Contrary to popular belief, however, only 10 percent of Korean-owned businesses in southern California serve primarily African American clients.[21] The rising tension between African Americans and Korean Americans, largely due to merchant-customer conflicts, played a major part in explaining the targeting of Korean-owned businesses during the riots.

KOREAN AMERICANS AND THE RIOTS

Immediately following the burning and destruction of April 1992, community and political leaders emerged calling for calm and healing. Many Korean American community leaders demanded "reparations" and financial aid in the wake of the riots. Politicians such as Mayor Tom Bradley, Governor Pete Wilson, and President George Bush moved to declare Los Angeles County an emergency disaster area. The Federal Emergency Management Agency (FEMA) and the Small Business Administration (SBA) began to offer assistance such as rental and mortgage aid, unemployment payments, tax adjustments, low-interest loans, and other forms of relief. Victims were required to fill out application forms to receive these benefits. As it turned out, the bureaucracy became yet another nightmare for Korean American victims. Staffing and paperwork were not designed to meet the needs of limited- or non-English speakers, and the sheer number of people in need was overwhelming. All of this was exacerbated by negative sentiments toward ethnic Koreans.

It soon became clear that there was a complete breakdown of the political infrastructure of the city. Los Angeles suffered from a lack of leadership among the ranks of elected officials—a void that, unfortunately, was filled by a quiet rage toward Korean Americans. The hostility was fueled by several factors: the shooting death of Latasha Harlins and the subsequent probationary sentence imposed on Soon Ja Du; the fact that the few meager assets in the neighborhoods of South Central, Koreatown, and Pico-Union districts were owned predominantly by ethnic Koreans; and the disgraceful images perpetuated by the media of Korean Americans as nothing more than rude, greedy, selfish merchants who refused to learn the English language.

In addition, former Chief of Police Daryl Gates had been at the helm of the Los Angeles Police Department (LAPD) for more than a decade. Under his leadership, police brutality had become a too-frequent occurrence that cost the city literally millions of dollars each year.[22] The philosophy and policies of the Gates administration drove community confidence in the police department to an all-time low.[23] The office of the Los Angeles County District Attorney also failed the public. District Attorney Ira Reiner had created a reputation for himself as a media hound. Consequently, he was ineffective in providing leadership as the head of the agency vested with the responsibility of enforcing the law through the courts. His apparent lack of commitment to crime prevention and community education about the criminal justice system took its toll.

And, indeed, the *Webster Report* (1992), a report on the causes, the events, and the aftermath of the riots, concluded that the LAPD had no plan to deal with the civil unrest that occurred on April 29, 1992. This fact was confirmed by the many Korean American victims who reported specific instances of indifference by LAPD officers who were called for help. Even in light of advance warnings, the LAPD had taken no steps to train officers, to obtain equipment, or to put any kind of written or oral plan together. In contrast, Los Angeles Sheriffs Office had tried for over a year to get the LAPD to come to cross-training and train for the possible civil unrest. Los Angeles Sheriff's Office had a plan in place for specific incidents, including what happened in April 1992. They were ready and put out an alert some one month prior to the verdicts in the Rodney King matter.

Another contributing factor was that local elected representatives failed to appreciate the effects of the dramatic demographic shifts in the city's population. There was little or no effort made to dedicate resources to assess the changing needs of the community. Nor were there any serious attempts made to bridge the widening gap between and among the cultures living in the city. The state of human and community relations in Los Angeles had deteriorated to an all-time low. Racial tensions were mounting, and no effective model existed for reducing or channeling the tension into action that could serve the communities in conflict.[24] For Korean Americans, the most dangerous part of that conflict was seen in the relationship between customer and merchant. Stories of "nasty" Korean American shop owners were used to fuel the rage of African American consumers, who had been deprived of goods and services in their neighborhoods for so long.

And finally, the media—always in a position to shape public perception of reality—did so in a way that proved to be extremely damaging to both the City of Los Angeles and particular Korean Americans. For example, coverage by the *Los Angeles Times* during the twelve months preceding the riot reveals that two-thirds of the articles printed about Korean Americans discussed the conflict between Blacks and Koreans.[25] There were at least twenty-six articles dealing with the Harlins-Du case, many of which contained the gratuitous reference to "a $1.79 bottle of orange juice," suggesting that Korean American merchants do not appreciate the value of human life, especially that of African Americans. This cruel, shortsighted shorthand for much more complex issues undoubtedly gave some individuals enough reason to target Korean American businesses following the acquittal of the police officers.

THE CHALLENGES CONFRONTING KOREAN AMERICANS

Korean American experiences during and after the 1992 crisis brought into focus several critical issues. These include questions about ethnic identity, the future of Asian American coalition building, and the challenges of ensuring the inclusion of immigrant experiences in community organizing and advocacy.

Korean Americans have been forced to reexamine their ethnic identity in the context of dramatic changes in race relations in America. Since *Sa-ee-Gu*, they have had the dubious distinction of having become the most visible segment of the Asian American community. It is clear that American-born Chinese Americans and Japanese Americans are uncomfortable with this fact because they certainly cannot, and do not, identify with Korean immigrant experiences. Likewise, Korean Americans are uncomfortable with this situation because there are so many infrastructure deficiencies within the community.

Many Asian Americans have tried to distinguish themselves from the Korean American community out of fear. Some have gone so far as to blame Korean Americans for causing conflicts with African Americans. Asian American activists, who strongly identify with the Black civil rights movement, condemned Korean Americans for being so "insensitive and selfish." Given these attitudes, it is unclear whether a pan–Asian American movement could ever be built.

IN SEARCH OF A NEW VISION

Historically, the assimilationist framework has been utilized as a justification for Asian exclusion, the rationale being that Asians were unassimilable and a racial threat to the white population on the West Coast. It was also used to measure the degree of "difference" between newcomers and the mainstream. Ironically, third- and fourth-generation Japanese and Chinese who integrated into mainstream society are often cited as examples of successful assimilation.

The Los Angeles riots deeply affected the development of Korean American identity and survival. On one hand, Korean Americans were told to assimilate and become "Americanized" so as to succeed in America. They believed in the American dream: if they worked honest and long hours, they would succeed. Yet, in the wake of the 1992 riots, Korean immigrants experienced the pitfalls of the assimilationist ideology. Many Korean Americans felt they had been victimized and used as scapegoats for larger societal failures. Korean Americans became the buffer (middleman minority) between dominant and subordinate populations.

Despite tremendous financial and psychological suffering, the riots taught many valuable lessons to Korean Americans. First, the crisis was a wake-up call creating a consciousness about what it means to live in a multiethnic society. Korean Americans now understand the price one pays for remaining silent and passive, isolated from the mainstream political process. They now realize the necessity of participation in political and social processes so that their needs and opinions can be articulated: political empowerment has become an urgent and immediate goal. Many Korean Americans have expressed a need for representation from and accountability of our political leaders. (It is no coincidence that six Korean Americans were elected into local, state and federal political offices during the 1992 elections.) More than ever, Korean Americans throughout the nation have begun to mobilize resources to empower themselves politically.

Second, the riots thrust Korean Americans into the dialogue about creating a multicultural America. Korean Americans no longer have to struggle to define who they are. The old stories of being asked whether one is Chinese, Japanese, and so forth, are gone.[26] Korean Americans now have the opportunity to actively involve themselves in cultural debate, to record history, to interpret the events and experiences of this generation, and to begin finding ways to integrate the Korean cultural heritage within a greater American culture.

Third, it is important to recognize that for the majority of Korean Americans indices of social instability in our cities held no significant meaning. This was partially due to the fact that the community functioned upon terms of self-reliance (often interpreted as being insular or obstinate). Concerning police-community relations, most Korean Americans had little contact with the local authorities, except in emergency situations; due to language barriers and institutional inadequacies, many avoided reporting crimes or complaining about the handling of investigations; forming a relationship with law enforcement agencies was certainly not a community concern before April, 29, 1992;

Korean Americans hold that police have a duty to protect, citizens have a duty to obey, and if ever the two interests diverge, the police are right. Korean Americans' change in attitude toward police and reevaluations about the inadequacy of services for limited- or non-English-speaking Koreans took place only after the riots of 1992.

Fourth, churches remain the single most powerful social institutions in the Korean American community. Following the April 1992 riots, churches became natural centers for disaster assistance, counseling, and community meetings. Many observers believe that the churches should contribute their resources and talent to shaping and transforming the Korean American community. They must now respond to the criticism about their lack of involvement in community issues. The previous excuse that "secular" problems do not fall within their sphere of responsibility can no longer be upheld.

And finally, the riots served as a catalyst for Korean Americans to consider seriously the notion of working together as a community rather than struggling as individuals. Countless meetings have been convened in the past three years to bring together first- and second-generation representatives. Mobilization of almost every social service agency in Koreatown resulted in combining many of them under auspices of the Korean American Inter-Agency Council. Whether or not these efforts will yield long-term working relationships is yet to be seen. What is important is that the riots of 1992 served as a catalyst to bridge the gap between first- and second-generation Korean Americans.

First-generation immigrants were mostly concerned with homeland politics and their own economic survival. Their experience is not unique at all. European immigrants also utilized "survival through solidarity" tactics to adjust to and seek incorporation into mainstream America. In order to survive in a hostile and strange environment, newcomers often establish ethnic enclaves. Korean immigrants are no different. However, one of the major differences between European immigrants and Korean immigrants is that the former cultivated some degree of economic and social contact with mainstream society. Korean immigrants have focused their social, political, and economic activities around Koreatown or Korean-immigrant voluntary associations, without direct and indirect contact with other communities. This must change.

During and after the riots, American-educated 1.5- and second-generation Korean Americans played an important role by representing Korean Americans in the mainstream.[27] Korean immigrants were grateful to young Korean Americans who spoke-up for the community. Due to language barriers, Korean community leaders were unable to articulate their concerns to the larger society.

At the time of the riots, 1.5- and second-generation Korean American had been making inroads into political, economic, and social institutions, but only for a short period. In the Los Angeles area, examples of this movement can be found in almost every part of community life. There were struggles for funding, for media access, for representation among various coalitions, and over leadership. Yet this limited engagement with government bureaucracy, negotiating with political representatives, and working in coalition with other non-Korean community-based organizations was a necessary foundation upon which Korean Americans could draw upon to respond in the aftermath of the burning, looting, and vandalism that destroyed the lives of so many families.

The Korean American community has learned that the first and second generations must work together. This will not be an easy task. There remain many issues that split along generation lines. Out of the crisis of 1992, the first, 1.5, and second generations were brought together to discuss and share their experiences and search for common ground. In their search of a new vision, Korean Americans must identify new leaders. The new leaders must possess qualities that can represent the Korean American community within a multiethnic society. The new leaders must also possess the skills to go beyond ethnic differences. They should build coalitions and alliances between different racial and ethnic groups based on common concerns and interests.

CONCLUSION

The Los Angeles riots marked the beginning of a new era in which the presence of Korean Americans was finally recognized by mainstream America. Today, the Korean American community is in search of a new vision that will return at least some part of the sense of dignity and hope to those who lost so much in April 1992. As we move through this period of history, we are awaking to the fact that we have a tremendous stake in the future of Los Angeles and other large urban centers across the nation. The Korean American community must play a pivotal role in the social change taking place in America today. No longer will it be confined to a junior or minor role. Rather, the Korean American community must be an active and strong force in shaping the infrastructure of a society that works for all. Though the events in Los Angeles during the spring of 1992 were wrought with violence and vengeance, Korean Americans have a choice in how they shall respond—more violence, deeper vengeance, or a new vision.

9

White Privilege: The Rhetoric and the Facts

Carolyn B. Murray and J. Owens Smith

White males occupy the most powerful and privileged positions in American society. They are in positions to make decisions that have major consequences for society. They dominate the large corporations, public bureaucracies, and other organizations. They look upon the machinery of state and local government as theirs to run as a matter of privilege on the one hand, and a matter of rights, on the other. In addition, they occupy the key command posts of the social and economic structures where resources and values are authoritatively allocated.

The irony of the privileged status of white males is that many of them are unaware that they occupy privileged positions. They feel that they occupy these positions because of their abilities and their subscription to American traditional values such as hard work, individualism, and internalization of the Protestant work ethic. They have become so comfortable with their privileged position that they view any attempt by government to adopt policies that will interfere with this privileged status as a violation of their sacred rights.

For example, white males view affirmative action and other civil rights programs as giving minorities an unfair amount of resources (e.g., jobs, positions in professional schools, and positions of power in government) at their expense. However, these prevailing sentiments overlook statistical data. Statistically, white males constitute 39.3 percent of the population but account for 82.5 percent of the *Forbes* 400 (persons worth at least $265 million), 77 percent of members of Congress, 92 percent of state governors, 70 percent of tenured college faculty, almost 90 percent of daily newspaper editors, and 77 percent of television news directors.

P. McIntosh points out that even though white men may grant that women are disadvantaged and that people of color (i.e., African Americans, Latinos, and Native Americans) are disadvantaged, they are unwilling to accept that they are privileged. White males' privileged positions do not allow them to see the contradiction in this thought pattern.[1]

In this chapter, evidence will be presented to support the contention that white males occupy a privileged status in society and that they do not recognize their privileged status. This phenomenon will be approached from a multidisciplinary and multidimensional perspective.

EVIDENCE THAT WHITES ARE PRIVILEGED

Historical Evidence

From the colonial period to the present, white males have come to occupy a privileged status in American society. This status was prescriptive from its inception. The framers of the Constitution recognized that the purpose of government was to promote the interest of the ruling class. Based on this philosophy, they structured the new government to ensure domination by upper-class white males. They achieved this goal by insisting that voting eligibility be based on property ownership. This requirement systematically excluded the masses who were without property.

Historically, the white male has been able to maintain his privileged status by "legally" controlling access to the ownership of property. Starting with the colonial period, property ownership was embraced by merchants, manufacturers, artisans, craftsmen, and farmers who were uprooted by the industrial revolution. During the seventeenth century, farm ownership was one of Protestantism's most sacred values. Land ownership represented not only a means of economic stability but also social status and prestige.

The relationship established between Blacks and whites best illuminates how the privileged status of whites was purposefully created by law. The dominant factor that distinguishes class in the American society is the ownership of property. The question that emerges here is what method white males used to limit access to the ownership of property.

The attempt to limit access to property began at the turn of the nineteenth century, when Congress passed the Land Grant Act. Special care was taken to ensure that land ownership in the Mid west was limited to whites. It was made clear from the beginning that free Blacks were not to settle in this territory. Whites in power adopted an exclusionary policy whereby special efforts were made "in the 1840s and 1850s to prevent Black immigration [to the Mid west] and to remove the Blacks who were already there."[2] For example, the states of Indiana, Illinois, and Oregon adopted laws prohibiting Blacks from entering their states. The political significance of a policy prohibiting free Blacks from participating in the "Free Soil" movement is that it prevented them from acquiring economic stability.

The exclusion of Blacks from participating in the ownership of land continued into the 1860s and 1870s. The major land program during this period was the Homestead Act of 1862, which gave white males 160 acres of land at little or no cost. Blacks were again excluded from participating in this give-away program.

The importance of land ownership as a determinant of economic stability was further manifested during the period between 1880 and 1910. Prior to this period, the government gave land to immigrants as an incentive to immigrate to an area. But the new immigrants who came during this period did not receive any land because no more land had been set aside for development. Without the right to acquire and possess property, groups such as Russian Jews, Poles, and Italians were impoverished for over two generations. They were unable to leave the slums until the era of the New Deal, when the federal government adopted laws to undergird their economic stability. The law that specifically helped them to escape the slums was the National Labor Relations Act (NLRA) of 1935. This act, for the first time, provided workers with a set of property rights and the right to collective bargaining. It took their rights to acquire and possess property off the goodwill of their competitors and adversaries and placed them on a principle of law.

The NLRA gave white workers the right to negotiate wages, conditions of employment, and other fringe benefits such as paid vacation, sick leave, medical benefits, and so forth. This protection provided workers with a sense of economic security whereby they could plan for the future. The NLRA also provided workers the right to establish a formal process of job upward mobility. Two processes were used. One of the processes was known as job enlargement. The most frequent practice European immigrant groups used to ensure mobility was to seize control of a certain sector of the economy through collective bargaining and, soon after, establish rules and regulations that protected job opportunities for themselves and their offspring. This process allowed fathers to establish a privileged status for their sons. They could, by law, guarantee their sons highpaying and skilled jobs at their respective places of employment. When jobs were not available, fathers had the liberty to create one through the process of job enlargement opportunities. Through this process, a group could legally prevent other groups access to these jobs.

The practice of enlarging job opportunities accented white male privileged status from the New Deal to the 1970s. In order to maintain their status, white males had to rearrange institutions to guarantee their privileged status as a matter of law. Whenever new job opportunities became available, they established rules and regulations to guarantee themselves the first right of refusal. This method was known as the equal division of labor and seniority. Equal division of labor applied when work was persistently irregular. When work was slow, employees were laid off according to seniority. Seniority came into play in the reverse manner whenever the workload increased. That is, the last to be laid off were the first to be rehired.

Seniority systems always worked against African Americans. They were last to be hired during the period of prosperity and the first to be fired during the period of austerity. This practice is very important to an understanding of the white male's privileged status. White males carried the supposition that their whiteness automatically entitled them to a status superior to that of African Americans. But this sense of superiority would have proved fruitless if it were not for the fact that they could obtain jobs that required the use of their minds and paid a salary that was higher than that of African Americans.

Another advantage that white males had over African Americans was their power to establish for themselves the exclusive right to be associated with jobs that required the use of the mind. It is often argued in the literature that white males achieved positions as craftsmen and artisans because of their racial superiority. But close examination of the New Deal legislation reveals that white males became skilled because the federal government granted them exclusive rights to job training. Their training was subsidized under the National Apprenticeship Act of 1937.

The original intent of the apprenticeship act was for the secretary of labor to bring together employers and employees to create an apprenticeship program. The unions seized control of these programs and began to establish rules and recruitment processes to favor themselves and their offspring. They purposefully excluded African Americans by law because otherwise Blacks would have been "equal" to whites.

Another policy the federal government established to ensure whites privileged status was the Davis-Bacon Act of 1952. Under the Davis-Bacon Act, construction companies that had contracts with the government were required to pay prevailing wages and fringe benefits to workers on federal government contracts for the construction of public buildings or public works. This act served as the cornerstone to various other federally assisted programs. By 1970, the "prevailing wages" concept had spilled over to approximately 60 other federally assisted projects. The political significance of the "prevailing wages" law is that wages were determined not by the free market but by law. This artificially raised workers' incomes higher than that earned in manufacturing and nonagricultural industries, thus giving these workers an economic advantage over the workers in these other sectors.

Because there was no antidiscriminatory clause to place African Americans civil rights to employment opportunities on a principle of law, the unions foreclosed to African Americans the freedom to seek jobs in the high-paying construction industry. The unions' discriminatory treatment, combined with the other prescriptive practices discussed above took a toll upon the status of African Americans. The unions admitted that they discriminated against African Americans but also defended the right to do so. They went so far as to include discriminatory clauses in their contracts, thus throwing the force of federal law behind their decision to inhibit the upward mobility of African Americans.

In short, white ethnic groups have used various instrumentalities of law to lock themselves into the mainstream of the American income redistribution system where high incomes and power are given. African Americans and other people of color (i.e., Native Americans, Latinos, and Puerto Ricans) have been purposefully locked out as a function of the unequal access to the mother lode of society's income redistribution system, and thus they have remained at the bottom of the economic ladder.

Present-Day Evidence

In spite of affirmative action legislation—government's proclaimed attempt at counteracting the discriminatory practices that have characterize labor practices—whites still enjoy unearned entitlements. Research findings from several recent studies sharply dispute recent claims that hiring practices are color-blind, and certainly do not support the perception that Blacks receive preferential treatment when seeking employment.[3] Moreover, of all races Blacks had the highest job loss rate in proportion to their job gains in the 1990–91 recession. Their percentage in the labor force also decreased.

Discrimination in employment has operated to systematically, though covertly, empower whites and put people of color at a disadvantage. For instance, employers commonly direct recruitment efforts to white neighborhoods to avoid recruitment sources that might result in a disproportionately inner-city Black labor force. In defense of these practices employers and researchers present data that indicate that the current earnings differential between Blacks and whites is more closely tied to differences in work-related skills than to labor market discrimination. However, several studies have found that when equally qualified Blacks and whites are considered for the same job, hiring and promotion decisions significantly favor whites. The effects of the privileged status of whites in employment are extremely detrimental to people of color.

Moreover, educational training has profoundly favored the white middle and upper classes. One of the most effective practices to ensure conferred dominance by whites is tracking, in which students are classified as bright, average, or slow learners for the purpose of appropriately training them for their future vocations. Blacks, Latinos, and other people of color are disproportionately placed in the lower tracks, in which the curriculum is qualitatively and quantitatively inferior to that used for the average and bright tracks. The fast tracks prepare students to enroll in universities. The average tracks prepare students to enroll in trade schools. The slow tracks are designed to channel students toward menial jobs as common laborers and the welfare system. Thus long before an individual applies for a position, his or her options have been determined, the results being that whites have been given another unfair advantage over people of color. In sum, the American caste system/racial stratification confers privileges to whites because of the their race.

The prescriptive privilege system permeates society. Whites are treated more favorably than persons of color by banks and savings and loans institutions, by the "justice system," in the housing market, which keeps persons of color concentrated in residential ghettos in central cities, and by car dealers.

In spite of this privileged position, many whites remain oblivious of their advantages and strongly maintain a myth of meritocracy. The structural forces that divide whites from people of color are based on complex beliefs and values. The forces that create the beliefs and values that divert the attention of most white Americans from seeing their privileged status are discussed in the next section.

WHY WHITES ARE BLIND TO THE FACTS

Distortions in Normal Cognition

Egocentrism in the Distribution of Resources

Any explanation for whites' unawareness of their privileged status should include a discussion of relevant aspects of human cognition (i.e., how people think, process information, and ultimately arrive at conclusions). When people are successful they have a tendency to perceive such outcomes as stemming from *internal* causes (i.e, their own traits), but bad or unsuccessful outcomes are perceived as stemming from *external* factors (i.e., ones beyond their control). With respect to judgments of fairness, egocentrism leads people to favor themselves in terms of what they perceive to be a fair division of available rewards. In other words, egocentrism leads people to conclude that they deserve more than is actually the case in many situations. Egocentrism leads one to conclude that (1) one's contribution is greater than is actually the case, and that (2) one therefore deserves a larger share of the credit or rewards.

In addition, there is a tendency for people to react more negatively to situations in which they receive less than they feel they deserve than to situations in which they receive more than they believe is fair. In short, people appear to be far more sensitive to inequity when it works to their disadvantage than when it works to their benefit. Moreover, people are more upset by inequity when it involves them directly than when it involves other unrelated persons. Therefore, solely on the basis of normal cognitive functioning, whites would not perceive their privileged status as such and would become upset by what they perceive as "unfair privileges" conferred on unrelated others (i.e., people of color). While this phenomenon is a reasonable explanation and most likely contributes to whites' inability to see that they are privileged, it does not completely explain the ignorance when reinforcements are so grossly lopsided in a person's or group's favor, as is the case with whites in general and white males in particular.

The Victim's Disposition

A phenomenon known as the fundamental attribution error further explains why whites are unaware that the grossly lopsided distribution of resources is due to their privileged status. According to the fundamental attribution error, people perceive others in terms of dispositional rather than situational causes. That is, people tend to perceive others as acting as they do largely because they are "that kind of person"— refering to their disposition. Thus, the many situational factors that may affect the behaviors of other people tend to be ignored. Indeed, people show this type of bias in situations where they know full well that others' actions were not under their own control. Relevant to the present thesis are the assumptions held about the underclass— mostly comprising people of color and women. It is supposed that the underclass condition is produced by the poverty of culture, which is explained in terms of the absence of moral virtues, a lack that keeps individuals from "deferring gratification, planning ahead, and making sacrifices for future benefit."[4] So social conditions—lopsided distributions of resources favoring white males—impacting the undeserving poor are ignored and instead they are blamed for a lack of character.

Self-Justification

The theme of the "undeserving poor" that permeates our society justifies unfairness. Two cognitive distortions that facilitate the maintenance of this belief are the just-world and victim-derogation hypotheses. The just-world hypothesis is the belief that justice always triumphs, with the good guys being rewarded and the bad guys being punished. So, even though the white ruling class has enslaved, exploited, raped, and oppressed people of color for hundreds of years, the just-world hypothesis leads an individual to rationalize and ignore whatever happens to others by deciding that the victim must somehow deserve his or her fate.

Perhaps the most unsettling type of distortion that occurs in such situations involves the tendency of persons receiving more than they deserve to derogate or devalue the persons they exploit. That is, such individuals often conclude that the victims of their unfair tactics actually deserve the treatment they are receiving. The psychological correlate of this treatment has been for whites to convince themselves that people of color are unworthy, subhuman, stupid, or immoral.

Both the just-world hypothesis and victim derogation result in a phenomenon known as self-justification. This phenomenon helps persons from feeling immoral if they enslave members of a group, deprive them of a decent education, or murder them. Moreover, whites low on the socioeconomic hierarchy also benefit from the presence of the undeserving poor in that they feel superior to somebody. The result is that Blacks, Latinos, and Native Americans are negatively stereotyped, allowing whites, without guilt, to exploit them for their resources (e.g., labor and land).

The Role of Stereotypes

Much of the recent literature on social cognition—how we perceive ourselves and others—has focused on stereotypes. Creating and holding stereotypes should not be viewed as a sign of abnormality. Rather, they reflect a human need to organize, remember, and retrieve information that might be useful as they attempt to achieve their goals and meet life's demands. Because people cannot respond to each individual piece of information to which they are exposed, people develop categories. Stereotypes, then, are categories about people. Categories in general, and stereotypes in particular, are shortcuts to thinking. People have to make so many decisions about behavior during a given day that they need guidance, hints, helpful rules, and so forth. Stereotypes, in part, serve this purpose.

Bias Perceptions in the Formation of Social Groups

A discussion of how people process information about their own group (in-groups) and out-groups is beneficial when answering the question of how it is that such a grossly unfair distribution of resources is not perceived as privileged by those who are advantaged. Furthermore, once categories are formed, the process of identification takes over, leading people to classify others into two categories—those like them-selves and those not like themselves. Such categories result in the creation of in-groups and out-groups. In-groups and out-groups facilitate the development of self-identities. In sum, people are who they are because they are not like others. This identification of others as being in the same or a different group has resulted in intergroup differentia-tion and discriminatory behavior and produced categorization error (overestimation of in-group similarities and the overestimation of between-group differences) as well as ethnocentrism, or evaluating one's own group as better than the out-group.

Clearly, in-group–out-group categorization leads to prejudice and discrimination. There is a close relationship between negative stereotypes and prejudice, since people have feelings (or prejudices) about various traits and beliefs. Stereotypes are the be-liefs (i.e., cognitions) that fuel the fires of prejudicial feelings and discriminatory be-haviors. Thus it is not surprising that whites hold negative stereotypes and prejudicial feelings about out-groups (e.g., African Americans, Latinos, and Native Americans) and actively behave in ways that put these groups at a disadvantage, all the while not consciously recognizing the bias and unfairness of such beliefs and actions.

False Consensus Bias

Another part of normal cognition related to the formation of in-group–out-group bias is the false consensus bias, in which people come to believe that their values, beliefs, and responses are common, appropriate, and based on the circumstances. On the other hand, they assume that out-group members' values, beliefs, and responses are uncommon, inappropriate, deviant, and due to the out-group member's disposition (e.g., personality, etc.). Whites think that their lives are morally neutral, normative, and average—and also ideal—so that even when they work to benefit others, their purpose is to facilitate the transformation of those others into becoming more like whites.

Information Processing Bias

Categorization of salient social groups is also an important encoding strategy, one that can influence the processing and retrieving of information acquired about indi-viduals. Furthermore, the extent to which the perceiver perceives an individual to be a part of a larger social entity can influence his or her causal attributions (i.e., interpreta-tions of cause and effect relationships) used to understand the person's behavior. Pre-existing stereotyping, if allowed to go unchallenged, acts as a filter for the new information. For instance, learning that Black Americans' unemployment relative to whites worsened during the 1980s is filtered through preexisting stereotypes and are translated into "more evidence that Blacks are lazy and just don't want to work." The new information is seldom stored without modification by preexisting beliefs. In sum, when whites receive factual information about the gross inequities within our society, they cognitively distort that information to fit a preexisting stereotype. Thus, they do not recognize their own privileged status, while rationalizing the systemic lack of opportunity for others.

Self-Serving Function of Prejudice and Reliance upon Stereotypes

Lastly, prejudicial attitudes are resistant to change because they serve clear functions for people. Some of these self-serving functions are: bestowal of rewards by society onto those who express prejudicial attitudes; the avoidance of punishment by expressing such attitudes; protection of a person's sense of self-worth; ego enhancement resulting from a person's belief that his or her culture, beliefs, in-group, and values are the correct ones; and providing a rationale for exploiting others and maintaining power. Today, a popular rationale for maintaining the status quo is a general consensus by whites that discrimination existed only in the past, and therefore previously oppressed groups need to stop blaming whites for their troubles. White males feel they are being pushed around to make up for past wrongs. Moreover, they believe that people of color "do not deserve the progress they have made."[5]

Short Sightedness of the Social Cognition Literature

Two shortcomings of the social cognition literature, its proponents would have us believe, are that human cognition occurs in a vacuum, and that racism is an individual act instead of a systemic bestowal of power and unearned privileges. On the contrary, though, prejudices and stereotypes are shaped and determined by societal thought and reinforcements. "Social categorization entails much more than cognitive classification of events, objects, or people. It is a process impregnated by values, culture and social representations."[6] Illustrating this process, and relevant to the present thesis, is the fact that the group in power (white males) defines who is superior and who is inferior as well as selects which characteristics (stereotypes) are emphasized in each group and what value, if any, is placed on those characteristics. Within the United States, white males are characterized (stereotyped) as the "thinkers" (possessing high intellect, using their minds), a stereotype highly valued in a technological society, while Black males are characterized as the "bodies" (aggressive, sexual, using their hands), a stereotype not only devalued but feared in a society plagued with violence and sexually transmitted diseases.

The stereotypes that become a part of one's cognitive schema are the ones expected, socially sanctioned, and positively reinforced in society for the benefit of the group in power. Some groups are negatively stereotyped until these stereotypical beliefs become part of the culture. The dominant group and even the stereotyped group internalize these stereotypes to various degrees. Thus, while normal cognition (e.g., categorization, false consensus bias, etc.) per se may propel an individual to behave in a biased manner to an out-group member, this behavior can be modified or totally eliminated. Moreover, definitional power can be employed to change or create positive or negative images. Thus, it is not surprising that with few exceptions, white students and students of color are exposed to a public school curriculum that distorts, ignores, and exaggerates evidence concerning the contribution of Europeans (whites) in a positive direction and those of people of color, especially Africans (Blacks) in a negative direction.

The Educational Agenda

Schooling in America does not train its constituency to see whites as oppressive, as unfairly advantaged, or as participants in an oppressive culture. To the contrary, the educational institution in America has taught whites to believe that their privileged status is morally right, due to objective means, and legitimate. The basis of this teaching is Eurocentrism. Eurocentrism is an ideology and practice of domination and exclusion based on the fundamental assumption that all relevance and value are centered in European culture and peoples and that all other cultures and peoples are at best marginal, and at worst, uncivilized.

It is not simply a question of teaching too little about cultures of people of color, but also of the content and attitudes taught, that is, falsehoods. For instance, in the textbook *Introduction to Psychology*, embedded in a discussion on "multiple intelligence," it is stated that "the development of logical scientific thought occurred late in the evolution of the human species (as an invention of the aftermath of the Renaissance)."[7] This statement, whether meant to deceive or written due to ignorance, perpetuates the belief that no other society had logical scientific thought prior to the Renaissance. And, while not saying it directly, the connotation is that intellectual sophistication was a European phenomenon.

The facts are that other civilizations made many scientifically sophisticated discoveries and inventions thousands of years prior to the Renaissance period. For instance, the scope and precision of the pyramids challenge the abilities of even today's engineers. A close study of the structure of the pyramids would convince anyone that the mathematical, geometrical, and astronomical data inherent in it is not accidental. In addition, when great civilizations other than European are mentioned, they are "whitenized." Egyptians are presented as looking like Elizabeth Taylor, when even the leading European scholars of that period described them as having "thick lips, broad noses, wooly hair, and [being] burnt of skin."[8] Moreover, Egypt, like the rest of northern Africa, is often not presented as even being in Africa, but rather as part of the Middle East.

This kind of cultural programming permeates the educational curriculum. Eurocentrism allows the masses to ignore or refuse to recognize unequal power in this society and its effects on people of color. There has been a progressive Europeanization of human consciousness and culture that is one of the major problems of our times. Europeanization of human consciousness and culture refers to the systematic transformation of the cultural consciousness of the world's people by Europeans through "education," religion (i.e., indoctrination), and the media (i.e., programming). Thus, whites are taught to believe that their privileged status is earned, the outcome of a fair system of reinforcements to be taken for granted.

The Social Sciences Agenda

A prime example of this programming has been the interplay between so-called scientific discourse and exploitation (e.g., slavery, colonialism, etc.). The social sciences legitimized exploitation by rationalizing racist practices on the grounds that the oppressed, the excluded, or otherwise victimized groups are inferior physically, intellectually, culturally, or in a combination of all three ways. For instance, from the nineteenth century through the early part of this century social Darwinists extended the interpretation of the biological theory of evolution into a theory of the development of a society of conflict in which the stronger and more advanced race would naturally triumph over the inferior and weaker race. Thus it was believed that social relations were circumscribed and constrained and that white male domination of people of color was inevitable. The social Darwinian theory received its maximal significance in the concept of the "white man's burden" and "manifest destiny," which had the political consequences of not only justifying and legitimizing racism and oppression but making it the responsibility of whites to control and dominate the "inferiors" (people of color). Thus, while this type of rationalizing is similar to cognitive distortions (discussed earlier in the section "The Victim's Disposition") in that both relieve guilt and responsibility for unfair treatment of others, it is more insidious because it is cloaked in the "objectivity" of science.

The most popular social scientific assumption of why persons of color remain marginalized is the assumption that they possess a fundamental weakness within their culture, community, and/or family. The press and policy makers, armed with social scientific dogma, have convinced most of the public that people of color are disadvantaged because of something wrong with the "victim" (e.g., a disregard for "family values," absent fathers, laziness, broken homes, bossy women, fatally wounded psyches, slavery, and so on). By focusing our attention on the effects—the victim's responses—we are diverted from the causes: racism, discrimination, segregation, and the powerlessness of the victims.

Every important social problem—crime, mental illness, civil disorder, and unemployment—has been analyzed within the framework of the victim-blaming ideology, and government policy has been constructed to change the victim. Ryan points out that victim blaming is "very subtle, cloaked in kindness and concern, and bears all the trappings and statistical furbelows of scientism; it is obscured by a perfumed haze of humanitarianism."[9]

Blaming the victim is quite different from the conservative ideologies that hold that Blacks and people of color are genetic inferiors. In addition, blaming the victim is more optimistic in terms of solutions (e.g., it spawned Head Start, Weed and Seed, etc). Even victims perpetuate these pseudoscientific tenets, and this further legitimizes and obscures the privileged status of whites.

In conclusion, victim blaming not only sustains the power of socioeconomic interests but also cements social identities under the guise of objectivity. Silence, denials, and even lies about privilege are key political and power tools. By keeping the masses unaware of gross structured inequality, unearned advantage and conferred dominance are protected.

Culture: The Hidden Agenda

"The structure and patterns of most Western institutions and social interaction are supported by several assumptions which lie at the basis of traditional Western culture."[10] Culture consists of those aspects of the environment that people make. Culture is transmitted from generation to generation, with the responsibility given to parents, teachers, religious leaders, and other respected elders in a community. Thus culture also consists of ideals, values, and assumptions about life that guide specific behaviors. Successful social adjustment, in effect, is the process of learning the habits, norms, and ways of thinking essential for fitting into the society of one's culture.

However, since culture as a rule is widely shared and accepted, there is little reason to discuss it, and therefore we are often not aware of its influence. Our own everyday sense of reality is constituted through interaction with others. It is such an integral part of how we experience the world that we generally lack the necessary distance and objectivity to see that interaction clearly. A socially derived set of assumptions, definitions, and typifications serves as the frame of reference that underlies the individual's perceptions, cognition, and behavior. That frame of reference functions as a lense, causing the individual to experience social reality according to the underlying rules of the culture. In turn, the person assumes that his or her values and behaviors are correct, valid, and best and that contrasting values and behaviors are inappropriate, invalid, and less efficient.

The components of the Western world view of interest to the present thesis are:

1. The individual as the primary unit, connoting individual responsibility to self, independence, and autonomy.
2. Competition as the driving force in society: winning is everything.
3. An orientation toward action, which translates into mastery and control over the environment and all of nature.

4. An emphasis on objectivity achieved through the scientific method, rational linear thinking, cause and effect relationships, and a quantitative emphasis.
5. An emphasis on status and power, which is measured by material and economic possessions, credentials, titles, and position.

Unfortunately, the underlying cultural assumptions on which these Western worldview components are based are infrequently addressed. The major philosophical tenet that drives the manifestations is dualism.

Dualism is the belief that the universe is comprised of opposing good and evil forces. With regard to humans, good is equated with the mind and evil with the body; the good is rational, morally right, and just, while the evil is emotional, violatile, destructive, and in need of control by the good. Christian theology as articulated by St. Augustine, Luther, and Calvin clearly reflects dualistic tenets.[11] The mind, spirit, or soul, is considered the source of moral control; the body, the mortal, is considered to be an inferior aspect of the person that must be made subject to moral control.

Furthermore, Western cultural thinking is hierarchical, as exemplified by the assumption that all beings can be ranked based upon their relative proportion of good and evil, or superiority and inferiority. Many people of color place value on at least some of the various qualities identified by the traditional Westerner as non-rational. The main nonrational qualities that are valued, varying from the culture of one person of color to that of another, are: (1) more intense emotional or aesthetic expressiveness, (2) rhythmic music and dancing, and (3) naturalistic religions and medical practices.[12] Consequently, Western man believes himself to be more rational, good, and superior than people of color, who are perceived as being less rational or more animal, bad, and inferior. Whites believe that people of color must be subjected to the rule of white men, who are rational and entitled to rule. People of color are kept at the bottom of the hierarchical structure by overt means (e.g., armed warfare) and/or covert means (e.g., educational tracking, labor laws, etc.). A few individuals from these groups are permitted to rise slightly from the very bottom of the hierarchy, but only to the extent that they adopt the value orientation of Western culture. Thus control of society is meant to remain in the hands of those of Western origin. Racism (i.e., institutional practices) is an established form of group oppression within Western society to ensure that it does.

Dualism and hierarchial thinking are also the cornerstone of Western social science in that Western culture is assumed to be superior to other cultures. As a matter of record, Western culture is considered identical to civilization, and the cultures of persons of color are considered to be in varying states of development, moving toward civilization. That the people of a culture should view themselves as culturally superior is certainly common, but not so common is the feature contained in Western cultural thinking that the superior should control the inferior. Such notions as the "white man's burden" and such practices as missionary imperialism are derived from this type of thinking. Thus according to Western thinking, exploitation, oppression, and even genocide are morally defensible.

In sum, dualistic thinking—the belief that the universe contains objective and opposing forces of universal good and evil and that the moral goal of mankind is to enable or ensure that the good control the evil—facilitates and sustains group oppression. Moreover, dualistic thinking perpetuates the belief that oppression of people of color (the evil) by whites (the good) is morally right, and even the white man's responsibility. Thus the privileged status of whites is not perceived by whites as exploitive or even unfair. To the contrary, it is perceived by many whites as a natural consequence of good prevailing over evil. The author Alex Haley was once asked by a reporter whether he thought that the enslavement of his great-great grandfather was a much better fate than the likely outcome if he had remained in Africa. Such arrogance and self-rightousness logically springs from dualistic and hierarchial thinking.

SUMMARY AND CONCLUSIONS

The overall thrust of this chapter was to demonstrate that white males occupy a privileged position but are unaware of it. Data and theories were presented to show that their privileged status is supported by institutional arrangements, for example, educational tracking, discriminatory lending practices by banks and savings and loan institutions, and so forth, and laws such as the Land Grant Act, the National Labor Relation Act of 1935, and the National Apprenticeship Act of 1937. Whites have justified their status as something that they have earned, based on meritocacy. But an examination of the historical data and present-day practices overwhelmingly disproves this false notion.

A small but influential number of whites, for example, social scientists, policy makers, and the press, work at making sure the myth of meritocracy is maintained. As we have demonstrated, the current social scientific theories, hypotheses, and assumptions that permeate the literature blind whites to perceiving themselves as privileged. These assumptions include "the white man's burden," "the undeserving poor," and others. Further perpetuating whites' unawareness of their privileged position is the fact that they are cognitively motivated (by means of egocentrism, fundamental attribution error, victim derogation, stereotyping, etc.) to accept the notion that they have received their status due to the inferiority of their victims—people of color.

Moreover, the impetus for the denial of their privileged status is embedded in Western cultural thought patterns, that is, dualism and hierarchial thinking. They have equated themselves with civilization and technological progress and equated people of color with primitive culture. These cultural values are structured to socialize the developing white male child to believe that he is superior by the mere facts of skin color and gender. The institutional arrangements (e.g., education system, labor market, etc.) are designed to assure him of this false sense of superiority genetically, culturally, and behaviorally. Consequently, white males are unable to discern that they are privileged because they believe they have earned their status due to their essential superiority. Their monopolization of the instruments for describing themselves as superior—media, higher education, and so on—keeps them totally oblivious of the facts (e.g., that they control most of the world resources at the expense of people of color).

In conclusion, perceiving people of color as the problem not only sustains the power of socioeconomic interests but also cements social identities under the guise of objectivity. Silence, denials, and even lies about privilege are key political and power tools. By keeping the masses unaware of gross, structured inequity, unearned advantage and conferred dominance are protected. Also, by seeing those who are the victims of their privileged status as inferiors, whites are relieved of the responsibility to do anything about the situation. This perception, moreover, legitimizes further exploitation of the victims.

10

Dialogue and Diversity:
Communication across Groups

Mary Jane Collier

The Constitution of the United States begins, "We, the people . . . ." But who are we? How have we changed since the writing of the Constitution? What keeps us together? How can we communicate with one another? How can we more effectively discuss issues about education, representation, or distribution of wealth? Do the concepts behind multiculturalism and pluralism, for example, diversity, political correctness, feminism, and affirmative action, help us or hinder us in our efforts to communicate more effectively with one another?

A multicultural society, by definition, includes diverse perspectives. Some say multiculturalism is necessary to overcome omnipresent discrimination, others believe multiculturalism and affirmative action unfairly give special privileges to minorities. Some say U.S. culture is too concerned with being politically correct (PC) and that political correctness is the adoption of a specific political agenda of left-wing liberalism. Others define political correctness as the use of language and the creation of policies that include all members of our society in the decision-making process. Wherever such issues are discussed and no matter with whom, such conversations quickly polarize into "us" versus "them."

The purpose of this chapter is to propose ways in which all of us—Asian Americans, European Americans, males, females, hetero/homo/bisexuals, older, and younger—can begin to talk with one another and understand one another. We all need to learn and to think about how we can effectively discuss politically controversial topics with people from other groups. To be effective, such discussion must allow all participants to feel they have participated.

There is one thing that all humans have in common. We all want to answer questions about who we are. Individuals in every country throughout the world are trying to answer questions like, Who am I? Who are my people? Who are you? How are we going to be with one another? What do I want? Who do I want to become? Are you with me or against me? Can we be friends? Are you going to help me or hurt me?

These questions are about identity. Who I am depends partly upon who you think I am, who you think I should be, and how you behave toward me, not to mention whether you think we can work together. Communication with others is the way we come to know who we are, separately and together.

I grew up in Colorado, where presently some are arguing that gays want special rights. I have taught in an inner-city high school where busing for integration was in effect for the first time. I have lived on a Navaho Reservation. I have been a professor at an ethnically diverse university campus in the heart of Los Angeles. Also, I have visited the Soweto township in South Africa as well as Belfast.

I am a white, middle-class woman who has learned that it's all about identity and power. I have learned that the answers to many of my questions can be found in dialogue with people who I initially believe are very different from me. I have also learned that dialogue is a dynamic process—sometimes threatening, sometimes engaging, but always a source of knowledge. I am a teacher of intercultural communication because I believe that through communication we can better understand each other, develop quality relationships, manage our conflicts, and create an environment of morality and peace.

In this chapter we will look at how we can improve the quality of our communication through an understanding of group identities. In order to do this, we must be sure we are using terms in the same way and understand some fundamental assumptions about the nature of people. We will first consider the communication process. Next, we'll look at different types of group and cultural identities. Then we'll explore particular differences in communication style that emerge in different cultural contexts.

After we have developed our understanding of the communication process within and across groups, we can then discuss how to become more effective communicators. This process of gaining communication competence has applications for members within a group and between members of different groups. Communication competence allows us to relate to one another more appropriately and effectively.

COMMUNICATION

"Communication" is the process of assigning meaning to verbal and nonverbal messages. It takes at least two of anything to communicate. Each additional person added to a communication event makes the event more complex and challenging.

When family members communicate with one another at the dinner table, more than one person typically speaks at once, not all messages are "heard" in the same way, and one sibling may miss another sibling pulling a face at him or her. At a work meeting to discuss affirmative action procedures in hiring, the supervisor may roll her eyes and use a sarcastic tone while saying to the group, "I fully support the policies of our company in this area."

As a conversation between two persons unfolds, the thoughts, feelings, behaviors, and interpretations of each participant may change from moment to moment. All of these are variables in the process, and each variable affects one or more of the others simultaneously. Both persons are linked into a kind of system in which each talks and listens and observes and behaves all at the same time. Why is this important? Because we tend to make assumptions about what the other person means. We make these assumptions to fill in the gaps in our understanding or listening attention. Sometimes we miss verbal or nonverbal messages that are being sent our way. We may forget that our verbal and nonverbal messages are influencing the other person. Our thoughts and feelings are not necessarily shared by or with the other person and can therefore lead to misunderstandings.

As you probably have already noticed, sometimes it is difficult to understand another person well. Sometimes you understand each other but disagree. A good way to summarize this problem is that meanings are created in people, not in messages. And people are different.

As communicators, we tend to assume that others understand what we say and do in the way that we want them to. Words and nonverbal cues connote different things to different people. Each individual is a composite of different experiences, beliefs, attitudes, values, and expectations. Each word or gesture is interpreted based on all those factors. Unemployment compensation connotes very different things to homeless individuals, displaced workers, owners of small businesses, Democrats, and Republicans.

Nonverbal cues are a frequent source of miscommunication. The nonverbal part of a message is very important, because we tend to focus on nonverbal cues when we want to know how a person really feels about something. If the verbal part of the message and the nonverbal part of the message are contradictory, for example, a person says, "Oh sure . . . . I have a great deal of respect for Mexicans" with a facial expression and tone of voice that is somewhat judgmental and condescending, an attitude of criticism is apparent even though the verbal content may seem positive.

Nonverbal cues like tone of voice, inflection, silence, eye contact, and body language are also indicators of relationship status. People who trust one another, feel intimacy, and desire a close relationship indicate their feelings not only by what they say but by what they do. Nonverbal cues are also a strong indicator of who is in control and who has greater power in the relationship. When some women complain that men are overly dominant and controlling they may be focusing on nonverbal cues such as talking for long periods of time, interrupting more often, and touching cues. Physical proximity, tone of voice, eye contact, and posture are all cues that can indicate who is in control of a conversation.

Every behavior occurs in a cultural context and will be interpreted according to the listener's cultural background. For example, an appropriate and sincere European American greeting to a friend may be a verbal, "Hi, how are you doing?" without a pause for a response. In Mexican American friendships, a sincere greeting would generally go beyond the verbal greeting. It might include sitting down together to hear how the other person's family is or how mutual friends are doing or hearing about anything that may be troubling the individual. Neither kind of greeting is more appropriate than the other; they are just different.

In summary, what you say and how you say it are only part of the communication process. Meanings are assigned by individuals, and the connotations and perceptions of each message may vary a lot or a little. We communicate in order to validate our beliefs, values, and attitudes and to get a sense of who we are. To become a more effective communicator, one must remember that nonverbal cues are signals about feelings and the status of the relationship but also that meanings are individual and are in people, not in the words, and that people make a lot of assumptions based on their experiences and background. When you think about it, it's a wonder we are able to understand each other at all.

As we have seen, communication is the process by which we get to know each other and develop relationships and our identity. Conversely, our group identities affect the way we conduct ourselves and interpret the conduct of others as we develop relationships with others.

GROUPS AND IDENTITY

Culture and Identity

Some groups develop a sense of culture. In this chapter we will approach culture from a communication perspective. Generally speaking, an anthropologist would study artifacts, tools, and art, among other things, to understand culture. A social psychologist would study the economic and political conditions that affect self-esteem and crime. From a communication perspective, we will focus upon the symbolic language codes and interpretations of the group.

From this perspective, culture is made up of a commonly used language code, shared interpretations for the verbal and nonverbal symbols in the language, and norms for what is appropriate and inappropriate behavior for members of the group. Furthermore, groups with a culture have a sense of history that is handed down to new members. In other words, persons are taught what it means to be, for example, Chinese American, and what are appropriate ways of behaving as well as what the history of the group is.

Cultural identity systems are mutually intelligible, commonly accessible to all group members, and deeply felt. So persons who identify themselves as Chinese American know and understand their history, traditions, institutions, and rituals, and are all able to talk about and enact what is expected and appropriate; they have a sense of identification and deeply held affinity with their group. People can't become Chinese American like they can change a religion or move to a new place; cultural identity is something that endures.

Types of Identity

As individuals we are members of many different groups. It is important to realize that there are many types of groups to which we belong and many group identities that each of us holds. International identity, nationality, gender, and ethnicity are examples of a few types of identity, along with geographical residence, physical ability, profession, support group membership, and neighborhood.

National groups differ in their identity and communication styles. Japanese have been described as collectivistic and group oriented, while U.S. Americans have been described as more individualistic. In work situations, for instance, U.S. Americans are more likely to ask, "What should I be doing?" while Japanese are more likely to ask, "What should we be doing?"

Men and women are also socialized, or taught to behave, in different ways. We are taught to "be good little girls" or to "be a man" at an early age, no matter what our particular national culture happens to be. There is a difference, however, between our biological sex and what many refer to as gender cultural identity. Gender is a socially constructed cultural style and can be designated as masculine and/or feminine. The societal norm is that men should act masculine and women should act feminine, but not all of us act or are comfortable with that norm. Most of us combine both masculine and feminine styles.

A final category of group identity includes those styles developed by ethnic groups. Sometimes this is discussed as racial identity. Many people assume that race and ethnicity are one and the same. Race, however, is simply a physical appearance indicative of genetically inherited characteristics like skin color and texture of hair. The original categories, Negroid, Caucasoid, and Mongoloid, were proposed by Western anthropologists in the nineteenth century. Given migration, centuries of intermarriage, and the analytical flaws and generalities of the original categories, racial identity is an outdated and overgeneralized category of identity. Still, persons do make attributions about others on the basis of appearance and what they think is race because we need to make sense of our environment and feel the need to predict the actions of others. Race is a quick means by which to predict attitudes, behaviors, and so forth because racial stereotypes and attributions are so familiar, having been reinforced through the media and our institutions in order to justify oppression and slavery. It is ultimately, though, an inaccurate indicator. For our present purposes, it will be more accurate and more useful to talk about ethnic rather than racial identities.

Ethnic identity is much more than just genetic ancestry. It is based on cultural heritage, rituals that have been handed down, language, and norms. Ethnic groups in the United States are those groups whose ancestors came from places outside the United States or preceded the creation of this nation (e.g., Native American Indians, African Americans, and Polish Americans).

Ethnic communication styles are a product of cultural heritage, history, and the national culture of residence, among other factors. Persons who are ethnic American are both ethnic and U.S. American. Many European Americans have lost their collective memory and active recognition of ethnic roots (from Germany or England, for example) and partly because of a position of sociocultural power, have come to define themselves as "non-ethnic." But they are an ethnic group.

In summary, there are many cultural identities that an individual can take up throughout his or her lifetime. This chapter will concentrate upon national, ethnic, and gender identities because these identities are a focus of substantial conflict in our society today. We will spend the remainder of this chapter clarifying the different types of cultural identities and outlining how intercultural communication, which validates identities, can be accomplished.

Properties of Cultural Identity

First, we will give attention to the properties or qualities of cultural identities that can help us understand our own cultural identity and that of others. Each of the properties will be highlighted with a suggestion of how we can apply knowledge of that property to improve our communication with others.

In the first place, each individual has many identities. One or more of these identities may become salient in a given situation. When I visited South Africa and the topic of women's rights came up with a group of men who were criticizing women executives, I found a feminist identity becoming salient for me. When people criticized the United States, I became primarily aware of my nationality as a salient identity. When speaking with a group of students with diverse ethnic backgrounds, diverse political views, and varying perceptions of "the New South Africa," my professional identity as a teacher/student of intercultural communication became predominant. Each person, then, is a combination of many identities, and depending upon the conversation and situation, one or more identities may become salient. To behave toward someone as though that person has just one identity (for example, Irish), for instance, is unfair to the individual and can lead to misunderstandings. (Is that person an Irish Catholic or an Irish Protestant?)

When you meet others for the first time, remember that the other person is more than just "Chinese" or "homeless" or whatever, just as you are more than just "U.S. American" or a "salesperson." The identity that you think is important for the other person may not be the same one that the other person thinks is important. The identity you find most salient may change depending upon the situation and conversation you find yourself involved in.

Second, people don't all agree about what it means to take on a particular identity. Not all U.S. Americans are alike. Not all Japanese Americans agree about how to be Japanese American. Many African Americans have written about how disturbing it is to be asked to speak for all African Americans.

People are simultaneously members of particular groups and unique individuals. Some Navahos are "old ones" who speak Navaho at all times and live in hogans in very traditional ways. Others speak both Navaho and English, attend traditional ceremonies and powwows, but also drive school buses or work on construction projects with non-Indians who live off the reservation. All members of a culture are not alike.

Third, identities are formed through communication with others. At least two processes are involved in identity formation and change. One part of identity is who *we* choose to be when we are with others. This is called avowed identity because it is the identity which is taken on by the individual. Another process is how others view us; this is called ascribed identity. An individual cannot take on or enact a cultural identity unless people who are already members of that group accept him or her into the group and communicate their acceptance. Cultural identity is group identity and is based on both avowed and ascribed processes.

The identity you ascribe to someone else may not be the same identity as the one she or he avows. And you may be defining the identity differently. Rosa may avow and Mike may ascribe to Rosa an identity as Mexican American. But Rosa may be proud of her Mexican heritage, Spanish language, and strong family bond, while Mike may be defensive, threatened, and critical of a lack of social mobility when he thinks of her Mexican American identity.

As human beings we need to make sense of our environment, including the people that we meet. We stereotype and overgeneralize attributions and assumptions about others because we do not have the time or resources to get to know each individual we meet. Stereotypes (ascribed identities of other groups) are reinforced in the media, educational institutions, family, and peer groups. All cultural groups are stereotyped, and all of us stereotype others.

However, as individuals, many of us do not like being labeled as similar to everyone else in the group. It is important to remember that when we stereotype, we make some dangerous assumptions about the similarity of everyone in a group and overlook individual differences. In addition, our stereotype of a particular group may not be defined in the same way as other persons' stereotypes.

Your view of yourself as a group member and individual is partly dependent upon how others treat you. Ascriptions are often stereotypes, which are always overgeneralizations.

Fourth, cultural identities are both enduring and changing. There are qualities of being a U.S. American that endure over the years, such as expecting certain individual rights, freedom of speech and religion, and some degree of materialism and access to technology; these have persisted for many generations. As well, some qualities have changed; women and ethnics now have the legal right to vote, hold office, own property, and so on. In addition, the identity of U.S. Americans as members of the most powerful and technologically advanced nation in the world is now debatable. Cultural identities include both change and continuity.

Communication Styles and Identity

People adopt identity through using a particular style of communication. We become a member of a group and identify who else is in the group or out of the group through what we say and do. Groups develop certain patterns or styles of communication based on the history of the group, its values, socioeconomic status, and external conditions. Each group develops its own set of verbal and nonverbal cues and its own set of norms (appropriate behaviors). A group also develops its own ideas about and rules for how cues are interpreted. Subgroups within each culture further diversify the values, norms, and meanings.

Thus a group expresses its cultural identity through its codes, its interpretations of those codes, and norms for use of the codes. The group develops its history through a process of teaching new members what is expected in the group. The history of the group is what gives a group a cultural identity and a quality that endures generation after generation. For example, gays and lesbians in the United States share codes of how to refer to each other, norms about supporting one another, values about the need to fight against discrimination and agreements about where to live. At the same time, the norms change as they are being taught. The debate in the lesbian community about the practice of "butching" is a reflection of changing norms.

Recognizing the different styles can be useful because we are constantly making assumptions about others' beliefs, attitudes, and values based upon what they say and do. While considering examples of communication styles in various groups, we must remember that these are general patterns of communication. Not every individual in the group behaves in the same way, nor is every individual in the group the same. We will consider a few examples of some dimensions of communication that characterize some cultural groups so that we can begin to recognize the differences and appreciate the different styles.

Frequently, researchers compare groups by looking at the communication style or the set of values that characterizes the group. Since the bulk of the research on these dimensions has illuminated national cultural identity, we will begin our discussion with examples of cultural styles.

One of the most common characteristics ascribed to U.S. Americans is individualism. Individualism means putting one's individual needs before those of the group. In the United States, individuals are responsible for their own success and achievement in education, the corporate world, and social relationships. Assertiveness, directness, and accountability for individual actions are all valued forms of behaving. "I" statements are quite common and are encouraged, and drawing attention to the self in appropriate ways is socialized in childhood games.

On the other hand, other national groups are more group oriented. In Japan, a person attributes his or her success to the support of family, the company, or the unit in the company. Sayings such as "the nail that sticks up is the first to be hit" summarize the need for a group orientation, some degree of conformity, and attention to others in the group. Indirectness may be used as a means of protecting the "face" of others in the group.

Another example of a difference across national groups is what Edward T. Hall calls high and low context.[1] Context is the extent to which groups emphasize the verbal part of the message or the nonverbal part of the message and, in a sense, whether the responsibility for interpreting the message lies with the speaker or the listener. A high-context culture is one in which members are more indirect, letting the context speak for them. Members of high-context cultures use fewer words and allow the environment, the status of persons who are present, their appearance, and tone of voice to convey the message. The listener is then expected to draw conclusions based on the nonverbal cues to ascertain the meaning of the message.

Mr. Shimizu, a Japanese executive, may say to Ms. Brown, a U.S. executive visiting Japan, "We may wish to take that course of action." This message could mean many things, depending upon Mr. Shimizu's status and position, who else is present, where the meeting or conversation is held, and the prior relationship developed between the two executives. If Ms. Brown wishes to understand the message as a Japanese would, she would need to decode all of the contextual cues.

Another stylistic category is the extent to which the group is relationship oriented. This relationship orientation can be seen in talk about relationships and the expression of concern about each person's feelings toward others in the group. It is also seen in a tendency toward inclusiveness, or an active concern that everyone in a group has the opportunity to share an opinion. The focus of this style is upon togetherness and community.

A group's competitive achievement orientation is sometimes described as the opposite of relationship orientation. People enacting this style negotiate their identities through job performance, completing tasks, and social performances like telling stories. They work, then, to increase their individual status and achievement. The style is also demonstrated in talk about activities and giving facts and evidence in an effort to persuade others. This style is characterized by talking about what one does rather than who one is. The United States has been identified as achievement oriented. Edward Stewart has described the United States as a "doing" culture rather than a "being" or "being-in-becoming" culture.[2]

Styles that characterize particular ethnic cultural identities have also been identified by researchers. Styles that African Americans have developed are the products of almost four centuries of slavery, exploitation, continuing racism, socioeconomic struggle, and pride. Generally speaking, within the African American ethnic culture, directness and assertiveness are valued, emotional expressiveness is appropriate, and "authenticity" or (having no hidden agendas) is important. Those identifying with Mexican American culture tend to emphasize relational trust and establishing a supportive climate and positive relationship prior to dealing with a task. In addition, Mexican Americans manage conflict through situational flexibility and relationship reinforcement. The family and support for it are common topics of conversation.

In their intercultural communication with European Americans, African Americans are sensitive to being stereotyped negatively and often feel a sense of victimization that can lead to conflict. Such perceptions of communication with European Americans are not unique to African Americans in the United States. Other groups who have experienced discrimination voice similar concerns.

In summary, recognizing the behavior others as a product of cultural style can be useful. This recognition can help limit quick negative judgments. It may be that we can all learn something from other styles.

INTERCULTURAL COMMUNICATION COMPETENCE

When people with different identities come together, the communication is to some extent intercultural. Communication competence means communication conduct (verbal and nonverbal) that is mutually (to all communicators involved) appropriate and effective. Effective communication occurs when both participants feel as if there is mutual understanding and each experiences some positive outcome. Communication occurs between people, so both (or all) persons must be involved in creating the rules for what is competent. For example, a Korean American employer is meeting with a Mexican American employee. Both individuals must share in deciding what should be talked about and who should be in control of the conversation in order for the communication to be effective. Both parties negotiate how to manage disagreements, how to solve problems, what constitutes appropriate praise, and what is meaningful, constructive criticism.

Competent communication implies that group members follow the norms that apply to the situation, topic, and relationship. Competence means more than just being polite. It is also behaving in ways that are mutually effective. Communication that is effective results in some positive outcome for both people. The outcome need not be the expected one; so long as it is positive, communication has been effective. For example, effective communication between two groups of workers trying to coordinate work schedules occurs when both groups end up with satisfactory schedules, when one ends up with a satisfying schedule and the other gets first choice on the next round of scheduling and when neither is satisfied with its schedule but both perceive that each has showed empathy for the other and concern for the company during the conversation, leading to a continuation of a positive working relationship.

Cultural competence also refers to the exhibition of appropriate and effective conduct with members of the group. Behaving in a competent manner for a first-time visit to an Alcoholics Anonymous meeting is relatively easy because the norms are explicitly stated at the beginning of every meeting.

Intercultural competence is much more complex and difficult to learn. Intercultural competence is when both people ascribe and validate the identities that the other person is avowing. In other words, if Jack wants to be appreciated as a father and Maria wants to be appreciated as Chicana, Jack and Maria should each validate and reinforce the preferred identity of the other. Jack and Maria have to figure out first how the other wants to be identified and then how to appropriately reinforce the other's identity.

When communicating with someone who has a different cultural identity, anxiety is perfectly normal. Not knowing the rules or what is expected is difficult, and trying out new behaviors can be risky. People who visit other countries usually experience culture shock which is a natural reaction to an unfamiliar language and surroundings and not knowing how to ensure that needs are met.

Cues and Labels of Identity

In a new situation, we may be faced with the question of which identity or identities are salient for the other person. We consciously and unconsciously take on identities; we align ourselves with each other by association, by selecting a particular label to call ourselves, by wearing a particular mode of dress, or by speaking a particular language.

Groups usually prefer to name themselves (African Americans) rather than using the label imposed by members of other groups (colored, Negro, nigger) because a name represents identity and who assigns the name represents power. Naming something gives it life.

How can you decide which labels or terms to use? First we must consider whether a label is ever necessary. Most people object to being labeled. It might be helpful if we all clarified with each other what label, if any, is acceptable and in what situations the label is appropriate. Further, it is important to remember that labels, just like cultural norms, change over time and that some people may object to labels, while others may be comfortable with several labels.

Avoid overly general labels, and when labels are necessary, ask insiders to talk about their understandings and preferences. If you use a label in talking about another group, clarify who is represented by the label and your reasons for using that label.

Language

Sometimes groups create their own language and restricted code to protect or to reinforce group identity. Language codes are a major part of identity. Not only are codes used as cues about identity, but they are also the means by which identity and norms are taught. For example, Mexican American children are taught about concepts of family, social roles and responsibilities, the importance of community, and ethnic heritage in Spanish.

In intercultural communication, there is the likelihood that more than one language is being used and/or terms used may be unfamiliar. This makes figuring out the identities of the other person more difficult. Each of us creates and reinforces our individual identity through language (ethnolinguistic identity). Researchers who have studied ethnolinguistic identity have found that groups who are adapting to a new culture and language tend to use the other group's language when status is an issue, when they see a large distinction between their in-group and the out-group, and when there is institutional (education, justice system, and political system) support to use the new language. It is natural and easiest to communicate in our primary language.

Power Issues and Intercultural Communication

All communication occurs within a context. Among other types, contextual elements may be economic, political, social, psychological, or relational. One of the most important contexts is that of socioeconomic power. Socioeconomic power describes the ability to influence and distribute or withhold resources and rewards, including the ability to punish or control. Perceptions of power impact the communication process in that if one person perceives that the other holds more power, the first may feel threatened. Members of groups who have experienced discrimination may fear that the group in power may withhold resources like jobs, houses in particular neighborhoods, or even friendships. The result of such powerlessness and fear can be avoidance or confrontation.

There are many bases or types of power. Satisfaction or dissatisfaction with power is one of the most important determinants of relationship satisfaction. However, the group in power gets to make the rules about how resources are distributed. In South Africa, for example, white Afrikaners control the overwhelming percentage of wealth (capital and property). Until recently, they created and enforced a system of government that excluded Blacks from any form of representation, any ownership of property, and any freedom to travel. A power differential that is as great as that between Black and whites in South Africa can greatly affect the possibilities for a relationship.

Each individual and each group has a need for power because we all need to have the capacity to influence others and our environment to some degree. Part of finding out who we are as a people and as individuals is finding out who listens to us and who is changed by us. Power and identity definition are inextricably linked, just as are modification and reinforcement. Living is all about the power to define ourselves for ourselves.

Every group wants to keep or build its power. The conduct of every cultural group reflects assumptions about power.

INTERGROUP POLITICS

Isms

Racism, sexism, ageism, homophobia, and so forth are all forms of oppression, and each is institutionalized, systematic, and based in history. Each ism applies to a different group. Racism means treating members of a race, such as whites, negatively and differently simply because they are white. Sexism means treating males or females in a discriminatory way; homophobia is not only discrimination toward homosexuals but also an irrational fear of homosexuality. Many people who are over 65 years of age talk about the unfairness of mandatory retirement laws, the overemphasis on youth and beauty in society, and the cold and sterile environment of nursing homes as examples of ageism in the United States.

Every ism is based on overgeneralization and negative stereotyping. Isms polarize people, pitting group against group and individual against individual. Isms are very common and very destructive to relationships.

An example about two colleagues on a school committee may help make this more clear. During a meeting the male remarks, "She is too emotionally involved in the issues to run the committee smoothly. After all, she is a woman." The female colleague, a self-avowed feminist, replies, "Can you believe him? Indicting all women as overly emotional! Is he living in the 1950s? And men wonder why we label them male chauvinists!" In this situation, both colleagues are overgeneralizing.

Women have been misjudged and mistreated by men in almost every culture on earth. Nonetheless, it can be destructive for women to try to take back power and make up for history by continually confronting men until they admit they are responsible for all the wrongs done to women. If the goal of women is to build positive relationships with the men they work with, accusations by women will most likely lead to more accusations, excuses, and rationalizations on the part of those accused. As we know from conflict research, defensiveness usually begets more defensiveness.

A possible way to avoid this quid pro quo of defensiveness may be to talk in terms of the personal consequences of sexism or racism. Dialogue about the privilege that accompanies being male (and/or white, heterosexual, physically abled) can also be beneficial.

Discrimination is a more specific form of oppression that denies the rights and privileges and constricts the behavior of particular persons because of their membership in a particular group. The key to a discussion, argument, or conflict about discrimination is to explain how and what discrimination is, how it functions, how it is reinforced, and the consequences it has for each of us in our role as oppressor or oppressed.

Prejudice is the attitude or set of attitudes that drives discrimination. Prejudice typically shows itself as a dislike for a group or an aversion to some aspect of the group members' values, beliefs, behaviors, history, or emotional states. It is an extremely negative evaluation that predisposes the judging party to avoid, criticize, or behave negatively toward members of other groups.

Prejudices also influence and are influenced by stereotypes held about particular groups. Prejudices and stereotypes relate to thoughts and feelings about other groups; discrimination refers to the treatment of a group at the hands of the prejediced. Stereotypes are sets of beliefs about characteristics attributed to members of a certain group. Stereotypes are overgeneralizations and oversimplifications. For instance, a stereotype of U.S. Americans might be that they are individualistic, self-oriented, materialistic, capitalistic, and ethnocentric. If a Korean executive held that set of beliefs about U.S. Americans, then routinely and probably unconsciously, the Korean would assume that all the characteristics were applicable to all U.S. Americans.

We make such generalizations about others because we don't have the time, will, or memory capacity to get to know every person we meet as a unique individual. We make assumptions and attributions about others because we have such a strong psychological need for closure.

Prejudice does serve a number of functions. It may serve an ego-defensive function. If I share my negative attitude toward Japanese Americans with another person, I am revealing my own standard of comparison, which has at its base the attitudes and values of my own group. The implied meaning of, "I just don't like Japanese Americans because they are _____" is, "Whew, aren't we glad we're not Japanese Americans because we are so much better people."

Sometimes prejudice serves a more utilitarian function. If I am a European American male who did not get a job I wanted, I might react by saying, "It's those affirmative action policies. Ethnic women have an unfair advantage. If the interviewers had just gone on the basis of who was best qualified, then I would have gotten the job." Prejudices help to rationalize or make sense of, in this case, rejection.

Conflict between groups is common, and disagreements are everyday occurrences in all countries and in all languages. The intensity of a conflict and the way in which individuals choose to manage the conflict differ. There are choices available enabling us to manage the conflict in a way that will save the relationship. Prejudices and stereotypes can polarize individuals and groups and make them dig in their heels and defend their positions. Consciousness of these issues and processes may help build understanding about another person's behavior. This, in turn, can diffuse the intensity of a conflict or argument when it is appropriate or help in the selection of an appropriate way to express a point of view.

If we all hold stereotypes (which we do) but don't like to be stereotyped by others, and if we all have prejudices (which we do) but don't like to experience prejudice, specifically what can we do in our communication practices to manage prejudice and stereotyping and talk about oppression?

STRATEGIES FOR INTERETHNIC OR INTERGROUP COMMUNICATION

Steps to Identify Intercultural Competence

One technique that can be used is to ask someone what the rules are and what you are expected to do in your particular role. Another idea is to observe the verbal and nonverbal patterns: What are people talking about? How are they beginning and ending conversations? How are they addressing one another? How close are they standing? What kind of tone of voice is being used? What are their facial expressions?

Another suggestion is to try out behaviors and evaluate others' reactions. If you find that people who are enacting another cultural identity are reacting negatively to your behavior, you may have violated their expected norms. I have found that if I explain my reasons for behaving in a particular way, for example, "I addressed you by your first name because that is how I would show that we are friends in my culture. What would be a more appropriate way for me to show respect and a desire for friendship in your group?" then others have a basis for understanding why I might have broken their rules and see that I have a desire to learn more about their community and culture.

For the rest of the chapter I am going to make several recommendations with regard to improving intercultural communication by recognizing the role of socioeconomic issues, power, and history on groups and their identity. These recommendations apply to members of all groups and can be applied to a variety of intercultural communication situations.

Acknowledge the Politics and Power Issues

One of the first suggestions I have is to remember that all communication is political and to some extent persuasive. Rarely is power equally shared in our relationships. Communication is situated in a social and political context. Group members whose history has included discrimination have that history as a part of their identity.

In Studs Terkel's book *Race,* an African American man describes that being Black in the United States is like owning and wearing one pair of ill-fitting shoes. Every step that is taken is a reminder that the shoes don't fit. Additionally, different African American people respond to wearing the shoes in different ways. Some try to hide the fact that the shoes don't fit. Some limp around but don't verbalize their discomfort. Others complain every so often. Still others complain loudly and demand to be given the opportunity to buy a pair of shoes that fit. However, each one knows, every moment, that the shoes don't fit.

If you are a member of the white European American group, acknowledge your white privilege. Persons who are white have a wide variety of options about what to do for a living, where to work, where to live, and with whom to socialize. Most people speak your language, and you will be represented by political candidates from your community. If you are a white male you are the most privileged of all, even with affirmative action. Why? Because the values that are taught and reinforced in all forms of the educational system, the media, and the political and justice systems reflect your values. White males still hold the majority of high-status positions in all types of organizations. I suggest that if an ethnic complains to you—a European American in the United States—the most appropriate response is, "You are right. I do benefit from my race, sex, and class, every day. What are things I could understand better about your perspective that will give us the best chance of getting along?"

Acknowledge that History Affects Current Privilege

There are some arguments and comments that are commonly made by persons in power about past history that are particularly destructive to relationships. In a study I recently conducted, I asked whites, Blacks, and coloreds from South Africa as well as a variety of ethnic U.S. Americans to make recommendations about how to communicate effectively with one another. Whites in both countries recommended to the other groups to forget the past and move on to a future orientation. They said that their ancestors were to blame for apartheid or slavery and none of the whites today voted those laws and practices into existence. Therefore, whites today aren't responsible.

There are a number of negative consequences to this kind of argument. Domination, oppression, and discrimination have occurred and are still occurring. To discount these by saying, "Let's move on to the future, let go of the past" is to discount the experiences of those who have been and who are discriminated against. In effect, this argument is saying, "As a white I am not responsible for your plight. So quit complaining and just work harder." Such an argument does a couple of things: it completely discounts white privilege, discounts history and the experiences of those who are discriminated against, and places responsibility on the ethnic group members to change the dominant social system.

A better strategy for white South Africans and U.S. Americans who choose to improve the quality of their interethnic relationships would be to acknowledge their privilege. Acknowledge the ongoing discrimination and oppression that exists. The other authors in this book have eloquently and definitively argued about the existence of discrimination against ethnics, females, and homosexuals in the United States. Communicate your view that racism, sexism, and homophobia are pervasive and violate the human rights of U.S. citizens.

In the same research study of South Africa and the United States that I conducted, the recommendations for Blacks and Asians in South Africa and ethnic group members in the United States included offering personalized descriptions of current examples of prejudice and discrimination. Current descriptions of experiences help dispel the notions that discrimination is something that existed in the past and contemporary discrimination is precluded by laws that protect all groups and all individuals. My respondents also noted that if your goal is to competently communicate rather than alienate, then your tone of voice, posture, and non-verbal cues need to be consistent with that relational goal.

Avoid Ethnocentrism

There is an important assumption that the culturally sensitive need to be cognizant of in conversations about potentially confrontational topics. This assumption is that one's own culture and one's own identity are the standards by which others should be judged. This is known as ethnocentrism. In the United States, as I have already described, European Americans are culturally taught to be individualistic. Documents such as the Constitution and the Bill of Rights reinforce the right of the individual to practice any religion, to speak out on any issue, to create a free press, and so forth. This presumes that autonomy, authenticity, and freedom are characteristics that describe the zenith of human development.

Such individualism implies that everyone starts out with the same resources. The myth that holds that if one works hard one can get whatever one wishes for is a myth because social class, race, sex, and physical ability all affect an individual's potential to achieve.

Presume Appropriate Similarity and Difference

Marsha Houston, an African American scholar of communication, lists three statements "that a white woman who wants to treat Black women with respect and friendship should never utter." The statements illustrate the importance of recognizing differences while maintaining a positive attitude toward the relationship. The statements are: (1) "I never even notice that you're Black," (2) "You're different from most Black people," and (3) "I understand what you're going through as a Black woman because (I'm Jewish, Italian, overweight, and so forth)." Houston cautions that the first statement presumes that blackness is something negative, the second that most Blacks are a particular way and that the person is somehow an exception to her ethnic group, and the third that both persons' experiences of discrimination are equal in character, frequency, and intensity.[3] It is important then, to check out understandings of similarities before presuming they exist.

Goals of Competent Communication

I have been making several assumptions about the motivations and goals of persons wishing to become competent intercultural communicators. I am assuming that an important goal of the interactors includes the development of mutually positive intergroup relationships. To be effective, you must want to be effective and be willing to put time and effort into the endeavor. Another goal I presume is a desire to learn about the other person's group identities in order to learn more about your own identities. One way to understand your own cultural identity is to view yourself through the eyes of an outsider. In intercultural conversations that are competent, both parties recognize the importance of being open to new information, new ways of thinking, feeling, and behaving. Only when we are confronted with new and different ways of being can we really see and know ourselves.

To illustrate the power of this assumption, consider the fact that many Navahos attend several different churches, including Protestant and Catholic ones, but also participate in traditional peyote ceremonies with their people and a medicine man. They are able to appreciate many religions and find ways to apply the diverse principles to one way of life. The Navahos still hold onto their beliefs about the origin of their people and the creation of the world, but they realize that, for instance, Jesus and Spider Woman stand for many of the same things. A medicine man might say that all religions are just a different road to the same place. This may be a new way to think about religion and spirituality.

Another critical assumption that we must agree upon is that there is no one set of "recipes" or "guaranteed strategies" that will improve the quality of the communication in every instance. All situations are different; all individuals are different; all relationships are to some extent unique. Goals, then, must be negotiated and modified as communication unfolds.

Specific Competent Behaviors

I have already addressed steps that can be taken to figure out what is appropriate and effective in a new situation. There are also general communication skills tested in international travel and interethnic conflict, which may improve the chances for a more satisfying experience. These skills are general ones and should be adapted to your preferred style, the topic discussed, the situation, the relationship you have with the other person, and your goals. Because there are so many different cultural styles and contextual variations, it is not possible or appropriate to provide specific examples of how to do each behavior. Each behavior will look a little different depending on both persons' personal communication style, the cultural identities that are salient, the situational context, the task at hand, and so on.

The first general skill is that of *display of respect.* This is the ability to show respect and positive regard for another person. In some situations empathy is most effectively communicated through non-verbal high-context means; in others, explicit verbal confirmation is more appropriate.

Empathy is a second skill. Empathy is the capacity to demonstrate that you understand the world similarly to the other person. Each individual involved in a conversation can benefit from putting him- or herself in another person's shoes. *Appropriate task orientation* refers to behaviors that involve the initiation of group problem-solving activities. Since all communication has a task and a relationship component, *relational skill* is also needed. You will need to negotiate the power and control and intimacy in each of your relationships.

A *tolerance of ambiguity* can be helpful in that intercultural contact includes high amounts of uncertainty and ambiguity. This skill can be demonstrated by reacting to new and ambiguous situations with little visible discomfort. *Information-gathering* skills will be essential in managing culture shock and developing positive relationships.

The *willingness to be open to new ideas and new relationships,* and the *capacity to be flexible* are also important. Some groups may expect less assertiveness or more directness, and so forth. No one expects a novice to demonstrate appropriate new skills completely. However, making a concerted effort to adapt (e.g., learning a new language) can be very effective. The more information you have about a group or an individual and the perceptions of cultural identities held the easier time you'll have understanding the perspective of the group or person.

Dialectic of Difference

We are all individuals, and we are drawn to many group identities. Group differences exist. There are many varieties of language, dress, food, religions, music, and art appreciated in the United States. It can be useful to think of these differences and similarities as a series of dialectics.

A dialectic is a juxtaposition of apparent opposites, like yin and yang. Yin and yang are forces that are both present in humanity and spirituality. Another example of a dialectic is interdependence and independence. Both dimensions are found in marriage and friendship, for instance. A satisfying interpersonal relationship for both partners will include both the element of independence and that of interdepence. At some points in the relationship, at the beginning stages of intimacy, for example, there may be more interdependence. But when the partners grow more successful in their respective careers, for example, there may be a trend toward more independence. There may be interdependence in decisions about financial investments and independence in decisions about clothing or automobiles. The relationship contains elements of both independence and interdependence.

Intercultural communication also contains elements that are dialectic. Groups are similar and different. A South African Black Zulu woman remarked to me once, "We can see the differences between the Blacks and the whites; the differences exist. We Blacks learn to see also with our hearts, and we can see heart to heart. I wonder if the Afrikaners have forgotten how to do so."

In conclusion, my call to you is to recognize that each person is a composite of many cultural identities. Our cultural identities exist in dialectic tension with our individual identities. Many factors affect who we are with one another, but recognizing that complexity is the first step toward understanding what it means to be human, and ultimately the first step toward forging a society wherein all can live together peacefully. Let the dialogues begin and continue.

Notes

INTRODUCTION

1. Aparicio, "On Multiculturalism and Privilege," 580, 582.
2. Omi and Winant, *Racial Formation in the United States*. For the discussion following, see Frankenberg, *White Women, Race Matters*, especially chapter 6.
3. Young, *Justice and the Politics of Difference*, 58–9.
4. See chapter 8, note 3.

CHAPTER 3

1. This chapter is based on a presentation made as part of a panel on "Racial and Ethnic Complexities in American Life" during the Sixteenth Annual Black Studies Conference held at Olive-Harvey College, Chicago, Illinois, on April 24, 1993.
2. For one insightful discussion see Taylor, *Multiculturalism*.
3. See the *Time* magazine special issue, "The New Face of America: How Immigrants Are Shaping the World's First Multicultural Society."
4. Wolf, "Perilous Ideas," 6.
5. Ibid.
6. Outlaw, "African, African American, Africana Philosophy," 86.
7. Hall, "New Ethnicities," 30.
8. Hall, "Cultural Identity and Diaspora," 223, 225.
9. Peter Gay, in speaking about the philosophers who were the architects of modern Western world making in his *Enlightenment*.

CHAPTER 5

1. Frye, "Oppression," 11.
2. Foucault, *Discipline and Punish*.
3. See Sher, "Groups and the Constitution," 256.

4. Heidegger, *Being and Time*.
5. See Altman, *The Homosexualization of American Society*.
6. Macpherson, *Democratic Theory*, chap. 3.
7. See Delphy, *Close to Home*.
8. See Ferguson, "Conceiving Motherhood," 1984.
9. Brown, "Mothers, Fathers and Children."
10. Alexander, "Gendered Job Traits."
11. See Ackerman, *Social Justice and the Liberal State*, chap. 8.
12. Roemer, *A General Theory of Exploitation and Class*, 122.
13. Reiman, "Moral Assessment of Capitalism."
14. Lugones and Spelman, "Have We Got a Theory for You!"
15. Fraser, "Social Movements."
16. See W. E. B. DuBois, *The Souls of Black Folk*, 45.
17. See Marable, *Race, Reform and Rebellion*, 238–41.

CHAPTER 6

1. The term "Latinos" is used here as an alternative to the term "Hispanics," a term developed by the U.S. Census to identify all Spanish-speaking and/or Spanish-origin populations in the United States. The terms Chicano and Chicana refer respectively to men and women of Mexican descent residing in the United States. Additional clarification of these terms can be found in Garcia, "Yo Soy Mexicano" and Hurtado and Arce, "Mexicans, Chicanos."
2. Garcia, "The Chicano Movement."
3. Young, *Justice and the Politics of Difference*, 59.
4. Quoted in Rodriguez, "Affirming Cultural Citizenship," 22.
5. Ibid.
6. Ibid., 22–23.
7. Barrera, *Beyond Aztlan*, 160.
8. Ibid.,160–175.
9. See Hayes-Bautista et al., *No Longer a Minority*, xii–xiii.
10. Ibid., 42.
11. Ibid., 44.
12. Chinchilla, Hamilton, and Loucky, "Central Americans in Los Angeles," 78.
13. Reported in Nazario, "Janitors' Suit Settled."
14. See Paget-Clarke, "Texas Seamstresses on the Move," 2.
15. See Buss, *Forged under the Sun*, 21.
16. See Gonzalez, "Chavez's Death," 1.
17. Cited in Gonzalez, "Arturo Rodriguez Talks," 1.
18. Taylor, "The Environmental Justice Movement," 23–25. See also Bullard, "Anatomy of Environmental Racism."
19. Young, *Justice and the Politics of Difference*, 53, 55.
20. See Buss, *Forged under the Sun*, 23.
21. de la Torre and Pesquera, *Building with Our Hands*, 2.
22. Ibid., 4.
23. Ibid., 5.
24. Chabran-Dernersesian, "Comments," 2.

25. Ibid., 3.
26. Young, *Justice and the Politics of Difference*, 56.
27. Pachon, "Obstacle to Empowerment," 77–87.
28. National Association of Latino Elected and Appointed Officials, *Unheard Voice*, 1.
29. Gomez-Quinones, *Chicano Politics,* 180.
30. Young, *Justice and the Politics of Difference*, 62.
31. See Bastian, *Hispanic Victims*, 1.
32. See U.S. Commission on Civil Rights, *Mexican Americans*.
33. American Friends Service Committee Immigration Law Enforcement Project, *Human Rights,* 9.
34. Ibid., 8.

CHAPTER 7

We thank Kelvin Santiago-Valles and Gladys Jimenez-Muñoz for suggestions that have given the chapter more layers of complexity than it had when they encountered it. We also keep our compañeros at the Escuela Popular Norteña in mind as we put these thoughts on multiculturalism down on paper. We have developed these ideas collectively and practiced them in the course of doing popular education together at La Escuela Popular. Our companeros/as include: Mildred Beltré, Dalida Maria Benfield, Geoff Bryce, Aurelia Flores, Ricardo Herrera, Paul Hyry, Manuel Herrera, Laura Dumond Kerr, Julia Schiavone Camacho, Lisa Tessman, Sarah Williams, Maritza Burgos, Suzanne LaGrande, Rob Gonzales, Elias Espinoza, and Laura Burns-Levison.

1. Rosaldo, *Culture and Truth,* 198.
2. Jordan, *Civil Wars*, 91–92.
3. Frye, *The Politics of Reality,* 164–5.
4. Pratt, "Scratches on the Face of the Country," 145.
5. Goffman, *Presentation of Self in Everyday Life.*
6. Quoted in Gwaltney, *Drylongso*, 110.
7. Ibid., 102–3.
8. hooks, *From Margin to Center,* i.
9. Yamada, "Invisibility Is an Unnatural Disaster," 40.

CHAPTER 8

1. In South Korea, important events are known by the date of occurrence. The terms "riot," "uprising," "insurrection," and "crisis" have all been used to describe the violence and destruction of April 29, 1992. All are probably fair descriptions. We use the term "riot" in this chapter to reflect our Korean American perspective on the events that took place in Los Angeles on April 29, 1992.
2. As of this writing, less than half of those losses have been replaced.
3. See Patterson, *Korean Frontier in America*, 69.
4. Ibid.
5. See Choy, *Koreans in America;* and Yang, "Koreans in America," 5–22; Patterson, *Korean Frontier in America*; and Bang, *Jae Mi Han In Wei Dok Nip Ung Dong.*

6. See Patterson, *Korean Frontier in America*; and Takaki, *Pau Hana*.

7. See Takaki, *Pau Hana,* 69.

8. Patterson, *Korean Frontier in America*.

9. See Choy, *Koreans in America,* and Bang, *Jae Mi Han In Wei Dok Nip Ung Dong*.

10. The Chinese Exclusion Act of 1882 prohibited immigration of Chinese laborers to the United States. It set the tone for later immigation of Japanese, Koreans, and Pilipinos.

11. See Takaki, *Strangers from a Different Shore*.

12. Picture brides are Asian women who came to the United States through the exchange of photographs during the early 1900s. Most came from Japan, Korea, and Okinawa. For more information see Yu and Phillips, *Korean Women in Transition*.

13. *Statistical Record of Asian Americans,* 572. Anti-Asian sentiment played a pivotal role in shaping and influencing America's national immigration policies. In 1882, anti-Chinese sentiment led to the passage of the Chinese Exclusion Act. Subsequently, all Asian immigration came to a halt with the passage of the National Origins Act of 1924. Korean immigrants, like other Asians, were denied eligibility to become naturalized citizens. Because of these institutionalized forms of discrimination, Korean immigrants remained invisible, isolated, and politically powerless in America. The number of Korean Americans remained relatively low until the passage of the 1965 immigration act. The elimination of racial preferences for European immigrants opened the door to Asian immigration, including that of Koreans.

14. See Kim, *New Urban Immigrants*.

15. For United States–South Korea relations see Cumings, *Origins of The Korean War;* Baldwin, *Without Parallel;* and Yu and Kandal, *Korean Peninsula*.

16. See Yu, *Korean Community Profile,* 3.

17. These data were compiled by the Korean American Inter-agency Council (KAIC), based in Los Angeles. KAIC is composed of social-service agencies, including the Korean Youth and Community Center, the Koryo Health Foundation, the Korean American Coalition, the Korean Health Information and Referral Service Center, and the Korean Family Counseling and Legal Advice Center. It was formed in May 1992 for the purpose of coordinating social service resources, assessing the needs of Korean American victims, and providing disaster assistance, where possible.

18. See Yu, *Korean Community Profile,* 3.

19. See Hurh and Kim, *Korean Immigrants in America*. However, Kim, *New Urban Immigrants*, 191, found that less than 40 percent of the Korean immigrants in the New York metropolitan area participated in churches.

20. See Yu, *Korean Community Profile,* for all the following statistics, and an excellent discussion in general about the Korean community.

21. Yu's survey found that the customer base of Korean-owned businesses in southern California is 48 percent white, 22 percent Korean, 17 percent Latino, and 10 percent African American.

22. In 1990 alone, the Police Misconduct Lawyer Referral Service (a non-profit, now named "Police Watch") received over 2,600 complaints against law enforcement agencies in the Los Angeles area. A total of 616 complaints concerned the Los Angeles Police Department. In 1991, there were 2,425 complaints against the LAPD as of mid-October. By about the same point in time, police brutality case settlements and judgments amounted to about $13,000,000.

23. The U.S. Department of Justice's Community Relations Service, Western Regional Office, convened a meeting among representatives of various ethnic communities on June 21–

22, 1991 to address the growing tensions, frustration, and fear of local law enforcement agencies, including the LAPD.

24. In 1986, the Black-Korean Alliance (BKA) was created to improve relations and reduce conflict between African Americans and Korean Americans in Los Angeles. By November 1992, the group had been dissolved. For more detailed discussion of the BKA, see Chang "Building Minority Coalitions."

25. See Chung, "Korean American Community."

26. Edward Chang relates: Two weeks after the Los Angeles riots of 1992, I was walking along the streets of downtown Atlanta. A passerby approached and asked me if I was Korean. My reaction was one of surprise. For the first time someone had asked me if I was a Korean American instead of Japanese or Chinese American. Does this mean that Korean Americans have finally made it into mainstream America? Does this represent a new set of challenges to a multiculturalism that is a form of resistance to oppression and racism? Korean Americans are beginning to question the viability of an assimilationist ideology. They were told to assimilate or face consequences. Does becoming Americanized mean being less Korean?

27. In the Korean American community, "second generation" refers to those born and raised in the United States. Those born in Korea who later emigrated to the United States with their parents are known as "1.5-generation." Although "1.5-generation" is a common term for Korean Americans, scholars disagree on how to define the term. Some believe "1.5-generation" refers to Korean children who came to the United States between the ages of eleven and sixteen. Others believe the term can be applied to Korean American children who spent some of their formative years in Korea.

CHAPTER 9

1. McIntosh, "White Privilege."
2. Fredrickson, *Black Image,* 133.
3. Thomas and Scott, "Studies Show Widespread Bias," 11.
4. Goldberg, *Racist Culture,* 169.
5. Gates, "White Male Paranoia," 48–53.
6. Tajfel and Forgas, *Social Categorization*, 114.
7. Atkinson et al., *Introduction to Psychology*, 476.
8. Carter, *Herodotus Histories Vol. II,* 104.
9. Ryan, *Blaming the Victim*, 6.
10. Hodge, Struckmann, and Trost, *Cultural Bases of Racism and Group Oppression*, ix.
11. Ibid.
12. Ibid.

CHAPTER 10

1. For a discussion of context, see Hall, *Beyond Culture,* 85–103.
2. See Stewart, *American Cultural Patterns,* 20.
3. Houston, "Black Women," 137–8.

Bibliography

Ackerman, Bruce. *Social Justice and the Liberal State.* New Haven: Yale University Press, 1980.

Alexander, David. "Gendered Job Traits and Women's Occupations." Ph.D. diss., University of Massachusetts, 1987.

Altman, Dennis. *The Homosexualization of American Society.* Boston: Beacon Press, 1982.

American Friends Service Committee Immigration Law Enforcement Project. *Human Rights at the Mexico-U.S. Border.* Philadelphia: American Friends Service Committee, Mexico-U.S. Border Program, 1990.

Anzaldua, Gloria, ed. *Making Face, Making Soul/Haciendo Caras.* San Francisco: aunt lute press, 1990.

Aparicio, Frances R. "On Multiculturalism and Privilege: A Latina Perspective." *American Quarterly* 46, no. 4 (1994).

Atkinson, R. L., et al. *Introduction to Psychology.* llth ed. Fort Worth, Texas: Harcourt Brace Jovanovich, 1993.

Baldwin, Frank, ed. *Without Parallel: The American-Korean Relationship Since 1945.* New York: Pantheon Books, 1973.

Bang, Sun-Joo. *Jae Mi Han In Wei Dok Nip Ung Dong: Korean American Independence Movement.* Choon-Chun, Korea: Han Rim University Press, 1989.

Barrera, Mario. *Beyond Aztlan: Ethnic Autonomy in Comparative Perspective.* New York: Praeger, 1988.

Bastian, Lisa D. *Hispanic Victims: Bureau of Justice Statistics Report.* Washington, D.C: Department of Justice, 1990.

Bernstein, Richard. *Dictatorship of Virtue: Multiculturalism and the Battle for America's Future.* New York: Knopf, 1994.

Breslin, R. *Understanding Culture's Influence on Behavior.* Fort Worth, Texas: Harcourt Brace Jovanovich, 1993.

Brown, Carol. "Mothers, Fathers and Children: From Private to Public Patriarchy." In *Women and Revolution,* ed. L. Sargent. Boston: South End Press, 1981.

Bullard, Robert D. "Anatomy of Environmental Racism and the Environmental Justice Movement." In *Confronting Environmental Racism,* ed. R. D. Bullard. Boston: South End Press, 1993.

————. ed. *Confronting Environmental Racism*. Boston: South End Press, 1993.

Buss, Fran Leeper. *Forged under the Sun*. Ann Arbor: University of Michigan Press, 1993.

Carter, Harry, trans. *Herodotus Histories Vol. II*. New York: Heritage Press, 1958.

Chabran-Dernersesian, Angie. "Comments." In *Building With Our Hands: New Directions in Chicana Studies*, ed. A. de la Torre and B. M. Pesquera. Berkeley: University of California Press, 1993.

Chang, Edward T. "Building Minority Coalitions: A Case Study of Korean and African Americans." *Korea Journal of Population and Development* 21, no. 1 (1992).

Chinchilla, Norma, Nora Hamilton, and James Loucky. "Central Americans in Los Angeles: An Immigrant Community in Transition." In *The Barrios: Latinos and the Underclass Debate*, ed. J. Moore and R. Pinderhughes. New York: Russell Sage Foundation, 1993.

Choy, Bong-Youn. *Koreans in America*. Chicago: Nelson-Hall, 1979.

Chung, John. "Report on Coverage of the Korean American Community by the *Los Angeles Times*." Report presented to the Korean American Bar Association Media Relations Committee, Los Angeles, June 1992.

Cumings, Bruce. *The Origins of the Korean War*. Princeton: Princeton University Press, 1981.

Cyrus, V., ed. *Experiencing Race, Class, and Gender in the United States*. Mountain View, Calif.: Mayfield Publishing, 1993.

de la Garza, Rodolfo, et al. *Latino Voices: Mexican, Puerto Rican and Cuban Perspectives on American Politics*. Boulder, Colo.: Westview Press, 1992.

de la Torre, Adela, and Beatriz M. Pesquera, eds. *Building with Our Hands: New Directions in Chicana Studies*. Berkeley: University of California Press, 1993.

Delphy, Christine. *Close to Home: A Materialist Analysis of Women's Oppression*. Amherst: University of Massachusetts Press, 1984.

DuBois, W. E. B. *The Souls of Black Folk*. New York: New American Library, 1969.

Estrada, Leobardo, F., et al. "Chicanos in the United States: A History of Exploitation and Resistance." In *Latinos and the Political System*, ed. F. C. Garcia. Notre Dame: University of Notre Dame Press, 1981.

Ezorsky, Gertrude, ed. *Moral Rights in the Workplace*. Albany: State University of New York Press, 1987.

Ferguson, Ann. "On Conceiving Motherhood and Sexuality: A Feminist Materialist Approach." In *Mothering: Essays in Feminist Theory,* ed. J. Trebilcot. Totowa, N.J.: Rowman and Allanheld, 1984.

Foucault, Michel. *Discipline and Punish*. New York: Pantheon, 1977.

Frammolino, Ralph. "A New Generation of Rebels." *Los Angeles Times*, 20 November 1993.

Frankenberg, Ruth. *White Women, Race Matters: The Social Construction of Whiteness*. Minneapolis: University of Minnesota Press, 1993.

Fraser, Nancy. "Women, Welfare, and the Politics of Need Interpretation." *Hypatia: A Journal of Feminist Philosophy* 2, no. 1 (1987).

————. "Social Movements vs. Disciplinary Bureaucracies: The Discourse of Social Needs." CHS Occasional Paper No. 8. Center for Humanistic Studies, University of Minnesota, 1987.

Fredrickson, G. M. *The Black Image in the White Mind: The Debate on Afro-American Character and Destiny, 1817–1914*. Middletown, Conn.: Wesleyan University Press, 1971.

Frye, Marilyn. "Oppression." In *The Politics of Reality*, ed. M. Frye. Trumansburg, N.Y.: Crossing, 1983.

————, ed. *The Politics of Reality*. New York: The Crossing Press, 1983.

Garcia, F. Chris, ed. *Latinos and the Political System*. Notre Dame: University of Notre Dame Press, 1981.

Garcia, John A. "The Chicano Movement: Its Legacy for Politics and Policy." In *Chicanos: The Contemporary Era*, ed. D. Maciel and I. Ortiz. Tucson: University of Arizona Press, in press.

———. "Yo Soy Mexicano . . . : Self-Identity and Socio-Demographic Correlates." *Social Science Quarterly* 62, no. 1 (1981).

Gates, D. "White Male Paranoia." *Newsweek* 121, 29 March 1993, 48–53.

Gates, Jr., Henry Louis, ed. *"Race" Writing, and Difference*. Chicago: University of Chicago Press, 1986.

Gay, Peter. *The Enlightenment: An Interpretation*. 2 vols. New York: Norton, 1977.

Goffman, Erving. *Presentation of Self in Everyday Life*. Garden City, N.Y.: Doubleday, 1959.

Goldberg, David T. *Racist Culture: Philosophy and the Politics of Meaning*. London: Blackwell, 1993.

Gomez-Quinones, Juan. *Chicano Politics: Reality and Promise 1940-1990*. Albuquerque: University of New Mexico Press, 1990.

Gonzalez, Christian R. "Chavez's Death Inspires Rebirth of UFW Organizing Efforts." *Hispanic Link Weekly Report*, 11 November 1993.

———. "UFW President Arturo Rodriguez Talks about Tomorrow." *Hispanic Link Weekly Report*, 11 November 1993.

Gonzalez, A., M. Houston, and V. Chen. *Our Voices: Essays in Culture, Ethnicity, and Communication*. Los Angeles: Roxbury Publishing Company, 1994.

Goodman, E. "The Difference Between Sexism and Suckerism." *Boston Globe*, 23 December 1990.

Gwaltney, John Lanston. *Drylongso: A Self-Portrait of Black America*. New York: Random House, 1980.

Hall, Edward T. *Beyond Culture*. Garden City, N.Y.: Doubleday & Co., 1976.

Hall, Stuart. "Cultural Identity and Diaspora." In *Identity, Community, Culture, Difference*, ed. J. Rutherford. London: Lawrence & Wishart, 1990.

———. "New Ethnicities." *ICA Documents: Black Film, British Cinema*. ICA Conference. (February 1988).

Hayes-Bautista, David, et al. *No Longer a Minority: Latinos and Social Policy in California*. Los Angeles: Chicano Studies Research Center, University of California, Los Angeles, 1992.

Hayes-Bautista, David E., R. Burciega Valdez, and Anthony C. R. Hernandez. *Redefining California: Latino Social Engagement in a Multicultural Society*. Los Angeles: Chicano Studies Research Center, University of California, Los Angeles, 1992.

Heidegger, Martin. *Being and Time*. New York: Harper & Row, 1962.

Hodge, J. L., D. K. Struckmann, and L. D. Trost. *Cultural Bases of Racism and Group Oppression*. Berkeley, Calif.: Two Riders Press, 1975.

hooks, bell. *From Margin to Center*. Boston: South End Press, 1984.

Houston, Marsha "When Black Women Talk to White Women: Why Dialogues are Difficult." In *Our Voices: Essays in Culture, Ethnicity, and Communication*, ed. A. Gonzalez, M. Houston, and V. Chen. Los Angeles: Roxbury Publishing Company, 1994.

Hughes, Robert. *Culture of Complaint: The Fraying of America*. New York: Oxford University Press, 1993.

Hurh, Won Moo, and Kwang Chung Kim. *Korean Immigrants in America: A Structural Analysis of Ethnic Confinement and Adhesive Adaptation*. Madison, N. J.: Fairleigh Dickinson University Press, 1984.

Hurtado, Aida, and Carlos H. Arce. "Mexicans, Chicanos, Mexican Americans or Pochos . . . Que Somos? The Impact of Language and Nativity on Ethnic Labeling." *Aztlan: A Journal of Chicano Studies* 17, no. 1 (1987).

Jordan, June. *Civil Wars*. Boston: Beacon Press, 1981.

Kim, Illsoo. *New Urban Immigrants: The Korean Community in New York*. Princeton: Princeton University Press, 1981.

Kinder, D., and D. Sears. "Prejudice and Politics: Symbolic Racism versus Real Threats to the Good Life." *Journal of Personality and Social Psychology* 40, no. 3 (1981).

Lugones, María, and Elizabeth Spelman. "Have We Got a Theory for You! Feminist Theory, Cultural Imperialism and the Demand for 'the Woman's Voice.'" *Women's Studies International Forum* 6, no. 6 (1983).

Maciel, D., and Isidro Ortiz, eds. *Chicanos: The Contemporary Era*. Tucson: University of Arizona Press, in press.

Macpherson, C. B. *Democratic Theory: Essays in Retrieval*. New York: Oxford University Press, 1973.

Marable, Manning. *Race, Reform and Rebellion: The Second Reconstruction in Black America, 1945–82*. Jackson: University Press of Mississippi, 1984.

Marshall, R. *The Negro and Organized Labor*. New York: Wiley, 1965.

McIntosh, P. "White Privilege: Unpacking the Invisible Knapsack." In *Experiencing Race, Class, and Gender in the United States,* ed. V. Cyrus. Mountain View, Calif.: Mayfield Publishing, 1993.

Moore, J., and R. Pinderhughes, eds. *The Barrios: Latinos and the Underclass Debate*. New York: Russell Sage Foundation, 1993.

Moraga, Cherrie, and Gloria Anzaldua, eds. *This Bridge Called My Back*. New York: Kitchen Table Press, 1981.

Murray, C. B., and J. Jackson. "The Conditioned Failure Model of Black Educational Underachievement." *Humboldt Journal of Social Relations* 10, no. 1 (1982/83).

————. "The Conditioned Failure Model Revisited." In *Race and Ethnicity: A Study of Intracultural Socialization Patterns*, ed. J. O. Smith and C. E. Jackson. Dubuque, Iowa: Kendall/Hunt, 1989.

National Association of Latino Elected and Appointed Officials. *The Unheard Voice of One Out of Every Four Californians: What Do Latinos Think about Anti-Immigrant Rhetoric?* Los Angeles: National Association of Latino Elected Officials, 1993.

Nava, Michael, and Robert Dawidoff. *Created Equal: Why Gay Rights Matter to America*. New York: St. Martin's Press, 1994.

Nazario, Sonia. "Janitors' Suit Settled." *Los Angeles Times*, 4 September 1993.

Oakes, J. *Keeping Track: How Schools Structure Equality*. New Haven: Yale University Press, 1985.

Omi, Michael, and Howard Winant. *Racial Formation in the United States: From the 1960s to the 1980s*. New York: Routledge and Kegan Paul, 1986.

Outlaw, Lucius. "African, African American, Africana Philosophy." *The Philosophical Forum* 24, no. 1 (1992).

Pachon, Harry. "Citizenship as an Obstacle to Empowerment in the Hispanic Community." *Journal of Hispanic Policy* 2, no. 1 (1986–87).

Paget-Clarke, Nic. "Texas Seamstresses on the Move." *Unity,* March 1992.

Patterson, Wayne. *The Korean Frontier in America: Immigration to Hawaii 1896–1910*. Honolulu: University of Hawaii Press, 1988.

Pratt, Mary Louise. "Scratches on the Face of the Country: Or What Mr. Barrow Saw in the Land of the Bushmen." In *"Race" Writing, and Difference,* ed. H. L. Gates, Jr. Chicago: University of Chicago Press, 1986.

Reiman, Jeffrey. "Exploitation, Force, and the Moral Assessment of Capitalism: Thoughts on Roemer and Cohen." *Philosophy and Public Affairs* 16, no. 1 (1987).

Rodriguez, Roberto. "Affirming Cultural Citizenship: Latino Scholars Examine Complex Issue." *Black Issues in Higher Education* 10, no. 9 (1993).

Roemer, John. *A General Theory of Exploitation and Class.* Cambridge: Harvard University Press, 1982.

Rosaldo, Renato. *Culture and Truth.* Boston: Beacon Press, 1989.

Rutherford, J., ed. *Identity, Community, Culture, Difference.* London: Lawrence & Wishart, 1990.

Ryan, W. *Blaming the Victim.* New York: Random House, 1976.

Sargent, Lydia, ed. *Women and Revolution.* Boston: South End Press, 1981.

Schlesinger, Jr., Arthur. *The Disuniting of America: Reflections on a Multicultural Society.* New York: Norton, 1992.

Sher, George. "Groups and the Constitution." In *Moral Rights in the Workplace,* ed. G. Ezorsky. Albany: State University of New York Press, 1987.

Smith, J. Owens. *The Politics of Ethnic and Racial Inequality.* 2nd ed. Dubuque, Iowa: Kendall/ Hunt, 1992.

Smith, J. O., and C. E. Jackson. *Race and Ethnicity: A Study of Intracultural Socialization Patterns.* Dubuque, Iowa: Kendall/Hunt, 1989.

Statistical Record of Asian Americans. Detroit: Gale Research Inc., 1993.

Stewart, Edward C. *American Cultural Patterns: A Cross-Cultural Perspective.* Yarmouth, Me.: Intercultural Press, Inc., 1972.

Sue, D. W., and D. Sue. *Counseling the Culturally Different.* 2nd ed. New York: Wiley, 1990.

Tajfel, H., and J. P. Forgas, eds. *Social Categorization: Cognitions, Perspectives, an Everyday Understanding.* New York: Academic Press, 1981.

Takaki, Ronald. *Pau Hana: Plantation Life and Labor in Hawaii.* Honolulu: University of Hawaii Press, 1983.

———. *Strangers from a Different Shore.* Boston: Little, Brown, 1989.

Taylor, Charles. *Multiculturalism and "The Politics of Recognition:" An essay.* Princeton: Princeton University Press, 1992.

Taylor, Dorceta. "The Environmental Justice Movement: No Shortage of Volunteers." *EPA Journal* 18, no. 1 (1992).

Thomas, J., and M. S. Scott. "Studies Show Widespread Bias against Blacks." *Black Enterprise,* August 1991, 11.

Time magazine special issue, "The New Face of America: How Immigrants Are Shaping the World's First Multicultural Society," Vol. 142, no. 21, fall 1993.

Trebilcot, Joyce, ed. *Mothering: Essays in Feminist Theory.* Totowa, N. J.: Rowman and Allanheld, 1984.

Trevino, Jessie. "The Political Game." *El Paso Times,* 14 January 1989.

Wolf, Eric R. "Perilous Ideas: Race, Culture, People." *Current Anthropology* 35, no. 1 (1994).

Yamada, Mitsuye. "Invisibility Is an Unnatural Disaster." In *This Bridge Called My Back,* ed. C. Moraga and G. Anzaldua. New York: Kitchen Table Press, 1981.

Yang, Eun-Sik. "Koreans in America, 1903–1945." In *Koreans in Los Angeles,* ed. E. Yu, E. H. Phillips, and E. Yang. Los Angeles: Koryo Research Institute, 1982.

Young, Iris Marion. *Justice and the Politics of Difference*. Princeton: Princeton University Press, 1990.

Yu, Eui-Young. *Korean Community Profile: Life and Consumer Patterns*. Los Angeles: Korea Times, 1990.

Yu, Eui-Young, and Terry R. Kandal, eds. *The Korean Peninsula in the Changing World Order*. Los Angeles: Center for Korean-American and Korean Studies, and California Sociologist, 1992.

Yu, Eui Young, and Earl H. Phillips, eds. *Korean Women in Transition: At Home and Abroad*. Los Angeles: Center for Korean-American and Korean Studies, 1987.

Yu, Eui-Young, Earl H. Phillips, and Eun-Sik Yang, eds. *Koreans in Los Angeles*. Los Angeles: Koryo Research Institute, 1982.

Index

About the Contributors

EDWARD T. CHANG is an assistant professor in the ethnic studies department at the University of California, Riverside. He received his Ph.D. from the University of California, Berkeley, where he specialized in the areas of Korean American–African American relations and immigration. Recently he served as a field reporter and consultant for "LA is Burning: Five Reports from a Divided City," a PBS program on the Los Angeles uprising of 1992. He is author of the Korean language book *Who African Americans Are.*

MARY JANE COLLIER is associate professor and chair of the department of speech communication at Oregon State University. She has coauthored with Michael Hecht and Sidney Ribeau *African American Communication: Ethnic Identity and Cultural Interpretation.* Her work has appeared in the *International Journal of Intercultural Relations* and *American Behavioral Scientist.* She has also served as the elected chair of the Division of International and Intercultural Communication of the Speech Communication Association.

ROBERT DAWIDOFF is a professor in the history department at Claremont Graduate School. He is author of *The Genteel Tradition and the Sacred Rage* and, most recently, coauthor with Michael Nava of *Created Equal: Why Gay Rights Matter to America.* He lives in West Hollywood.

JOHN A. GARCIA is a professor of political science at the University of Arizona. His primary areas of research are American politics, elections and political participation, and minority group politics, focusing especially on Latinos. He is coauthor of *Latino Voices: Perspectives of Cubans, Mexican Americans, and Puerto Ricans.* Recently he was appointed to the Executive Council of the American Political Science Association.

DEAN A. HARRIS is publisher of Bifocal Publications, a producer of anthologies focusing on contemporary issues. His current project is a collection of essays on white privilege. In addition, he is director of The Civic Dialogue Project, a civic-education organization that publishes the e-letter *Left Out.*

CHERYL ZARLENGA KERCHIS is a doctoral student in public policy at the University of Pittsburgh's Graduate School of Public and International Affairs. Her research interests include democratic theory and policy analysis, U.S. welfare and employment policy, and urban poverty.

MARÍA LUGONES is an educator and feminist philosopher. She teaches at the Escuela Popular Norteña in New Mexico and directs the Latin American and Caribbean Studies Program at State University of New York, Binghamton. She works on the interconnection between the theory and practice of overcoming oppression.

CAROLYN B. MURRAY is currently an associate professor in both the psychology and ethnic studies departments at the University of California, Riverside. In 1990 she received a Distinguished Teaching Award from that institution. She was also recently honored as the Riverside County-wide YWCA Woman of Achievement in Education. Professor Murray has been awarded by the National Institute of Child Health and Human Development a four-year grant to study the socialization processes of African American families.

ANGELA E. OH is in private practice in Los Angeles with the law firm of Beck, De Corso, Barrera, and Oh, which specializes in criminal defense. In 1993 she was asked to chair Senator Barbara Boxer's (D–Calif.) federal judicial nominations committee for the central district of California. During that year she also served as president of the Korean American Bar Association of southern California.

ISIDRO ORTIZ serves as chair of the department of Mexican American Studies at San Diego State University. He is the coeditor of *Chicano Studies: A Multidisciplinary Approach.* He has also published articles and book chapters on diverse aspects of Chicano and Latino politics. His current research focuses on political strategies of Latino elites and Chicano antiracist activism in California.

LUCIUS T. OUTLAW was born, raised, and educated through high school in Starkville, Mississippi. He earned his doctorate in philosophy from Boston College. He has been a visiting professor at Howard University, Spelman College, and Hamilton College. Presently, he is T. Wistar Brown Professor of Philosophy at Haverford College in Pennsylvania.

JOSHUA PRICE is an activist and educator affiliated with the Escuela Popular Norteña in New Mexico. He also works and writes on violence against women in the United States.

J. OWENS SMITH is a professor in the ethnic studies department at California State University, Fullerton.

PAULA TIMMERMAN is a graduate student in sociology at San Diego State University. Her research interests include the political and socioeconomic issues of Latinos, relationships of power, and evaluation research. She is currently working on an evaluation project for the Vietnam Veterans of San Diego.

IRIS MARION YOUNG is a professor at the Graduate School of Public and International Affairs at the University of Pittsburgh. She is author of *Justice and the Politics of Difference* and *Throwing Like a Girl and Other Essays in Feminist Philosophy and Social Theory*. She is on the editorial boards of a number of scholarly journals, has taught at Australian National University, and has been a board member for the Pittsburgh Peace Institute.

ISBN 0-89789-455-3

EAN

90000>